*The philosophy of Popper*

# The philosophy
# of Popper

T. E. BURKE

MANCHESTER UNIVERSITY PRESS

Copyright © T. E. Burke 1983

Published by
Manchester University Press
Oxford Road, Manchester M13 9PL, UK
*and*
51 Washington Street, Dover,
New Hampshire 03820, USA

*British Library cataloguing in publication data*

Burke, T. E.
   The philosophy of Popper.
   1. Popper, Karl R.
   I. Title
   192        B1649.P64

   ISBN 0–7190–0904–9
   ISBN 0–7190–0911–1 Pbk

*Library of Congress cataloging in publication data*
applied for

*Library of Congress catalog card number*
83-080361

Photoset in Plantin by
Northern Phototypesetting Co., Bolton
Printed in England by
Butler & Tanner Ltd
Frome and London

# Contents

|   | |  |
|---|---|---|
|   | Preface | *page* vii |
| 1 | The philosophy of philosophy | 1 |
| 2 | The philosophy of science | 37 |
| 3 | Relativism and truth | 82 |
| 4 | Historicism | 132 |
| 5 | Freedom and values | 174 |
|   | Notes | 210 |
|   | References | 217 |
|   | Index | 219 |

# Preface

Over a long career, Sir Karl Popper has made such varied and extensive contributions to philosophy that it would be futile to attempt to cover, and comment on, them all in a single book. Fortunately, he is lucid enough to have no need of a self-appointed interpreter; his own works are by far the best sources of information about the content of his thought. Accordingly, in what follows I have not attempted any comprehensive survey, but rather an exploration and development in some depth of a small number of Popperian ideas — ideas about philosophy itself, about science, about truth and relativism, historicism and freedom.

The attempt at development, as well as exploration, requires no justification; indeed, despite the fact that it sometimes leads us a long way from the texts and along lines which Popper himself would scarcely approve, it is this which provides the main justification for a book about him. For what makes something a major original work in philosophy — and doubtless in other fields as well — and therefore worthy of secondary studies, is just that it provides a stimulus and a starting-point for development. Such a work, characteristically, gives a classic statement of some central problems in its field of interest and of *one* way, at least, of tackling them, and thereafter becomes a point of reference, a landmark by which other subsequent research fixes its positions and determines its directions of progress.

By this standard, Descartes' *Meditations*, or Kant's *Critique of Pure Reason* is manifestly a major original work. And, by the same standard, some of Popper's writings must surely count as well. Consider, for example, *The Logic of Scientific Discovery*. The problems it poses and the solutions it offers are essentially simple; they belong, in substantial part at least, to the realm of what is obvious once it is pointed out. But, once they have been pointed out, it is also obvious that every serious student of the philosophy of science must take account of them. And, over many years now, much that is liveliest and most creative in this field has been written in response to Popper. The response has, of course, often been critical, and, as we shall see, the criticisms have often been severe and, in some measure, successful. Yet, while few of those qualified to publish an opinion would say, without reservation, 'I agree with Popper', a great many have felt constrained to explain how and why they disagree, to locate their own positions by reference to his. And even if sustained criticism ultimately wrecks the distinctively Popperian conception of science, it is likely still to endure as one of those wrecks that mark the channel through which all later research must pass – and in the long term, perhaps, no philosophical theory can hope for a better fate than that.

Similar claims may be made for the major works of political and social theory, *The Poverty of Historicism* and *The Open Society and its Enemies*. They can be, and have been, effectively criticized on many grounds. But there is no denying the importance of the issues they raise – an importance extending far beyond the realm of academic discussion – the issues between historicism and belief in freedom, totalitarianism and the open society. And neither can it be denied that Popper has made one of the most sustained and serious attempts of our time to analyse and expose what he sees as the essential errors of historicism in general and its Marxist variety in particular, and to develop an alternative conception of social development – and that these issues are increasingly discussed in Popper's terms and with reference to his theories. Accordingly if we want to enter such discussion at any level above that of mere emotional reaction or political propaganda, then, whatever out critical reservations, his are among the handful of books to which we must, perforce, pay attention.

How we respond to any original work and what lines of development we pursue, at any given time, will of course depend on what work we find already done in this field and what outside interests and preoccupations we bring to it. The present study begins with a comparison between Popper's conception of philosophy itself and that of his older contemporary and fellow-countryman, Wittgenstein, and finds a remarkable area of agreement underlying their surface differences. Then, after a survey of Popper's philosophy of science and some of the main critical reactions it has evoked, relativism emerges as a central theme; and considerable space is devoted to showing how, despite his fervent disclaimers, relativism both intellectual and moral is inherent in Popper's thought – and to exploring ways in which it might be eliminated or rendered innocuous. Another important theme then emerges from our analysis of the concept of an open society – the nature, and the conditions for the realization, of freedom.

In any study which covers an author's contributions to several distinct fields of interest, it is almost obligatory to demonstrate in them some element of unity-in-diversity, some single overall pattern. Hence perhaps a temptation to thrust unity upon him, even where he shows little evidence of having achieved it. But with Popper, fortunately, no forcing is needed. There is no difficulty in showing how the characteristic features of his theory of knowledge determine, in essential part, characteristic features of his political and social thought. Indeed from the body of his works one might say that something like a distinctive Popperian view of the whole human condition emerges – in brief, a conception of man as cast into an alien environment, in itself neither hostile nor friendly to him, which owes him no livelihood and no certainties, and which he can master only through his capacity endlessly to invent theories and policies, to test them, or let them be tested, to destruction, and then to invent again; a being whose survival and success depend on his own imagination and adaptability in a never-ending sequence of problem-situations. In the last analysis, it is this overall picture of humanity that we must endeavour to assess.

This study has grown out of seminars in which, over the past few years, I have discussed Popper's work with final year students at Reading University. Initially, to some academic colleagues, it seemed a surprising choice of subject; and until very recently at any rate, it has not been widely represented in university courses. Yet, in classes covering a variety of twentieth-century thinkers, I have found that it is very often Popper who stimulates the keenest debates and furnishes the favourite topics for essay-writing. At the least, he offers novel, arresting and boldly presented ideas to criticize; and even comparative newcomers to philosophy have little difficulty in discovering interest and importance in his themes.

I should like to thank the students, as well as colleagues on the academic staff, for many interesting discussions on Popper and the problems raised by his work. I should also like to thank Miss Joan Morris for the patience and skill with which she has produced a model typescript from a much-corrected and often barely legible manuscript.

# 1

## The philosophy of philosophy

### 1

I believe that the function of a scientist or a philosopher is to solve scientific or philosophical problems, rather than to talk about what he or other [scientists or] philosophers are doing or might do. Any unsuccessful attempt to solve a scientific or philosophical problem, if it is an honest and devoted attempt, appears to be more significant than a discussion of such a question as 'What is science?' or 'What is philosophy?' ... *We are not students of some subject matter but students of problems.* And problems may cut right across the borders of any subject matter or discipline.[1]

The title of the address from which these sentences are quoted – 'The nature of philosophical problems and their roots in science' – would seem to commit Popper to the view that there are some things worth saying about the distinctive character of philosophical *problems*, at any rate. But the questions that the layman, understandably enough, sees as the first and most obvious ones to put to a philosopher, questions like 'What is philosophy?' 'What is it about?' 'How is it done?' are, according to Popper, the wrong questions to ask. They arise from misunderstandings, and attempts to answer them as thus stated are unlikely to yield anything interesting or enlightening.

Doubtless it is at first sight surprising to find a philosopher dismissing as futile discussion about the nature of philosophy. We can readily accept that a painter or a musician is more happily and effectively employed in painting or composing, than in generalizing about the nature of visual art or of music. But a philosopher as such surely stands in a different relation to his discipline. He, after all, is characteristically occupied with the systematic cultivation of self-consciousness about his conceptual equipment; and the concept of philosophy itself should scarcely be made an exception. But Popper's

point is that to put our questions in this form, What is philosophy? etc.,
is in effect to start from what he calls 'the naive belief that there is an
entity such as "philosophy" . . . and that it has a certain character or
essence or "nature" '.[2] It is to suppose, in other words, that there is
some quality or set of qualities which distinguishes everything which is
genuinely philosophical from everything which is not, and the
explication of which would provide our layman with the kind of
answer he expects to his first question at least – for example, that
philosophy is the systematic study of a specific subject matter, or the
systematic application of a certain method of enquiry. And from this it
is a short and obvious step further to suppose that the discovery of this
essence, or essential nature, is perforce the first move in the whole
historical development of the subject, or in any individual thinker's
mastery of it.[3]

But, in Popper's view, there is simply no such discovery to be made,
no essence of philosophy – or, for that matter, of physics, history, or
any other discipline – which can be defined in terms of a unique subject
matter, method, or anything else. And its absence is no serious
handicap to the genuine researcher, whose aim is not to 'do'
philosophy, physics, or whatever, properly so called, but to tackle some
specific problem, which for some reason seems interesting or
important, but any method that seems promising. Whether his efforts,
or any publications that result from them, should be classified as
philosophy or as something else is a question which may, for practical
reasons, occasionally concern university administrators or librarians;
but to the researcher as such it is of only marginal interest. So long as
he can make some progress on the problem in hand, it matters little to
him whether it carries him across the boundary between two
recognized academic disciplines or indeed whether there *is* any
generally acceptable or satisfactory way of defining such a boundary.

In his 1958 preface to the English edition of *The Logic of Scientific
Discovery*, Popper, after reaffirming that 'there is no such thing as an
essence of philosophy, to be distilled and condensed into a definition',
goes on to say, 'A definition of the word "philosophy" can only have
the character of a convention, of an agreement'.[4] In other words, the
boundaries of what is properly called philosophical are a matter of
decision rather than discovery, the collective decision of those
concerned in such matters presumably – and a decision which could
vary from one generation, or one environment, to another. We *agree*
about what for us is to count as philosophy. And, again, this agreement

is a comparatively unimportant one – unless, as Popper goes on to warn us, it imposes needless restrictions on the range of topics or problems that members of the philosophical profession are prepared to tackle.

Such an appeal to convention requires, however, some qualification. We shall find the notion of convention cropping up in various forms and contexts throughout our discussion, but a few preliminary points may be made here. First, there is no simple either–or distinction to be drawn between decision and discovery. We can only make, teach or use conventions by exploiting the human capacity to recognize non-conventional relationships. For example, we teach an infant, as his first word, the use, say of 'cat' to indicate a certain species of domestic animal. And in so doing we teach him a convention. But we can only do so if he is able to recognize, without benefit of conventions, the similarities between the sounds we make on the various occasions when we say 'cat' to him, and likewise the similarities between the things we point to when we say it – similarities which are, perforce, non-conventional, simply *there* for him and us to discover. And while it is undoubtedly right to insist on the importance of convention in determining which similarities – or other relationships which are likewise non-conventional – are exploited, and how they are exploited, in the development of our language, we have to remember that all conventions are necessarily thus grounded in the non-conventional. Hence, it would seem that, even if we accept Popper's point that the definition of 'philosophy' can only be a matter of convention or agreement, we can still give our layman the kind of answer he wants to his question about the nature of philosophy – i.e. an indication of whatever features current convention has agreed shall distinguish what is to count as genuine philosophy from what is not – and spare him a lecture on his naiveté.

Also – though this is not the place to discuss the issue at any length – it is hard to accept some of the implications of the 'social contract' view of meaning suggested by such talk of conventions and agreements. No one is likely to suppose that there is literally a formal agreement, drawn up at some gathering of those suitably qualified, which fixes, at least for the time being, the definition of 'philosophy', or any other word. But even to say it is *as if* there were such an agreement is to imply, among other things, that the correct use of the word, and hence the range of things to which we can properly apply it, is something predetermined for us by what is the done thing, or the accepted thing, among those who use it already. In other words, learning to use a word correctly is like learning etiquette, or learning how to participate in some ritual, ceremony, or traditional game, the rules of which may never actually have been written down but are none the less widely understood and obeyed; and the learner masters them by taking careful note of what is done and approved by those more experienced than himself, and modelling his behaviour on theirs.

But although our use of, say, the word 'philosophy' is powerfully influenced by what our predecessors have done with it – and indeed has to be if we are to make ourselves understood – these analogies are, at least, over-simple and over-restrictive. Their chief disadvantage, for our present purposes, is that they focus attention too exclusively on the relation of *similarity*. To model our use of the word 'philosophy' on that of our mentors would be, presumably, to use it of things similar to those of which they use it, or, more specifically, sufficiently similar to pass muster with whatever audience we have in mind. (By the same token, if we wish to embark on careers as philosophers, properly so called, we should do things similar – in subject matter, method or whatever – to those that have been done by people commonly recognized as philosophers in the past.) And the only criterion of *rightness* of use would be the achievement of the appropriate degree of similarity. Conventionalism thus understood is to this extent conservative, an application of the principle of doing what was done the last time, or at any rate something as like it as possible.

But clearly similarity, (to any degree or in any respect) to some approved exemplars is not our only (and perhaps it is not even our most likely) reason for calling some piece of research or writing philosophical. Suppose, for example, we have a generation of philosophers who are predominantly metaphysical in the grand manner, developing from *a priori* principles systems purporting to cover the whole of reality – and then there is a reaction in which their successors attack the entire enterprise from the standpoint of radical empiricism or linguistic analysis. Now, granted that we call the work of this second generation 'philosophy' also – though we can of course imagine some diehard metaphysicians who would question its right to the title – it is clearly not on grounds of *similarity*, in subject matter or method, to what went before. Rather it is on grounds of *relevance*. A metaphysician, or anyone interested in his work, must take account of any serious study of the foundations of knowledge, language, or anything else, which challenges the very feasibility of metaphysics.

The positivist or the linguistic analyst has something to say which is vitally relevant to the metaphysician's characteristic concern, has posed a question which he cannot refuse to answer. This, surely, is why we group them together as practising the same discipline, or working in the same field of interest, and why, even if we belonged to the generation for which metaphysics provided the standard exemplars of philosophy, we should regard such reactions as philosophy also − not because we have noted any similarity between them.

Doubtless there are many other grounds as well for grouping together works that are *prima facie* very different under the single heading of philosophy. And if our layman asked, as he might well do, why the works of, say, Descartes, Hume, Hegel, Nietzsche and Wittgenstein are all called philosophy, the only adequate answer would be to trace for him the specific historical links between them. The only justification for the claim that Descartes and Wittgenstein, for example, were working withing the same discipline lies in the history of the development of European thought between the early seventeenth and the early twentieth centuries. Sometimes of course an appeal to similarities *would* be the right answer, or part of it − for example, if we were asked why ethics and aesthetics are parts of a single discipline. But the points to be made are that the unifying relationships are too many and too complex to be reduced to a neat one-sentence formula, and that simply to say it is a matter of convention is of little help. (We may notice also in this connexion how we should not account for the emergence of psychology or of mathematical logic as disciplines distinct from philosophy in terms either of the discovery of new essences, *or* of the making of new conventions − declarations of academic independence, as it were. Rather we should have to show how lines of research with a common point, or area, of origin diverge until exponents of one have (almost) nothing to say which is relevant to the professional concerns of exponents of the other, when they no longer have to take account professionally of each others' results, and stop arguing with each other, when, to use a fashionable modern term, dialogue between them ceases. It is then, roughly speaking − and we can only speak roughly here − that we begin to think of them as working in different disciplines.) So, to the general enquiry about what is or is not philosophy, it would seem that the safest and most satisfactory response we can give is to direct the enquirer to a fairly detailed history of thought, and leave him to it for some considerable time.

**2**

Such an account of the unity of philosophy, trying as it does to do justice to its essentially complex and loosely-knit structure, preserves a substantial measure of *freedom* for philosophers to react to earlier thought in whatever way seems to them most promising. And doubtless this freedom is what Popper wants primarily to insist on when he denies that they are bound by any permanent essence of their chosen discipline, and speaks instead – though for the reasons just indicated rather misleadingly – of conventions or agreements. It is, as we shall see, a characteristically Popperian view that in the development of any human interest, theoretical or practical, there is at every stage this element of choice, and hence an impossibility of predicting its future character and progress from its past. And philosophy is no exception.

But to what elements in earlier thought does any particular philosopher, or school of philosophy, react? Popper's central thesis, in the address quoted earlier, is that, if we are to avoid a descent into pedantry and triviality, these must extend a long way beyond the usual content of university courses in philosophy. For

every philosophy, and especially every philosophical 'school', is liable to degenerate in such a way that its problems become practically indistinguishable from pseudo-problems, and its cant, accordingly, practically indistinguishable from meaningless babble. This, I shall try to show, is a consequence of philosophical inbreeding. The degeneration of philosophical schools in its turn is the consequence of the mistaken belief that one can philosophize without having been compelled to philosophize *by problems which arise outside philosophy* – in mathematics, for example, or in cosmology, or in politics, or in religion, or in social life ... *Genuine philosophical problems are always rooted in urgent problems outside philosophy, and they die if these roots decay.*[5]

Hence an education which (unlike Popper's own[6]) encourages the student to concentrate on 'pure philosophy', and does not equip him to trace its origins in other fields of interest defeats its own purpose. (What do they know of philosophy who only philosophy know?) We may recall here Collingwood's theory that it is impossible to find out what someone meant by his statements, however lucidly they may be expressed, unless we know first what questions these statements were intended to answer.[7] And, according to Popper, if a student is introduced to the writings of Plato or Aristotle, Descartes or Kant, in isolation from the whole cultural and indeed political and religious situation within which they worked, and which gave rise to the questions they were trying to answer, then however assiduously he studies, he has little hope of understanding them. And, given the way in which philosophy is usually taught,

the student's chance of discovering the extra-philosophical problems (mathematical, scientific, moral and political problems) which inspired these great philosophers is very small indeed. As a rule, these problems can be discovered only by studying the history of, for example, scientific ideas, and especially the problem-situation in mathematics and science during the period in question; and this in turn presupposes a considerable acquaintance with mathematics and science. Only if he understands the contemporary problem-situation in the sciences can the student of the great philosophers understand that they tried to solve urgent and concrete problems.[8]

Without such understanding he simply acquires an elaborate array of intellectual apparatus, but nothing on which to use it. So it is not surprising if he directs it inwards upon his medium of expression, or upon the study of philosophy itself. Nor is it surprising if he is driven to the conclusion that such a study can do little more than clear up confusions of its own making, and has no serious function within the total economy of human thought — a conclusion which raises questions inevitably about why anyone should want to be a philosopher, and, as C. D. Broad once remarked, why any institution should want to employ him if he does.[9]

The specialization of modern university studies must, on this view, be unfavourable to philosophy, imposing on it an autonomy which it cannot sustain. Only in rare circumstances will such studies encourage anyone with the requisite background knowledge to turn his attention to it (unless we are prepared to regard it simply as a second career, or retirement occupation, for scientists, mathematicians, and the like, who have run out of ideas in their own fields). However, it is hard to think of many figures among those generally recognized as major original philosophers of the past who have not had more than an amateur's, or a schoolboy's, knowledge of some field of interest outside philosophy itself. And while Popper's emphasis on mathematics and science may be due in part to his own personal interests, there is little doubt that these have been the most favoured fields, at any rate among European philosophers from Descartes onwards.

It might be said that, however much we insist on the dependence of philosophy of extra-philosophical knowledge, there are still several of its traditionally recognized branches for which anyone with a reasonable standard of general education, academic or otherwise, has sufficient expertise. For example, we are all (presumably) moral beings, familiar with the making of moral choices and moral judgements, and this is all the relevant background knowledge an intending moral philosopher can have. We have all, as a necessary condition of being able to discuss any philosophical problem, as much proficiency in the use of language as we need for the philosophy of language. If we share P. F. Strawson's view that the chief concern of metaphysics is with the 'massive central core of human thinking which has no history . . . categories and concepts which . . . are the commonplaces of the least refined thinking'[10] we must all be equipped for metaphysics as well. And, however ignorant we may be of systematic science, we must be familiar with the basic processes of exploring and finding out about our environment, and of making and assessing claims to knowledge and truth, i.e. sufficiently qualified to cope with epistemology (or a substantial part of it) as traditionally understood.

And doubtless some notable works of what can fairly be called philosophy *have* been written out of a knowledge of human life, or of the world, that owed little to any specific branch of academic learning. But none the less, it is at least open to question whether ethics etc. *are* really as wide open to anyone with nothing more than a modicum of general education, and a clear head, as the previous paragraph suggests. The issue turns on the sort, or sorts, of dependence holding between philosophy and extra-philosophical knowledge.

Much of what we generally recognize as philosophy is, in an obvious sense, secondary to, or parasitic on, some other range of human interests or responses to the world, theoretical or practical. It is not simply philosophy, but philosophy *of* something, of science, mathematics, language, morals, politics, religion, or whatever it may be. The actual practitioner of science, say, or politics is perforce *using* a complex range of intellectual equipment, concepts, methods, presuppositions, standards, values; but even when he is using it skilfully and successfully he may, to use a well-worn analogy, be as little aware of it as he is of the bones and muscles on which his physical activity depends. Such a range of equipment is itself quite often referred to as 'a philosophy' – when we speak, for example, of the philosophy underlying a certain policy, or way of life, or of a political party rethinking, or needing to rethink, its philosophy. In this sense, no-one, whatever his field of interest, has a choice between having a philosophy and doing without, but only between having an implicit and having an explicit one. Can philosophy, in the sense of the characteristic activity of professional philosophers, be seen then simply as the *explication* of the philosophies implicit in other human concerns, what we called earlier the systematic cultivation of self-consciousness about out conceptual equipment?

No doubt philosophers *are* often engaged on something of this sort, endeavouring to bring to light and attention the things that workers in other fields simply take for granted. Whence perhaps one popular idea of the philosopher – someone who complicates comparatively straightforward discussions about, say, whether expenditure on space research is ever justified, or whether psychology or sociology can claim to be genuinely scientific, by raising questions like 'Doesn't it depend on what you mean by "justification", or by "scientific", or whatever?' And the clarification of key terms in the relevant vocabularies must, of course, be an important part, even if not the whole, of the process of explication. More generally, the function of philosophy, thus understood, is essentially *descriptive*. The philosophy of science, or morals, or politics, is simply its history – or perhaps sociology or anthropology – with a particular slant, i.e. not primarily concerned to record what is overtly done and said, or in what circumstances or with what result, but rather with how these key terms and concepts are used, with what is taken for granted, with what methods are being used, what criteria of success or failure applied, etc.

Unlike natural science, it is not a matter of delving for new facts, but simply of noticing, and noticing the influence of, things that have always lain open to view. The response that it characteristically seeks from the reader is one of *recognition* – 'Yes that is indeed what we do, even though I have never taken account of it before'. And that such description is the main, if not the whole, business of philosophy has, of course, been widely accepted. This is, in effect, philosophy as characterized in some of the most widely known and influential Wittgensteinian dicta, for example in the *Philosophical Investigations*:

We must do away with all *explanation*, and description alone must take its place . . . The problems are solved, not by giving new information, but by arranging what we have always known.[11]

And, a few pages later:

Philosophy simply puts everything before us, and neither explains nor deduces anything. Since everything lies open to view there is nothing to explain . . . The work of the philosopher consists in assembling reminders for a particular purpose.[12]

Or, even more explicitly, in the *Remarks on the Foundations of Mathematics*:

What we are supplying are really remarks on the natural history of man: not curiosities however, but rather observations on facts which no one has doubted, and have only gone unremarked because they are always before our eyes.[13]

These quotations are worth keeping in mind, for we shall have much to say later about the real points of dispute (and agreement) between Wittgenstein and Popper over philosophy. It is not, as we shall see, that Wittgenstein was an exponent of a brand of 'pure philosophy' – whatever that might be like – which took no account of other disciplines or fields of interest. Obviously there must be something already there, about which to frame descriptions and assemble reminders; and Wittgenstein's technique has, of course, been widely applied, by himself and others, to the fields of various 'philosophies of . . .', of mind, religion, social science, etc. Nor is it that Wittgenstein thought of the exercise as one to be performed merely for its own inherent interest. The reminders are assembled, and the descriptions framed 'for a particular purpose'. Rather, to oversimplify somewhat, we shall find them at odds over what the purpose is, over what is the point or value of embarking on philosophical enquiry at all, and what effects can be achieved thereby.

For Popper, as is evident from the passages quoted earlier, the relationship between, for example, science and its philosophy is *not* simply that the one provides a convenient field for the gratuitous curiosity of the other, but neither needs it nor is affected by it. A philosophy which, in Wittgenstein's phrase, 'leaves everything as it is' would not be worth bothering about. The 'real problems' of philosophy, the 'urgent and concrete' ones, are those forced on it by problems arising within science (or whatever the relevant extra-philosophical field may be). The only important or non-trivial philosophy of a given field is a response to some *crisis* within that field – and hence the relation between them is not a one-way dependence, but rather an inter-dependence. A (serious) essay in philosophy is an attempt to resolve a crisis – and hence presumably it must be judged by its success or failure, first of all in diagnosing the nature of the crisis, and then in finding a way out of it.

But to speak of the philospher's problems as being 'rooted in' or 'inspired by' those of science, mathematics, etc. still leaves it unclear just what kind of problems are characteristically his. After all, there is surely some point in saying that whatever difficulties science may get into, the practising scientists themselves are the best people to deal with them; and it is not altogether easy to picture them as waiting helplessly for a rescue-party of philosophers, even philosophers well versed in the history of science. Part of the answer to this is, once again, that the important differences are between problems rather than professions, that the development of science from time to time gives rise to philosophical problems and that anyone who tackles these, regardless of his professional qualifications or status, is *ipso facto* embarking on philosophy. But this, of course, still leaves unexplained at what points – or if 'points' suggests an exactitude which is here unattainable, in what areas – such problems arise. In trying to answer this, we may start by looking briefly at Popper's examples of philosophical problems, and also at some provided by his own original work.

In the address already quoted, he takes as his first example the Platonic theory of Forms or Ideas, which, he claims:

cannot be properly understood except ... in the context of the critical *problem situation* in Greek science (mainly in the theory of matter) which developed as a result of *the discovery of the irrationality of the square root of two*.[14]

Popper gives an intriguing, if somewhat speculative, account of the origins, and resolution, of this crisis. The principal stages would seem to be something as follows: From a few examples of the role of numbers, or numerical ratios, in musical harmony and in the construction of some simple geometrical figures ('square numbers', 'triangular numbers', etc.) the Pythagoreans had leaped to the decidedly rash conclusion that the essences, or essential natures, of all things were to be sought in their appropriate numbers or ratios. The atomism of Democritus took over, or at any rate shared, the Pythagorean view that the essences of things are very different from their surface appearances, to be discovered by an effort of thought rather than sense-experience. And, whatever appearances there may be to the contrary, all change and development consists essentially in the rearrangement of unchanging atoms. These atoms, and, most importantly, the ultimate elements of the space and time which they occupy, are indivisable finite units; and hence the essence of anything, its structure at any stage of its development, or the successive structures through which it passes in the course of its life-history, are in principle amenable to numerical expression. Thus 'Pythagoreonism and atomism in Democritus' form were both fundamentally based on arithmetic; that is to say, on counting'.[15] Then, at some point in the fifth century, B.C. – its exact history is unknown – came the discovery of *irrationals*, the discovery that for example, the length of the diagonal of a square of unit side, i.e. $\sqrt{2}$, cannot be expressed as a ratio of any two natural numbers, however large. Tradition has it that drastic measures were taken by the Pythagoreans to suppress the demonstration of this thesis, but in the long term it had to be accepted that there were some elements in the field of geometry, and *a fortiori* of cosmology at large, that could *not* be 'based on arithmetic' in the required sense.

According to Popper, it was Plato who realized, or realized most clearly, the implications for science of the discovery of irrationals.

He realised that the purely arithmetical theory of nature was defeated, and that a new mathematical method for the description and explanation of the world was needed. Thus he encouraged the development of an autonomous geometrical method. It found its fulfilment in the 'Elements' of the Platonist Euclid.

It was Plato also who

gave in the *Timaeus* a specifically geometrical version of the formerly purely arithmetical atomic theory; a version which constructed the elementary particles (the famous Platonic bodies) out of triangles which incorporated the irrational square roots of two and of three.[16]

The theory of Forms then, can be seen as a generalization of Pythagoreanism, a continuation of the quest for the underlying essence of things, which has freed itself from the exclusive preoccupation with numbers, and numerical ratios. Triangles incorporating irrationals, and hence irrationals themselves, were specifically admitted to the realm of Forms; and their discovery was one reason, at any rate, for the generalization.

Earlier, in *The Open Society and its Enemies*, Popper had presented the theory of Forms as, in part at least, Plato's response to the political turmoil in the Greece of his time.[17] (There is, of course, nothing inconsistent in the two accounts; Plato might well have intended to kill two problems with one theory.) Plato saw contemporary society as an example of the Heraclitean flux, unending restlessness and change;

indeed Popper suggests that both Heraclitus and Plato, in extending the notion of flux to the whole spatio-temporal order of things, were generalizing from their unhappy experiences of social turmoil. And for Plato at least, this was not merely change but degeneration, a descent into ever-worsening chaos and corruption. But such a process must, presumably, start from something not yet degenerate, from an ideal origin or prototype of society, something like the Golden Age of legend. This is transformed in Plato's philosophy into the Form or Idea of the state – and this in turn into a particular case within the general theory of Forms, according to which *all* the furnishings of the spatio-temporal world are more or less imperfect copies of ideal prototypes. Of this ever-changing spatio-temporal world, only subjective and unrealiable *opinion* is possible; genuine *knowledge* of it is impossible, rather as a definitive map of a network of channels and sandbanks, with change with every wind or tide, is impossible. Parmenides, another major influence on Plato, had already maintained that knowledge could only be of the eternal and unchanging. But he had contrasted the eternal so sharply with the spatio-temporal world of everyday experience as to leave whatever knowledge we might attain of the one with no bearing whatsoever on the other. For Plato, on the other hand, the eternal world is the world of his Forms or Ideas, and this *is* related to the spatio-temporal world, the world of everyday experience, as providing the ideal prototypes or examples which it strives to copy. If we can achieve knowledge of Forms, such knowledge *has* a vital relevance to our dealings with the everyday world; in particular knowledge of the Form of the state, and of qualities like justice, temperance, etc. which it should embody, is the first essential for any programme or reform, any attempt to get back to the original perfection. Knowledge of the ideal is a necessary, even if not a sufficient, condition for its realization. And thus the theory of Forms emerges not, or not only, as an attempt solution of philosophers' problems about the nature of knowledge, but as part of Plato's long-term proposals for dealing with the social and political crises of his time.

Popper goes on to offer, more briefly, Kant's *Critique of Pure Reason* as a further example of a philosophical effort to solve 'an inescapable problem which arose out of the contemporary situation in science'.[18] (The problem in this case, however, seems to have been raised not simply by contemporary science but by a philosophical reaction thereto.) Kant, in common with most of the intellectual world

of his time, and for a century after him, saw in the achievements of
Newton 'a *unique* event . . . in the history of thought, one which could
never be repeated: the first and final discovery of the absolute truth
about the universe . . . Mankind had obtained *knowledge*, real,
certain, indubitable and demonstrable knowledge'.[19] But Kant saw
also the force of Hume's argument that our claim to knowledge of the
universe can have no other basis than particular observations and
experiments, and that it is logically impossible that these should ever
yield indubitable and demonstrable knowledge of universal laws.
Whence the central problem of the *Critique*: How is pure natural
science possible? which, according to Popper, means simply: How is
Newtonian science possible? – a point vital to the understanding of the
whole enterprise, but one which the reader unversed in the history of
thought might well miss. Kant's solution is, of course, that embodied
in his Copernican revolution, i.e. the thesis that knowledge of the
fundamental structure of the world of experience is possible because
the experient mind is such that it does not merely *discover* this order
piecemeal from particular observations, but *imposes* it upon all
contents of experience. And once we have discovered, as Kant believed
himself to have done, what that imposed structure is, then we can
claim with certainty that all phenomena must conform to it, simply
because we cannot see them otherwise.

The problems which Popper himself tackled in his first major work,
part of which became *The Logic of Scientific Discovery*, were closely
related to that of the *Critique*. The work was, he tells us, 'devoted to
two problems – the problems of induction and of demarcation [i.e. of
science from non-science or pseudo-science] – and their
interrelation'.[20] (Whence its original title – *The Two Fundamental
Problems in the Theory of Knowledge*.) We shall of course have much
more to say about it in later chapters, but for the moment we are
concerned simply to notice how it also can be presented as a
philosophical response to an extra-philosophical crisis. Popper
describes very lucidly the situation in which he first began to think
about these problems as a young student in Vienna during the chaotic
period after the First World War and the collapse of the Austrian
Empire, 'a time of upheavals, though not only political ones',[21] when

the air was full of revolutionary slogans and ideas, and new and often wild
theories. Among the theories which interested me Einstein's theory of
relativity was no doubt by far the most important. Three others were Marx's

theory of history, Freud's psycho-analysis, and Alfred Adler's so-called individual psychology.[22]

Popper was closely associated with Marxists of various political shades and parties, and for a brief period regarding himself as a Marxist. ('The encounter with Marxism was', he tells us, 'one of the main events in my intellectual development'[23] – and we shall see the force of this statement later on.) The impact of Freud and Adler appears to have been of less importance for Popper personally, despite the experience of working (as an unpaid part-time assistant) in Adler's child-guidance clinics, but they still presented a challenge to man's whole view of himself and his motivations, and to his claims to rationality, that had to be met.

For our present purpose, however, the important point is that the exponents of these theories claimed for them the status and prestige of *science*. The various diagnoses of existing human ills offered by Marxism, psychoanalysis and individual psychology, and their various policies and prescriptions for improvement, were professedly grounded, not merely on dreams or ideals or what human life might or should be like, but on the scientific study of what it is like. If it could be sustained, this claim was obviously an important one, since a genuinely scientific analysis of a situation, and any predictions or prescriptions based thereon, demands acceptance by every rational being as such, regardless of his preferences or individual interests. But this claim was just what Popper found increasingly hard to accept – and hence his search for the lines of demarcation between genuine science, as represented by the work of Einstein, and these suspect claimants to the title. Accordingly to a widely accepted view, science was distinguished by its inductive method, by its patient accumulation of observational data in support of its generalizations. But, in the first place, Popper accepted that Hume, despite his critics, had been fundamentally right in pointing out that such data can never be logically sufficient to establish the truth of an unrestricted generalization, and that, if science as such is committed to using them thus, its foundations are permanently insecure. Also, the Marxist or the psychoanalyst (or indeed the astrologer) has no difficulty in compiling impressive lists of observational data favourable to his characteristic theses – and in showing that apparently unfavourable data are not really so. It was this last point, this invulnerability, or capacity to explain anything whatsoever, that Popper seized on as separating such theses from genuine science. A genuinely scientific thesis must put itself at risk; it must have implications, the more detailed and precise the better, about just what the observational data would be, under specific conditions, and if the data are otherwise, then it must be scrapped or modified. This was the condition that Einstein's theory satisfied, and the other theories mentioned failed to satisfy. Quite generally '*the criterion of the scientific status of a theory is its falsifiability, or refutability or testability*'.[24] Science has to abandon any claim to be a body of truths established once and for all; its theories can at best have the status of well-tested conjectures rather than established truths. And the science, or scientific knowledge, of any period of history can be nothing more than those conjectures that have thus far survived systematic attempts at refutation. The value of this demarcation lies not only, or primarily, in its inherent interest as a possible answer to a time-honoured philosophical problem, but in the light it throws on such questions as 'Is Marxism (or whatever) really a science?' and 'What authority would it have even if it were?'

There is little difficulty in seeing Popper's major contributions to the philosophy of politics, *The Poverty of Historicism* and *The Open Society and its Enemies*, as written in response to a related but even more acute crisis, presented by the rise of totalitarian regimes in several major European states, and, more immediately, the outbreak of the Second World War. Popper's native Austria had been occupied by the Nazis, and Popper, working in New Zealand, decided that these books were to be his 'war effort'. (It is interesting to note that even at that time he seems to have regarded fascism as a much less serious long-term threat to human freedom than Marxism, and it receives much scantier treatment in the works in question.)

I thought that freedom might become a central problem again, especially under the renewed influence of Marxism and the idea of large-scale 'planning' (or 'dirigism'); and so these books were meant as a defence of freedom against totalitarian and authoritarian ideas, and as a warning against the dangers of historicist superstitions.[25]

Very briefly, their starting-point was an attempt to show how Marxism and fascism alike drew an essential part of their inspiration from *historicism*, i.e. the doctrine that it is the task of the social sciences (in a wide sense) to bring to light general laws of social and political development which, in conjunction with sufficient data about the current situation, would enable us to predict the future course of such developments, somewhat as the astronomer predicts eclipses – and hence that the only policies for action we can reasonably adopt are those aimed at hastening, or lessening the birth-pangs of, the inevitable. Drawing on the basic principles of the theory of knowledge that he had explicated in his earlier work, Popper set himself the task of showing that the whole historicist programme is fundamentally misguided, that the analogy with natural science is a false one, and that it is in principle impossible to discover any general laws which could provide a scientific basis for long-term historical prophecy. (Just how he attempts to do this we shall discuss at length in a later chapter; again, the point here is simply to notice the extent to which Popper's own work exemplifies his view of philosophy as a response to extra-philosophical crises.)

## 3

The examples given are, I hope, sufficient to illustrate what Popper has in mind. It would, of course, be entirely at variance with his anti-essentialist standpoint, from which we started, to suppose that we could derive from these any completely general account of the essential character of philosophy as such − or to set ourselves to discover, by hook or by crook, for every major original work in the history of philosophy, the extra-philosophical crisis to which it was a response. No doubt there are many works widely accepted as meriting this description which would not fit at all readily into the pattern; they may, for example, have been responses to situations in which the most urgent task for philosophy was not the resolution of crises in other fields of interest, but the clearing-up of confusions within philosophy itself. And Popper indeed commits himself only to saying that philosophy, or a particular philosophical 'school', is 'liable to degenerate' through inbreeding, i.e. if it cuts itself off for too long from extra-philosophical stimulation, and is content to generate its own problems.[26] We might perhaps develop his 'root' analogy a little, and suppose that the root outside philosophy may sustain not only the original trunk, but to some extent at least branches growing from it, and twigs from the branches − but that these grow thinner and the fruit on them smaller, the further they are from the root, until sound husbandry eventually requires drastic pruning or re-planting.

We have, at any rate, seen grounds for saying that the crisis-and-response pattern can be traced in *some*, even if not all, important developments in the history of philosophy. (I do not think it at all

unreasonable to include Popper's own achievements in this class.) And
with our examples in mind, we can now return to the topic of the *kind*
of crisis and the *kind* of response in question. No doubt the histories of
both science and politics (to restrict ourselves to the main fields which
the example cover) are marked by a great variety of crises. Indeed, in
politics at least we should risk a charge of irresponsibility if we *ever*
denied that there is a current crisis. But presumably the vast majority
of such crises, and the ways in which they are met (or evaded) belong
*simply* to the histories of science or politics, and provide no – or at any
rate no important – role for philosophy. Reflecting, however, on the
first example quoted, which he himself labels 'Plato and the crisis in
early Greek atomism', Popper comments:

I believe that we can at this stage see fairly clearly why Plato's achievement
(although it has no doubt its physical, its logical, its mixed and its non-sensical
components) was a philosophical achievement . . . What we find in Plato and
his predecessors is the conscious construction and invention of a new
approach towards the world and towards knowledge of the world. This
approach transforms an originally theological idea, *the idea of explaining the
visible world by a postulated invisible world,* into the fundamental instrument
of theoretical science . . . Is this idea about the invisible structure of matter a
physical or a philosophical idea? If a physicist merely *acts* upon this theory, if
he accepts it, perhaps unconsciously, by accepting the traditional problems of
his subject as furnished by the problem-situation with which he is confronted
. . . then I should not call him a philosopher. But if he reflects upon it, and, for
example, rejects it (like Berkeley or Mach), preferring a phenomenological or
positivistic physics to the theoretical and somewhat theological approach,
then he may be called a philosopher.[27]

So again, we have the philosopher presented as someone who
characteristically reflects upon, and presumably attempts to explicate,
those fundamental ideas about, or approaches toward, the world
which the practising scientist simply acts upon, and accepts
unconsciously or implicitly. But in Popper's account of the matter, he
does *not* merely describe the sub-structure of ideas and leave
everything as it is. He undertakes nothing less than 'the conscious
construction and invention of a new approach towards the world and
towards knowledge of the world'. This, obviously, is not merely an
exercise in innovation for its own sake. It is rather something made
urgently necessary by the fact that the actual use, in the practice of
science, of the present approach, the present sub-structure of ideas, has
brought to light some flaw in it, some element of arbitrariness,
incoherence or over-simplicity, and that the further development of

science depends on the discovery of a remedy. A crisis generated, in essential part at least, by such a flaw, one which a scientific practice characterized by the use of the sub-structure in question is *ipso facto* incapable of resolving, but which is resolved by replacement or modification of that sub-structure, becomes, then, a paradigm example of philosophy.

Obviously, such an account leaves a considerable area of indeterminacy between the realm of science proper and that of its 'sub-structure', (or 'fundamental ideas', or 'approaches' towards the world or knowledge). Our practising scientist, at work on a specific piece of research, presumably acts upon, or accepts unconsciously, not only such things as an all-embracing atomistic or phenomenological view of his subject matter, but also many of those findings of earlier science which have long since come to be regarded as elementary and non-controversial, and are presented as such in the basic text-books. These also may on occasion prove to contain flaws of various sorts, generating crises which can be resolved only by fairly radical revisions and re-appraisals. How radical, it may be asked, do they have to be to count as philosophy? But here again the answer is that we are looking for a clear-cut boundary line where none has ever been drawn, or needed to be drawn. What matters is that the crisis should be resolved, (and science freed to continue its development) not in what academic discipline or department this is accomplished. It is, for example, one of the least important aspects of Einstein's achievement whether anyone judges *his* revisions of earlier ideas so radical as to constitute philosophy rather than science. (We can, of course, if we wish, play safe by calling him, as in the title of his 'Library of Living Philosophers' volume, a 'philosopher-scientist'.)[28] By tradition, philosophy concerns itself with those ideas, etc. which are most general and widely applied, those which, if not topic-neutral, are at least highly topic-versatile; as to *how* general and *how* versatile, our only real guidelines (whenever we feel obliged to decide on such matters at all) are the precedents provided by the history of philosophy – and our own discretion in applying them.

For the moment at any rate, the above examples and reflections thereon may suffice as an explication of Popper's 'crisis-and-response' conception of philosophy. But before we go on to consider possible lines of criticism of this conception, I want to return briefly to a point raised earlier, i.e. while we may be able to demonstrate fairly convincingly such interactions between philosophy and science or politics, at various crucial points in their development, can we trace a similar pattern of relationships in, say, moral philosophy or in substantial areas of metaphysics and epistemology? Here of course we have to keep in mind the warnings given a few pages back about the danger of generalizing from a small group of examples, and setting out to find a suitable extra-philosophical crisis for every major philosophical work, a danger increased by the fact that history often leaves us room for speculation about the motivation − or the 'real' motivation − behind a given work. In some of those branches of philosophy, which *prima facie* appear to provide scope, or refuge, for the philosopher who cannot claim to be more than an intelligent amateur in any field but his own, we may well find no trace at all of the pattern in question. For example, Strawson's 'descriptive metaphysics'[29] almost by definition precludes revisions or innovations for any purpose; its aim (apart from inherent interest) is rather to show that certain earlier revisions, like Cartesian dualism, were for various reasons unnecessary or unworkable. Strawson's 'central core of human thinking which has no history' presumably has no crises either, and comes under no pressure from crises arising nearer to the periphery. And something similar holds of much that is taught as theory of knowledge (− though Popper would argue here that a theory of knowledge which separates itself from the philosophies of science, mathematics, history, etc. i.e. the philosophies of all our systematic programmes of increasing knowledge, thereby abandons all the important problems about it, and serves only to exemplify the degeneration of philosophy). Ethics, however, may be in a different position. For it is at least plausible to suppose − even if impossible to demonstrate − that major contributions to ethical theory *are* made in response to crises generated by, for example, encounters between cultures with widely differing moral codes, or new ideas of man and his role in the world like those introduced by evolutionary theories, or a decline in religious belief which deprives morality of one of its traditional supports. And it might be instructive to test this supposition on, say, utilitarian, or existentialist contributions to ethics.

Again, of course, Popper is not committed to saying that *all* genuine philosophy conforms to the crisis-and-response pattern; and if some branches of the subject, or particular works, generally recognized as philosophy, do not, he has no need to reclassify them. Such conformity is not for him the criterion of philosophy as such. It does, indeed, seem to be his criterion of what is *important* in philosophy, so that to say that the most important philosophical works are responses to extra-philosophical crises is in effect an analytic truth rather than an historical generalization. But we can scarcely take exception to this. Importance is relative to some standpoint – important to whom, or for what? And if Popper succeeds in showing that philosophy can sometimes interact, in the way indicated above, with other interests and disciplines, and can play and indispensable role in the economy of human thought, instead of merely satisfying aimless curiosity, or solving puzzles of its own making, we cannot quarrel with him for regarding this as what makes it important. What matters is whether he *does* succeed in showing that it plays such a role.

**4**

He has, as we have seen, offered historical examples; and we have found more, which seem equally apt for his purpose, in his own work. But could these, perhaps, be presented in quite a different light?

For example, we may grant that the Pythagoreans and atomists of early Greece were seriously upset by the discovery of irrationals – and that philosophy might have helped to resolve their difficulty. But surely, we might go on to argue, what they needed in the way of philosophy was clarification of the scope and limits of the different disciplines or fields of interest in question, clarification of what separated arithmetic (at any rate as they understood it) from geometry, mathematics in general from natural science, and science from metaphysics and religion. More specifically, they needed someone to point out the inherent dangers of inductive generalization (as well as the extreme rashness of the one that seems to have produced the number theory in the first place,) and, best of all perhaps, a Greek Popper to point out that any generalization about the nature of reality, or of any part thereof, can only have the status of a conjecture, and that a refuting case, far from being deplored, should be welcomed as a stimulus to more adequate conjecture. If the philosophy of the time had been capable of drawing such lines of demarcation, no doubt the gains to Greek thought would have been considerable; the discovery of irrationals would have ceased to be a disaster, and become merely an interesting development in pure mathematics; and research in this and other fields would have been free to pursue its proper course unhampered by misunderstandings about what that course was. But the Platonic theory of Forms, if, or in so far as, it is simply the Pythagorean number theory doctored to allow for the awkward irrationals, fails to diagnose the real sources of the difficulty. It may have given some help to geometry by releasing it from the arithmetical straight-jacket, but it still leaves natural science looking for the wrong things in the wrong direction, i.e. for eternal truths enshrined in the realm of Forms, rather than for likely conjectures to be tested by systematic observation.

Again, we might say, the idea that genuine knowledge can only be of an eternal, unchanging realm is simply the product of mis-analysis of the concepts of knowledge and change – and that the best service philosophy could render here would be an attempt at correct analysis. There are serious misunderstandings also underlying the notion that the Form or Idea of the State is something there to be discovered, by any process of analysis, or that, once discovered, it is in any way authoritative on questions of how human societies ought to organize themselves, or that it embodies an ideal towards which actual societies must progress, or from which they have degenerated. Here again a Greek Popper would have been invaluable, this time to call attention to the errors of essentialism and historicism, and to the vital differences between natural and social science. But the Theory of Forms, as presented in the example in question and as Popper goes on to point out, is merely a product, and a further source, of such errors.

As for the example of the Kantian theory of knowledge, though Popper denies that the problem it purports to solve is a 'linguistic puzzle' or a 'pseudo-problem', he does admit that it is a 'mistaken problem'.[30] The mistake in question was over what science, or more specifically, Newtonian science, had achieved; it lay in supposing that the characteristic results of such science were established truths of unlimited generality. And when Hume showed that induction from particular observations is theoretically incapable of establishing the truth of such generalizations, there was clearly a problem about how it *was* established, the problem which Kant set himself to answer. But once we have realized, with Popper's help, that the generalizations of science are *not* established truths, but merely conjectures which can be falsified but never conclusively verified, then Kant's problem disappears. If he had been able to see more clearly what science actually did – though no doubt Popper is right in allowing that it would have been very difficult for him to do so at that comparatively early point in the history of modern science – he might have saved himself the trouble.

In short, the tasks which philosophy could usefully have performed in these historical situations, as distinct from the tasks it actually attempted, were, roughly speaking, those assigned to it by Wittgenstein in his later works. (We have to keep in mind, however, that Wittgenstein was as reluctant as Popper to set out the essence of philosophy in a formal definition. We must rely for guidance on his various examples and aphorisms, and where these lead us is by no means always beyond dispute.) The characteristic Wittgensteinian sources of philosophical confusions and problems are clearly in evidence – mistaken ideas about how certain philosophically sensitive terms actually function in discourse, failure to distinguish clearly between the rules and objectives of different language-games, and hence mistaken assimilation of game *A* to (the perhaps superficially similar) game *B*, with resultant problems when we discover that players of *A* cannot keep the rules or realize the objectives of *B*. And the only way to deal with such problems is not to tackle them again as originally stated, and hope to show still greater ingenuity than our predecessors in solving them, but rather to go back and ask whether such problems need ever have arisen in the first place, or whether if we take sufficient care to expose and avoid mistakes like those mentioned, they simply no longer arise. If the criterion of a 'real' problem is that it is *not* one generated by mistakes about how some elements of our linguistic equipment actually function in discourse, and can *not* be dissolved by the exposure of such mistakes, then it has yet to be shown that there are 'real' philosophical problems.

Popper of course insists, both in the address on philosophical problems and in his autobiographical essay, in explicit opposition to Wittgenstein, that there *are* real philosophical problems, and that an interest in such problems is his sole reason for being a philosopher. In the latter work he records that some exchanges in this topic between himself and Wittgenstein at the Moral Sciences Club in Cambridge in 1946, led (on the part of Wittgenstein) to heated words and door-slamming.[31] A calmer discussion might, however, have brought to light a considerable measure of agreement. And, before we go on to try to specify in general terms the relationship between them, it is highly interesting and instructive to notice how our examples of Popperian philosophy, drawn from Popper's own original work, can equally well be presented as almost classic examples of Wittgensteinian philosophy.

Thus, in the field of philosophy of science, Popper was faced with one of the time-honoured philosophical problems, 'the problem of induction', on which his predecessors had expended much time and ingenuity without discovering any satisfactory solution. His response was, in essence, that it was both futile and unnecessary to tackle the problem in the form in which it was traditionally stated. Hume had shown once and for all that inductive generalization was in principle incapable of performing the task assigned to it. But contrary to what earlier philosophers supposed, this is no reflection on the credentials of science, for science simply does not deal in such generalizations. Its characteristic use of sentences of the 'All *xs* are *ys*' form may look on the surface like (purported) statements of established fact; but more careful examination shows that their real function is to formulate conjectures, the truth of which can not and need not ever be established. The traditional problem of induction is thus shown in effect to have arisen from a misunderstanding of how certain key sentences in works of science function. Once this has been clarified the problem ceases to trouble us.

Obviously, when put in these terms, Popper's treatment of the problem accords very closely with our general outline of Wittgenstein's account in his later works of the role of philosophy. And obvious parallels can be shown with specific examples of Wittgensteinian thinking, for instance in the field of philosophy of religion. There have been long-standing problems over (purported) theological statements about the existence and nature of a deity, problems about how, or whether, such statements could be verified − or, for that matter, falsified. They were not about any possible contents of experience; and, when considered in the role of quasi-scientific hypotheses to explain features of the world of experience, it was hard to avoid the conclusions that they fulfilled this role very badly − or, more strictly, that they could not fulfil it at all. The Wittgensteinian solution, as illustrated in well-known essays by Braithwaite[32] and Phillips,[33] and in some fragmentary but intriguing notes from Wittgenstein himself,[34] was not to seek still more ingenious ways of establishing the truth, or falsity, of the statements in question. Rather it was to point out that, despite appearances to the contrary, they did not play, in actual religious discourse, the roles here assigned to them. Instead they should be seen as formulations of a commitment or dedication to a certain way of life and a certain pattern of values − or, alternatively, of a kind of overall, guiding 'picture' of reality and man's place within it. Either way, they lack truth-values, and no question of their verification or falsification arises. Again, once we have corrected the initial error about how the crucial sentences function in their appropriate context of discourse, (the language-game which is their original home) the traditional problem is seen as simply a product of misunderstanding, and no longer demands an answer as it stands.

Something of the same pattern can be traced in Popper's critique of historicism. Here also a long sequence of distinguished thinkers are alleged, in effect, to have let themselves be misled into the error of assimilating, on the basis of surface similarities, social science to natural science. Hence the quest for general principles of development which would enable us to predict, say, revolutions as the astronomers predict eclipses, seemed in principle feasible. Popper undertakes to show that it is not, by pointing out the inherent differences in their subject matter, which make it impossible for social science to set itself the same objectives as natural science, or to reproduce the special conditions under which the natural scientist can (sometimes) make unconditional long-term predictions. The refutation of historicism hinges on the claim that, given a sufficiently careful description of the relevant disciplines, and drawing of the demarcation-lines between them, the temptations of historicist programmes disappear.

## 5

Clearly, then, our examples, including those drawn from Popper's own work, can be shown to vindicate Wittgenstein's view of philosophy as readily as Popper's. Even if we grant the stimulus provided by some extra-philosophical crisis in each case, it would still seem that the only responses which are both recognizably philosophical *and* useful in resolving the crises, are simply clarifications of misunderstandings about how the relevant pieces of linguistic equipment function, or how the relevant language-games are played. When philosophy tries to offer anything more, for example the Platonic theory of Forms, or the Kantian system, then, according to Popper's own account, it merely multiplies confusions. In effect, for Popper and Wittgenstein alike, the task of good philosophy is to drive out bad, to expose and correct the errors that have given rise to its problems and the host of strange theories devised to solve them.

Yet it would, I think, be grossly unfair to Popper to present him as nothing more than an unwitting disciple of Wittgenstein, or to treat his criticisms of Wittgenstein's conception of philosophy as merely mistaken. If there is a sense in which Popper's work illustrates that conception, there is a sense also in which it develops it, and gives it a new interest and importance. How it does so becomes increasingly clear when we start to consider the various ways in which philosophy might set about the essentially *descriptive* task which Wittgenstein assigns to it. For any subject-matter, after all, there are indefinitely many descriptions; and which we count as good or bad, correct or incorrect, depends, in important part at least, on the purpose for which we undertook the description in the first place. So when we require of philosophy 'description alone' or how the philosophically sensitive terms or sentences function, of how the relevant language-games are played, we still leave open the question of what sort of description is in order here, or what is to count as correct or incorrect. And it is here, I think – to put the point somewhat dogmatically – that we are liable to get a better and more illuminating answer from Popper than from Wittgenstein or any of his immediate followers.

The impression which, at any rate, is commonly gained from these is that philosophy, i.e. good or regenerate philosophy, is little more than a humble exercise in linguistic sociology, patiently observing and noting how this or that term is used, this or that language-game played, taking care not to criticize or correct but, in the famous Wittgensteinian phrase, to 'leave everything as it is'. There is simply no standpoint from which philosophy *can* criticize or correct; how the term is commonly used, or the game commonly played is *ipso facto* the right way, since there is no other criterion of rightness. Specific errors can, of course, be made; but the philosopher has no special competence to notice or correct them, and there is no external standpoint from which he can criticize any use or practice as a whole, no Archimedean point, as it were, from which he can try to shift it. Indeed, his present descriptive task is made necessary by the attempts of earlier (bad or unregenerate) philosophy to take language away from the everyday tasks it performs quite adequately, and send it off on ill-advised holidays. But once we have identified these tasks, and learnt to confine our language to them, then we should be able to stop philosophizing,[35] since the traditional problems no longer arise, and the traditional solutions lose their point.

Compared to the tasks it set itself in the past, this doubtless seems a timid and unexciting programme for philosophy; and we can sympathize with Popper's protest that, if he thought this were really all it could achieve, he would have no interest in being a philosopher.

Yet, at the same time we cannot deny the reasonableness or the importance of the reminder that, whatever originality we may aspire to in our view of the world or of our own position within it, we are still perforce users of a common language, and that every work of philosophy is part of the literature of such a language. And – if we lay aside the possibility of some kind of inexpressible mystical vision – there is no way in which our thinking can ever escape from our language and its limitations. In the English-speaking philosophical world at least, it is Wittgenstein more than anyone else who has stimulated this self-consciousness about our role as language-users, who has, we might say, replaced the Cartesian starting-point 'I think' with 'I speak'. And while from 'I think' nothing may follow but my own existence as a thinking being, when we work out the requirements for developing, teaching and using a language, we find the range of possible world-views severely restricted and pedestrian commonsense reasserting itself. Thus, for example, as a Cartesian I may consider, as a possibility at least, that I am perhaps the only thing that there is, that all that I call the world may be mind-dependent in the way that dreams and illusions are. But as a Wittgensteinian I find such speculations immediately halted by such questions as: 'Is speech not necessarily a *social* phenomenon, so that as a condition of being a speaker (and having the means of framing solipsistic hypotheses) I must *ipso facto* be one among a community of language-users?' and 'Has "I" not got the function of directing attention to one thing among many, distinguishing the I from everything that is not I, so that "I am everything that there is" robs it of its function?' and 'Would it not be sheer misuse of terms like "dream" and "illusion" to apply them indiscriminately to all experiences?' and 'In short, from "I speak" does there not follow, not merely "I am" but "The world and society are as well" – or, more simply, "I speak, therefore we are"?'

We need not pursue these questions here – though we shall find ourselves later on faced with similar questions about the conditions for saying the things that we say, and meaning what we mean thereby. The point of introducing them here is simply to remind ourselves that there is much more than mere pedantry, or lack of speculative boldness and imagination, underlying this Wittgensteinian preoccupation with language. Words do *not* always travel well between familiar and unfamiliar contexts. Meanings *can* be lost in transit. And it is at least a useful policy, if nothing more, to check, in the case of common words transported into the rarefied atmosphere of philosophical problems and theories, whether they have been able to keep their meanings intact or not. And doubtless the finding is, in some cases at least, that they have not; that with familiar words and impeccable grammar we are quite literally talking nonsense. And hence, despite the derogatory sound of the title, the value of our 'sociology of language'. (We may perhaps usefully recall here how sociology, as ordinarily understood, while offering no adventurous plans for social revolution or an ideal state, may still demonstrate the complex structure of society, the interdependence of its elements and the difficulty of altering one without another, in a way that provides salutary warnings, if nothing more, for would-be revolutionaries or utopians.)

None the less, there are, clearly, some difficulties and ambiguities about the Wittgensteinian programme as thus outlined. These indeed could, and frequently have, provided material for substantial treatises in their own right; but we may be content here to note briefly a few points relevant to our immediate purpose. Consider, for example, the guiding *analogies* in the *Investigations*, the comparisons of language to a set of tools to be used, or a set of games to be played (replacing the famous 'picture' analogy which dominated the *Tractatus*). That they represent important insights is undeniable. But, quite generally, the point of drawing an analogy, of asking someone to think of $x$ as being like $y$ or $z$, has to be that $y$ and $z$ are in some way simpler or easier to understand than $x$. (Otherwise how could they assist our efforts to understand $x$?) Hence, they must, it would seem, *lack* some features which $x$ has, must in some respects be more limited or less subtle. So, while it is no doubt illuminating to consider the ways in which speaking a language is like using tools or playing games, it is also advisable to consider the ways in which they are not. For example, a game like chess or tennis is governed, and in part at least identified, by a set of *rules*, specifying the required equipment, the permissible moves, the criteria of success and failure, etc. The rules are known and observed by any competent player as such, taught to beginners, and set out comprehensively and authoritatively in the official handbooks of the game. And clearly, any correct description of the game must include a statement of these rules (or at least the most important of them). And we could in principle arrive at such a description by observing and questioning competent players, noting what instructions they offer beginners – perhaps if we are very conscientious taking on the role of beginners ourselves – or consulting the official handbook, or the governing body of the game. But if, as philosophers of science or religion, we set out to describe correctly the relevant language-games here, how much of this can we expect to hold? Granted that these are *disciplined* activities, is it merely an innocuous expansion of this to call them rule-governed activities – where this implies that, like other games just mentioned, they have each a distinctive set of rules specifying permissible moves, objectives, etc.? Does competence here also depend on knowing and observing such a set of rules? Could we, even in principle, draw up a comprehensive statement of them; and could we arrive at such a statement by observing and questioning practising scientists or believers, consulting the classics of science or theology, taking courses in elementary science or attending Sunday school? It will, I think, become clear when we reconsider our examples with such questions in mind, that, whatever the parallels, the task of describing how science or religion is practised differs in some very important respects from that of describing how a game is played.

Or, again, how like is it to describing the use of a set of tools? There are various questions we can ask about how something is used – for what purpose, in what way, in what circumstances, etc. But when we are concerned with the use of pieces of *linguistic* equipment, with terms or sentences, we have to draw one crucial distinction, which is absent when we are dealing merely with saws or hammers. When we ask 'How is this used?' we can be thinking either of our (convention-sanctioned) criteria for its correct use, or about the effects we produce, the claims or commitments we make, when we use it. For example, if we ask how our sentences embodying unlimited generalizations – those of, or reducible to, 'All $x$s are $y$s' form – are used in scientific discourse, then it may well be correct to reply that we make statements by the use of such sentences when we have a suitably lengthy and unbroken run of favourable experimental results (observations of particular $x$s which are $y$s) and, perhaps, when it is consistent with the main body of our scientific theories as well. Something of this sort may well be our *criterion* for such use of the sentences in question, i.e. the set of conditions under which we license ourselves, as it were, to use them thus. But we could reply to the question also by saying simply that we use such sentences to claim that every $x$ is a $y$, that this is the *commitment* we undertake in using it. And the distinction is, philosophically, a highly important one. For there is, clearly a logical gap between criterion and commitment here; the one could be satisfied but the other not, i.e. if all observed $x$s were indeed $y$s etc., but some unobserved *x*s were not. And it is in this gap that scepticism takes root. Other similar examples can readily be found. We may explain gently to, say, our Cartesian sceptic how terms like 'dream' and 'waking experience' are used, i.e. the criteria for their proper (conventionally accepted) use. We may point out to him further that without such criteria for distinguishing between the two he could never have formulated his problem in the first place; and hence that his doubts over whether all his experience may not be a dream are self-answering. But may he not reply: 'Yes, I am well aware of the normal criteria, but what worries me is that, when I claim something as part of waking experience, I commit myself to more than simply that the appropriate criterion has been satisfied; my grounds for what I say are doubtless *conventionally* sufficient, but it does not follow that they are *logically* sufficient?'

In philosophy it is, if nothing more, a useful rule of thumb that to every argument there is an equal and opposite counter-argument; and we should not assume that the sceptic has necessarily the last word here. We shall have much to say about scepticism in later chapters. But for the moment we are concerned simply with the bearing these considerations have on the question of what kind of *descriptions* are demanded of philosphy. To return to the example of Popper's account of science: it seems sufficiently clear that, whatever part Popper's knowledge of the history and practice of science may have had in its construction, it is *not* simply a summary of patient observations of what scientists do or say. Take, for example, his central assertion that scientific theories are '*genuine conjectures* – highly informative guesses about the world which although not verifiable (i.e. capable of being shown to be true) can be submitted to severe critical tests'.[36] This is, certainly, presented as a description of science, a statement about what it is actually like. And yet, as is evident from its content and context, it has not been arrived at by noting what scientists do or have done, or by questioning them about what they think they are doing. Popper is presumably well aware that, on the evidence of what scientists actually do or say, there are many scientific theories – like these set out in elementary text-books – which they characteristically treat, and speak of, as established truths rather than conjectures; and that, if the issue were raised, they would certainly want to distinguish between the central core of theories thus taught and treated as established truths, and a (probably much smaller) periphery of those which, because they are new, little-tried, or in various ways off-beat or eccentric, *are* regarded as genuinely conjectural. But Popper is, apparently, quite undismayed by the fact that his account of science is at variance, not only with that given by earlier philosophers, but also with that accepted, at least tacitly, by the scientists themselves and by the educated public at large over many generations. So whatever descriptive task he is engaged in, it is certainly very different from that of explicating the rules and objectives of chess or tennis.

Perhaps the most striking point of difference is that he is preoccupied, not with what, as a matter of history or sociology, scientists do or profess to do, but what, as a matter of logic, they *can* and *cannot* do. The essential point is not that scientific theories are actually assigned the function of conjectures by those concerned in such matters, but that this is the only function which they (i.e. if they take the form of unlimited generalizations) can justifiably be assigned. The empirical study of nature, by a process of piecemeal observation, *cannot*, logically, establish the truth of unlimited generalizations; but under favourable circumstances it *can* yield conjectures, which stand up to a great deal of testing and which may even be true, though we can never know for certain that they are. Hence, even granted that most scientific theories are not normally presented or treated as conjectures, there are none the less good grounds for saying that this is what they *are*, simply because this is all they can be.

Similar points, we should note, can be made about our Wittgensteinian accounts of the functions of religious discourse. Again, it seems obvious that very few of those who have, down the centuries, engaged in such discourse would themselves have given any such accounts, or would have recognized them as true if some philosophical precursor of Wittgenstein had put them forward. The considerations which give rise to them are not primarily concerned with what believers do, or think they are doing. Rather, the essential point is that statements about a reality transcending sense-experience cannot be verified, or falsified, as those about possible sense-experiences can. And hence, whatever anyone may think about them, they *cannot* function as quasi-scientific hypotheses. But there are other possible functions, like those mentioned above, which they *can* perform.

Is it misleading, then, to call such philosophy 'descriptive' at all? Our examples of Wittgensteinian philosophy of religion have certainly been accused of claiming merely to describe religion when they are in fact proposing its radical reform.[37] And, as we have just seen, the appeal to description, coupled with a too-literal interpretation of the 'game' and 'tool' analogies, is liable to suggest at least misleading models or paradigms of description. But, as we said earlier, the term 'description' can cover a variety of things. We are not, surely, abandoning *de*scription in favour of *pre*scription when we say, in effect, 'No matter what appears to happen, or is thought to happen even by the participants, in this or that field of interest, this is really what does happen'. After all, it is the business of correct description to tell us what really happens, or what is really the case, as distinct from what appears to be the case. And this is what Popper and the Wittgensteinian philosophers of religion alike profess to tell us, i.e. despite all appearances to the contrary, since this is all that scientists, or believers, can do, then *ipso facto* this is what they are really doing. So thus far at least, their descriptive role would seem to be sustained.

None the less, their examples are radically at variance with the idea of philosophy as a humble under-labouring kind of study of how terms are used or language-games played, which it undertakes primarily for the purpose of avoiding its own past errors, and otherwise does not presume to correct or criticize. In a sense, we have still a philosophy which leaves everything as it is; it does not propose to science new topics or techniques of research; or to the churches a new reformation. But there is also a sense in which it is much more willing to interfere in other disciplines and interest than was the older philosophy against which it reacts. That philosophy, broadly speaking, was prepared to take over uncritically, say, the scientists' own conceptions of their discipline, and of the functions of the characteristic formulae used within it. Philosophy then found its task in explicating and attempting to resolve the problems inherent in those conceptions. But whether its conclusions were essentially Humean or Kantian – whether it was content simply to point out to science the logical flaw built into its procedures, or whether it offered to make it logically respectable at a price – there was no question of thinking again about the nature of science or about how its formulae actually did function. Everyone, philosopher, scientist and educated layman alike, knew, or thought he knew, what science was; so the philosopher could go on to puzzle with Kant over how it was possible, or perhaps with Hume over whether it was really possible at all.

Our revised philosophy works in the opposite direction. It starts with these inherent problems, and, in effect, takes them as evidence that we have *all* been wrong about the nature of science. It is not simply a matter of errant philosophers, through ignorance or misguided ingenuity, mistaking something that has been perfectly well understood all along by the practising scientist or his commonsensical lay public. If it is, for example, a mistake to suppose that scientific generalizations (very often) function as purported statements of established truths, then it is a mistake which has certainly been made, at least implicitly, by a great many people other than philosophers. It may create a specific *problem* only, or primarily, for philosophers, since it is they who notice its disquieting consequences and search for a means of avoiding, or living with, them. But they have no monopoly of the initial error. Nor have they a monopoly of its unfortunate effects. However little inclination practising scientists may have to philosophize about science, clearly their work cannot remain permanently unscathed if they start with (even tacit) misconceptions about what they are trying to achieve, what their predecessors have achieved, what they may call in question and what they must accept as established, etc. (Several eminent scientists have, in fact, testified to the influence of Popper, not only in changing their overall picture of their discipline, but in changing their practice of it as well.[38]) And, given the role of science in everyday affairs, it is obviously not a matter of indifference whether the layman treats the content of current scientific text-books the way his ancestors treated Holy Writ; or whether he realizes (if Popper is right) that what the expert tells him on the television screen, or the doctor or psychiatrist in the consulting room, can never have any higher authority than that of a conjecture which has thus far resisted refutation.

It is here that the examples provided by Popper are particularly valuable. They show most clearly that, even if Wittgenstein is right to compare philosophy with therapy, it is none the less much more than the treatment of its own self-inflicted injuries; that it adopts rather than generates the errors which give rise to its characteristic problems; and that these same errors can produce serious crises in extra-philosophical fields of interest. The same lessons can of course be learnt, even if somewhat less explicitly, from our example of Wittgensteinian philosophy of religion. If it is a mistake to suppose that sentences like 'God made the world' or 'God is love' have the function of stating purported truths about reality, then it is a mistake which has certainly been made by many who are wholly innocent of philosophy. And while the systematic exploration of its consequences may as such be philosophy, philosophy is not such an isolated phenomenon that the ordinary believer remains unaffected. He also may be, and indeed often has been, troubled by the lack of sufficient evidence for the truth of his beliefs or by apparent evidence for their falsity; and if such worries arise from a misapprehension about the nature of religious belief, it is obviously important that he should know. So, if it is the philosopher who undertakes the task of clearing up such misapprehensions, what he says has, in principle, a relevance extending well beyond the circle of his professional colleagues.

We can now appreciate the precise sense in which, as Wittgenstein put it, the philosopher's 'description gets its light, that is to say its purpose, from the philosophical problems'.[39] This is something much more specific than merely saying that he approaches his descriptive task with the traditional problems in mind. As we have already noted, he *starts* his examination of science, religion or whatever from an awareness of such problems. And his aim is, in effect, to describe it in such a way that it no longer gives rise to these problems, even at the cost of a radical departure from earlier and widely-accepted descriptions thereof. What counts here as a *correct* description, or an identification of the *real* function of a piece of linguistic equipment is, in brief, one which leaves no room for the time-honoured problems. To go back to what was said earlier about the logical gap between criterion and commitment, we might say that (in some important cases at least) this is achieved by redefining the commitment in such a way as to eliminate the gap. Thus, it is sufficiently obvious that Popper starts from the old problems about induction and its role in science, and that for him the great merit of his conjectures-and-refutations account of science is that it avoids these problems. More specifically, the problems, as we have already noted, arose in the gap between any criterion the scientist could have for saying anything of the form 'All *x*s are *y*s' and the commitment which he, apparently, undertook in saying it. And the solution is, in effect, to let the criterion determine the commitment; if he has logically sufficient grounds only for putting forward conjectures (often, of course, well-informed and well-corroborated conjectures) then *ipso facto* that is what he is really doing, that is all the commitment he really undertakes.

Similarly, if religious discourse, or certain characteristic elements thereof, commits us to assertions about how things are in some transcendent realm, then evidently there is a gap between the commitment and any possible criterion we could have for making it, a gap in which, again, some ancient philosophical problems have taken root. But, if the commitment is simply to a set of values (or a way of life, or a way of seeing or responding to the world) the gap and problems alike disappear. So, since this is the only kind of commitment which, logically, we *can* make in this field of interest, it has to be the one we *really are* making. Other examples can readily be found as well. If statements about someone else's thoughts or interests or desires commit us as to what takes place in a private realm to which he alone can have access, then, clearly, no behavioural criteria can provide us with adequate cover, and we are faced with the Problem of Other Minds. But suppose we take such statements as empirical generalizations about his behaviour or likely behaviour in certain situations; or, more subtly perhaps, we claim that even if thought, desire, or any other 'mental activity' or 'mental state' is not to be identified *with* a certain pattern of behaviour, it is identified *by means of* such a pattern, so that behaviour can, in principle, provide logically sufficient grounds for ascribing it. Or, again, if the task of philosophy itself were to offer us knowledge beyond the reach of science about the structure, origin, or purpose of the world, there are obvious problems about the grounds on which it could possibly do so. But suppose its task is only to 'assemble reminders' or rearrange what we already know, to enable us to see why our apparently deep and intractable problems need never have arisen . . . and so on.

Of course, the object is not simply to fix our descriptions of the relevant fields of interest in the way that makes life easiest for philosophers. The alternative descriptions, however long and widely accepted, *did* have built-in, insoluble difficulties; and, as we have seen, even if only philosophers have directly faced them, they can make their presence felt (and often with serious and far-reaching consequences) in extra-philosophical thought and practice as well. More specifically, in the examples considered at least, we might say that the difficulties arise from logically overreaching ourselves, from attempting to do, or supposing that we can do or have done, what is strictly a logical impossibility (like establishing the truth of an unlimited generalization from particular observational data). And, while doubtless the philosopher *is* attempting to alter, say, the scientist's conception of his own discipline, his presumption in so doing has the justification that it is grounded, not primarily upon considerations about what scientists do or say (about which he almost certainly knows less than they do) but upon essentially *logical* considerations about what can or cannot be done (where he is, or ought to be, on his home ground). Altering the conception of science so as to avoid philosophical problems is thus, *ipso facto*, altering it towards a more realistic appreciation of what can, and cannot, be accomplished within it.

There has, of course, been no lack of critics to argue that these revised accounts of science, religion, etc. are themselves in various ways mistaken or inadequate. And I am not concerned to defend them here. In the following chapters we shall indeed consider at some length the reasons why Popper's conception of science, however valuable an insight it represents, will not do as it stands. And, more generally, we shall find that the programme of bridging the gaps between criteria and commitments runs into serious difficulties. But the immediate point is simply to illustrate an approach to philosophy which (despite their obvious differences in temperament, idiom, extra-philosophical interests, etc.) is in essentials shared by Wittgenstein and Popper. It is to Wittgenstein that we owe its classic statement, especially in the *Investigations*, and hence it can no doubt be properly identified as Wittgensteinian. But it is Popper who has most effectively corrected the impression that such philosophy is perforce a limited and self-absorbed study, endlessly preoccupied with its own medium of expression because it has nothing else to discuss. It is he, we might say, who has added a new dimension to it by showing that, even if it performs only the functions Wittgenstein assigns to it, it still plays an essential role in many, extra-philosophical, fields of interest. To begin with, undoubtedly they appear to represent two rival views of philosophy, clearly and uncompromisingly opposed to each other; and it may be that, as a matter of biography, this is how they saw themselves. But what this discussion has, I hope, shown is that (in the manner of Hegel's dialectic) what appear at first sight simply as opposites can be shown to complement and support each other.

# 2

# *The philosophy of science*

*1*

Science is not a system of certain, or well-established statements; nor is it a system which steadily advances towards a state of finality. Our science is not knowledge (epistēmē): it can never claim to have attained truth, or even a substitute for it, such as probability.

Yet science has more than mere biological survival value. It is not only a useful instrument. Although it can attain neither truth nor probability, the striving for knowledge and the search for truth are still the strongest motives of scientific discovery.[1]

Most of the issues which will concern us in this and the following chapter are raised, at least by implication, in these few sentences. We may start from the one on which all the others ultimately depend, i.e. the role assigned to the concept of *truth*. Despite serious difficulties, which we shall have to discuss at length further on, Popper insists that he has never changed his mind about this. His ideas about the nature of truth have developed importantly, mainly under Tarski's influence – of which more later – but, as the last sentence quoted makes plain, even in this first essay in the philosophy of science, he was clear that, whatever the correct analysis of the concept might be, truth was still the goal of scientific research. Twenty years later we find him again arguing against instrumentalism, and in support of the doctrine of Galileo that 'the scientist aims at a true description of the world, or of some of its aspects, and at a true explanation of observable facts'.[2] And, in his latest major work in this field – 'Our main concern in science and in philosophy is, or ought to be, the search for truth.'[3]

It is this conviction, primarily, that determines his problems about the philosophy of science and the range of possible solutions. Had we been able to accept instrumentalism, or any other theory which held that science was *not* essentially a search for truth, the whole field would have appeared in a very different light. As it is, his efforts are directed by two ideas, simple in themselves but far-reaching in their implications – that science is seeking truth, and that it can never have logically sufficient grounds for claiming to have found it.

Part of the problem had, as we have seen, been given its classic statement by David Hume – notably in the famous third part of Book One of his *Treatise of Human Nature*. Hume has argued in defence of

these two principles, *That there is nothing in any object, considered in itself, which can afford us a reason for drawing a conclusion beyond it*; and, *That even after the observation of the frequent and constant conjunction of objects, we have no reason to draw any inference concerning any object beyond those of which we have had experience*[4]

No doubt these principles were – and have continued to be – rejected or ignored often enough to justify Hume's lengthy defence of them, and his attempts at a psychological explanation of why they are so difficult to accept. But the essential logical point is simple and, it would seem, incontrovertible, i.e. that from the truth of the statement that this particular $x$ is a $y$, or even that every $x$ hitherto observed has been a $y$ (granted that $x$-ness does not logically entail $y$-ness) nothing follows about whether or not any other (hitherto unobserved) $x$ is a $y$, or *a fortiori* whether every $x$ is a $y$.

It is this elementary point of logic, taken in conjunction with the basic principles of an empiricist theory of knowledge, that gives rise to the time-honoured 'problem of induction'. For granted that our only means of finding out about our world is by observation, i.e. the disciplined use of sense-experience, and that all such experience can only be of particular things in particular situations, then our science, in the sense of a systematic or organized body of knowledge about the world, can be developed only by the use of such observations of particulars. But such observations, however assiduously collected and recorded, cannot by themselves furnish logically adequate grounds for prediction about future states of the world, or for unrestricted generalizations. (They cannot even show that the future will *probably* exhibit one feature rather than another, or that a given generalization *probably* holds.) Hence, in so far as it puts forward such predictions and generalizations, science – despite its reputation as a paradigm example of logical thinking – characteristically claims more than it is logically entitled to claim. It walks by faith as much as religion does – and is much less honest and clear-sighted about the need to do so.

Popper is no doubt right in saying that the way in which the problem of induction struck Hume, and his successors over several generations of thinkers, was determined, in important part at least, by the outstanding success of Newtonian physics. It was very difficult not to assume that physics had already yielded established truths of the highest generality. And, on empirical principles, these generalizations, telling us precisely what would happen in any situation that satisfied certain specific requirements, anywhere or at any time, could have no stronger or wider foundation than a handful of observations made in one very small region of space and time. Induction *did* work, and work astonishingly well. The question to be answered was What made it work, what had to be true of the world, or the mind of the observer, or the relation between the two, to account for its success?

We can, of course, follow the line of the Humean sceptic and admit — or even revel in the claim — that there *is* no defensible answer; that we may find a psychological explanation for our confidence in such generalizations, and that without such confidence not only science but everyday life would be practically impossible, but that it simply has no logically adequate basis. And no doubt such scepticism can take some credit for its honesty, for its refusal to fake explanations where none can be found. On the other hand, this is credit very cheaply gained, if we propose to go on making practical use of inductive reasoning even after we have undermined its logical foundations, and if we admit no obligation even to try to revise a view of the world and of ourselves which leaves the success of such reasoning inexplicable. But supposing we admit such an obligation, what form, or forms, could our revision take? It would seem, to put it very briefly, that it must supplement, or reject, the atomism embodied in the first of Hume's principles quoted above, i.e. the idea of a world made up of 'objects' which are logically independent of each other, so that there is no valid inference from the existence of any one such object to the existence of any kind of environment of others, and that we are in effect marooned on the one present at any given moment, with only irrational faith or habit to assure us of the existence of any other. We might, for example, simply supplement such atomism by an appeal to theology, i.e. to the idea of an intelligent and benevolent Deity who imposes order *ab extra* on elements which have no inherent connections with each other. This is the solution which in principle appears to have been adopted by Berkeley, a generation before Hume; and indeed the general idea of using theology to underwrite natural science has a long history.

Alternatively, we might seek the principle of order within the mind of the observer, as in Kant's Copernican revolution, i.e. try to show that the rational mind as such must *impose* certain kinds of order on all its contents of experience; and hence that the world *as experienced* (though not as it is in itself) must invariably exhibit such order, simply because we cannot see it otherwise. Or we might develop a view of the world, and its elements, which replaced Humean atomism with some internal principle of order, as in the various 'dialectical' philosophies of nature, or Whitehead's 'philosophy of organism', i.e. the present situation is seen as something *necessarily* linked to a past and a future, thus furnishing grounds, in the essential nature of the things we are dealing with, for expecting continuity (or continuous development) of characteristics from past to future.

There are thus various doctrines, not obviously incoherent, which appear to provide in principle a means of explaining the successes of induction. They offer us, we might say, the major premises required to make inductive arguments logically respectable – for example, the premise that Divine Providence has so ordered things that the regularities in nature which have occurred in the past will continue to occur in the future.

The Humean sceptic has, of course, lines of counter-attack at his disposal. He can demand to know just what major premises *would* actually serve our purposes? The specimen suggested above is open to objection, since we should not want to claim that *every* pattern or regularity is repeated. But, then, exactly what balance between repetition and novelty do we want, or need, to postulate, and can it reasonably be claimed that belief in Providence is sufficient to guarantee this? (Theism does not manifestly make the world safe for science.) Or, even if we are willing to adopt the whole Kantian apparatus of forms and categories – and accept the limitations of their application to the world of phenomena, with the resultant difficulties over how we can have a *shared* world or a *shared* science, or indeed any kind of inter-subject communication whatsoever – would it perform the task for which it was designed? For example, even granted we cannot but think of the phenomena presented to us as causes and effects, this in itself could not suffice to account for our success in formulating general causal laws. These would require also that the data provided by experience – or some of them at any rate – must fall into classes sufficiently clearly distinguished, and into patterns sufficiently simple and stable, for our recognition. And it is quite conceivable that it should not be so. Hence Kant's system still leaves us, in this respect, at the mercy of experience. (Incidentally, it is not even true to say that if the world of our experience *were* too complex or too rapidly changing for science as we know it, human survival would not be possible either. Most of the patterns and regularities which science has brought to light have after all been just within the grasp of the most gifted human beings, living in environments favourable for research; the rest of the human species, and all other living species, have demonstrated the possibility of surviving indefinitely in a world they are incapable of understanding scientifically.) With regard to the concepts of a world developing dialectically, with the momentum provided by a succession of internal conflicts and their resolution, or of a Whiteheadian world where each phase is essentially a process of self-creation from the material furnished by the past and provides in its turn material for the self-creation of the next generation, these leave us with fundamentally the same problem, i.e. how do these postulated general patterns actually account for the kind of specific patterns which are the concern of science to explore? Is it not a condition of their unrestricted generality that they should be so flexible and loosely defined as to be consistent with virtually any world imaginable?

Further, even if it is granted that one or more of these suggestions, *if true*, would provide the desired guarantee, there are obvious difficulties over how any of them could be shown to be true. According to the sceptic, we have a very restricted choice of methods, in effect the choice of being impaled on one or other of two prongs of a fork. Either these vast generalizations about nature, man and God are grounded on the data of experience, in which case we have once again, and in a particularly obvious form, the problem of the logical inadequacy of such grounds to support the generalizations in question. Any such 'justification of induction' is inevitably circular. Or, alternatively, if what we are doing is giving the results of analysis of our own concepts, no such analysis can yield any information about what concepts are actually instantiated, i.e. about what the world is actually like. Other ways of establishing the required general principles have indeed been tried. Thus we might claim that they are just seen or grasped by some kind of intuitive insight (Descartes' 'clear and distinct apprehension') or that acceptance of them is inherent in the very nature of the rational mind (Kant's conception of the synthetic *a priori*). But then, clearly, from the premiss 'We cannot help believing that $S$ (even where "we" comprises the whole of humanity)', nothing follows about whether or not *S* is in fact true; and, in any case, how is the premiss itself supposed to be established as true?

Again, of course, the sceptic need not be allowed the last word. It can be objected that his restriction of permissible ways of establishing truths to the two mentioned is arbitrary and unproven – and, more specifically, his case for treating pure mathematics (long regarded as an embodiment of general truths *not* empirically established) as consisted essentially of analytic truths has never been fully made out, and that there are powerful theoretical reasons for thinking that it could not be. Also the operation of, on the one hand, grounding or basing statements on sense-experience, and, on the other, arriving at them by analysis of concepts, have never, it may be said, been rigorously defined. Terms like 'grounded' or 'based' are after all merely metaphorical, and it is far from obvious which of the indefinitely various relationships between our statements and our experience they cover and which they exclude. Or, while the term 'analysis' suggests rigour, on the strength of its mathematical and scientific uses, in practice what is called conceptual analysis more often depends simply on an ear for what is or is not said, on an Austinian patience and sensitivity with the nuances and variations of linguistic usage, than on any closely defined rules of procedure. And in the face of demands for explanations or justifications, we can always draw attention to the quite general point that any explanation or justification must perforce appeal to something accepted without explanation or justification. To object to *any* such acceptance shows only failure to think carefully about the nature of what we are demanding. So in the case of induction what *are* we permitted to accept which is more manifestly true or right, less in need of explanation etc., and which does not covertly assume the validity of unductive argument? Unless he is prepared to answer this question, to allow the essential apparatus for explanation, etc. to remain in service, the sceptic's demands become pointless.

Such, very roughly, have been the lines (or some of them) along which the issue of induction has been discussed since the time of Hume. What, according to Popper, has been accepted largely without discussion in the supposed key role of induction in our lives, which is what has given point and urgency to the whole debate. It was simply taken for granted that these controversial leaps from particular observations to (purported) general truths constituted the essential method of all our sciences – and also indeed of all the unsystematic accumulation of lore, by the help of which we, and all living creatures that rise above the level of instinct, find our way about in the world. In some respects it is, of course, a reasonable enough assumption. Granted that man finds himself in a world not of his own making and under no obligation to conform itself to his ideas of how it must or ought to be, what *can* he do other than look about him, and make the most of the little he can observe? And Popper in effect accepts this view of the human situation. What he rejects are the traditional views of the functions of both the inductive method and the concept of truth in our dealings with the world – and consequently, the view of science as distinguished from other human activities by its strict and systematic use of induction. As we have seen, he holds that Hume was substantially right in pointing out that induction, in the relevant sense, involves a logically invalid argument from *some* to *all* – and all the ingenuity expended on the problem since this has not succeeded in showing otherwise. If we argue inductively, our premisses, even if impeccably true, are logically insufficient to show that our conclusion is true, or even probable – and that is that. But then since, contrary to widespread belief, our science and our everyday lore do *not* rely on induction, this is no great catastrophe. The interesting problem for the philosophy of science (and epistemology in general) is to determine how they *are* in fact developed – and what follows about their scope and limits.

## 2

First of all, what are Popper's grounds for claiming that we do not, in fact, in science or everyday affairs, rely on induction in the way traditionally supposed – a different issue, of course, from that of whether we should be logically justified if we did? His claim, put forward in many forms and contexts from the opening section of *The Logic of Scientific Discovery* onwards, is made in the most sweeping and emphatic terms in a lecture delivered in 1953:

Induction, i.e. inference based on many observations, is a myth. It is neither a psychological fact, nor a fact of ordinary life, nor one of scientific procedure.[5]

It is, however, as he acknowledges a little earlier in the lecture, a myth so deep-rooted and persuasive that his attempts to expose it as such have rarely been taken seriously. He describes how he encountered this difficulty when he first tried to do so to an English audience, at a meeting of the Aristotelian Society in 1936, when Russell had argued that an (unsupported) principle of induction simply had to be adopted as a 'limit of empiricism'. In Popper's view this was in essence a Kantian response to Hume's critique, so:

I said first that I did not believe in induction at all, even though I believed in learning from experience, and in an empiricism without those Kantian limits which Russell proposed. This statement, which I formulated as briefly and as pointedly as I could with the halting English at my disposal, was well received by the audience who, it appears, took it as a joke, and laughed.[6]

And, half a lifetime later, at the beginning of *Objective Knowledge*, we find him complaining of very similar reactions from a new generation of thinkers who had still failed to see the significance of his work.[7]

These reactions are not, indeed, altogether surprising. If it is granted that we learn from experience, and that the empiricism, which says that this is the only way in which we learn the nature of our world, is substantially correct, then how can we dispense with induction? Given only our experience of particular things in particular situations, then surely there is no way we can make ourselves general maps of our environment, no basis for expectations, other than these dubious leaps from 'All observed *x*s are *y*s' to 'All *x*s are *y*s.' Popper's answer, in effect, is that, however plausible this may appear at first sight, it gets the stages of knowledge-acquisition in the wrong order, i.e. it proposes that *first* come observations, understood as mere registering of stimuli, by a mind still innocent of all 'maps', expectations, theories, etc., and *then*, from a sufficient base of such observational data, a venture into generalization. But such pure observation, made with a totally innocent eye as it were, is not only psychologically but logically impossible, at variance with the very nature of observation.

the belief that we can start with pure observations alone, without anything in the nature of theory, is absurd . . . Observation is always selective. It needs a chosen object, a definite task, an interest, a point of view, a problem. And its description presupposes a descriptive language, with property words; it presupposes similarity and classification, which in its turn presupposes interests, points of view, and problems . . . For an animal, a point of view is provided by its needs, the task of the moment, and its expectations; for a scientist by his theoretical interests, the special problem under investigation, his conjectures and anticipations, and the theories which he accepts as a kind of background.[8]

To illustrate his point, Popper reminds us of the man who devoted his life to 'observing' (i.e. anything and everything that came under his notice) and then bequeathed his vast collection of findings to the Royal Society, in the vain hope that they had value as 'inductive evidence'. He records also how he once told a class of students to observe carefully and write down what they had observed – to bring home to them the point that until they were told *what* to observe, the instruction simply could not be obeyed. In a later work, he quotes from Darwin 'How odd it is that anyone should not see that all observation must be for or against some view' and goes on to elaborate:

Neither 'observe!' (without indiction of *what*) nor 'observe this spider!' is a clear imperative. But 'observe *whether* this spider climbs up, or down, as I expect it will!' would be clear enough.[9]

These conjectures, expectations, etc. – the wealth of terms which Popper introduces here is somewhat confusing, but perhaps justified by the wealth of possible preconditions of observation – are not chosen or adopted at random. They in their turn may be variously influenced by earlier observations – for example, they may have been developed to account for what was puzzling or unexpected in those observations. But even though this suggests a chicken-and-egg situation

There is no danger here of an infinite regress. Going back to more and more primitive theories and myths we shall in the end find unconscious, *inborn* expectations. The theory of inborn *ideas* is absurd, I think; but every organism has inborn *reactions* or *responses*; and among them, responses adapted to impending events. These responses we may describe as 'expectations' without implying that these 'expectations' are conscious. The new-born baby 'expects', in this sense, to be fed (and, one could even argue, to be protected and loved).[10]

Popper goes on to say that we might quite reasonably speak of 'inborn knowledge' here. If we do, however, it has to be 'knowledge' in an inverted-commas sense, since as he admits, and indeed insists, any such expectations, even if shared by the whole of mankind, carry no guarantees against disappointment.

In brief, then, from our earliest encounters with the world we are always looking for something, or attempting something. Kant was right in claiming – in contrast with the early empiricist view of the percipient mind as something passive, the Lockian 'empty cabinet' or 'blank sheet' – that it is essentially active, operating on every subject-matter presented to it. His only error lay in supposing that it could *impose* order on them, instead of merely *seeking* it. In the development of our science and our everyday lore about the world, there is no place for the passive reception of Humean 'impressions', or the cumulative effects of their repetitions in producing expectations or general beliefs. Not only is it faulty psychology to maintain that the existence, or the strength, of such expectations, etc. is always a function of repetition – though Popper argues that it *is* faulty – there is a point of logic involved as well. For there is no *absolute* sense in which a certain set of experiences are repetitions of some prototypical experience, or in which they are all experiences of '*x*s' where '*x*' is some general term. On the contrary,

they are repetitions only from a certain point of view. (What has the effect upon me of a repetition may not have this effect upon a spider.) But this means that, for logical reasons, there must always be a point of view – such as a system of expectations, anticipations, assumptions, or interest – *before* there can be any repetitions; which point of view, consequently, cannot be merely the result of repetition.[11]

In other words, whether we see two things to be the same or different, depends on the respects in which we compare them. Suppose, for example, a teacher writes some figures on the blackboard and tells his pupils to do the same as he has done. Merely by looking at what they put down in their exercise-books, we could not tell whether they had obeyed the instruction or not. Our judgement on this would depend also on what we took the purpose of the lesson to be – are the pupils supposed to reproduce exactly the shapes of the figures on the blackboard, or merely the order in which they occur without regard to individual styles in forming them, or to apply the mathematical technique they illustrate to fresh examples . . .? Quite generally, our judgements of sameness and difference are determined, in essential part, first by the range of concepts, of possible points of comparison, available to us, and then by which of these we are interested, for whatever reason, in applying in a particular case – and also, in some cases at least, by the degree of rigour with which we apply them. The judgements are not made for us, or imposed on us, by what is simply given to us in experience; they are made as a result of looking for, or expecting, or wondering about the possibility of, some common feature.

What follows, then, is not merely that we should not rely on induction – because it sins against logic – but that we could not, even if we wanted to, i.e. if by 'induction' is meant the process of receiving, with an open and inactive mind, various impressions of experience, and being determined by the repetition of certain patterns among these impressions to expect a recurrence of such patterns in the future. We may indeed persuade ourselves that this is how it happens, but only because our own activities of selection and decision are so common and all-pervasive that they can readily be overlooked. According to Popper, we start our conscious lives with certain primitive interests and expectations, and enlarge and develop these in response to their fulfilments or disappointments. It is difficult indeed – once this point is made – to envisage what it would be like to accept all our experience in a totally disinterested spirit, to which no one element of it mattered more than another. Perhaps the mystic, by a supreme effort of self-discipline or self-negation arrives at something of the sort. But if so, it is understandable why he finds his vision strictly indescribable. For description inevitably requires selecting certain aspects or elements of our experience, and classifying or comparing them by reference to certain standards or prototypes (our colour-charts, etc.) and ignoring the rest. Total impartiality, accepting everything in and for itself, as it were, without reference to any particular interests, would demand total silence, indeed total inactivity.

Many of our interests may, however, have to be modified or abandoned, many of our expectations may be disappointed, many of our theories or hypotheses may be shown to be untenable by our experience of the world. There is, as we have seen, no guarantee that the world will conform to them. However important our own activities of selection and decision may be, we can only select from, and decide whether or how to use, the raw materials which experience furnishes, the things, the qualities and the relationships which we actually find. (We may recall here what was said in the previous chapter about the essential role of non-conventional relations in the development of conventions.) Experience still has the last word. And Popper in fact sees our whole intellectual development as an unending process of adjustment and modification of these interests, expectations and theories under the pressure of experience.

the growth of our knowledge is the result of a process closely resembling what Darwin called 'natural selection'; that is, the *natural selection of hypotheses*: our knowledge consists, at every moment, of those hypotheses which have shown their (comparative) fitness by surviving so far in their struggle for existence; a competitive struggle which eliminates those hypotheses which are unfit. This interpretation may be applied to animal knowledge, pre-scientific knowledge, and to scientific knowledge. What is peculiar to scientific knowledge is this: that the struggle for existence is made harder by the conscious and systematic criticism of our theories. Thus, while animal knowledge and pre-scientific knowledge grow mainly through the elimination of those holding the unfit hypotheses, scientific criticism often makes our theories perish in our stead, eliminating our mistaken beliefs before such beliefs lead to our own elimination.[12]

Thus, at the pre-scientific state, we must perforce hold, and act on, many 'hypotheses' – the inverted commas acknowledging that, despite the learned term applied to them, these may be no more than rules of thumb, or expectations never precisely formulated or indeed never formulated at all – about how things are in the world, with implications as to what we should find under specific circumstances. But we do not force the issue by systematically seeking out such circumstances, to see whether or not they do in fact vindicate our hypotheses. We are content to wait until they arrive. When we do undertake such a systematic search, deliberately challenging the world to eliminate our hypotheses, and giving it every opportunity for doing so – by formulating the hypotheses and working out their implications as precisely as possible, and then looking for or constructing the relevant experience-situations – then we have passed to the stage of science. This stage, as Popper points out, has the biological advantage of making our hypotheses suffer in our stead, by eliminating the unfit or erroneous ones under laboratory conditions rather than when our lives depend on them. (Unfortunately, however, it also extends our capacity to create hazards to life *pari passu* with our capacity to avoid them.)

## 3

If there is indeed no such thing as induction, as Popper tells us, then the character of natural science has been long and widely misunderstood. It has been very commonly supposed that it is precisely the systematic use of induction that distinguishes natural science from other disciplines like pure mathematics and metaphysics. So, if Popper is right, a radically new account of science, making no appeal to induction, has to be found.

It may be said, and perhaps with some reason, that his taste for the dramatic has led him to overstate his case. Granted, an effective case has been made against one simplistic version of induction – *first* repetition among observational data and *then* generalization based on these. But even if we must start with some expectation, hypothesis or whatever, adopted without benefit of observational evidence, as a precondition of either repetition or observation properly so-called, may we not *then* accumulate observational evidence in its support? Is it not the aim of our natural science, and of less systematic explorations of the world as well, to transform these expectations and hypotheses so far as possible into established truths? And how else can we do this other than by patiently seeking out the relevant data? We may concede Hume's original point that, in the case of unrestricted generalizations, our observational data can never be logically sufficient to establish truth. But none the less do we not, for want of anything better, in effect make the requisite act of faith and use them in this way?

I do not think that Popper, in order to make his essential points, has any need to deny that induction thus understood is very often used. Indeed, his 'pseudo-scientists' characteristically produce impressive masses of data in support of far-reaching generalizations. But (despite what was said in the passage quoted at the beginning of this chapter), in Popper's view, the object of science, or indeed of any serious response to the world, is *not*, simply and without qualification, truth. If our aim were merely to make true, and only true, statements, regardless of their content, our task would be easy. We have only to be very cautious, or very vague. Anyone, even Descartes in his most sceptical phase, could have an indefinitely long list of indubitable truths for the making, if he were prepared to fill it with statements like 'I am now aware of a coloured patch . . . of a sound', etc. (The whole point about 'impression' or 'sense-datum' statements indeed is that they are ultra-cautious; they are designed to commit the speaker to nothing beyond the present experience, so that nothing else is relevant to their truth-value and hence capable of proving them false.) Or, like Popper's 'pseudo-scientists' we could frame generalizations so vaguely-worded and so flexible that virtually any situation which could arise will support them. But, of course, if we thus sacrifice the content of our statements to the desire for truth at any price, we sacrifice as well their interest, and their theoretical and practical importance. We cannot indeed rest satisfied with statements which are not true, or the truth of which is suspect. But, generally speaking, we are in search of statements not only true but, from some standpoint, important as well, and such statements tend to be highly exact, complex and unobvious in content. The price to be paid for dealing in such statements is that only in exceptional and fortunate circumstances are they likely to be true; usually they allow too many hostages to their subject-matter, too many ways in which the world may fail to conform to them, or they to the world, to have much chance of unqualified truth. They are not of course made at random. (The indefinitely various ways of arriving at them, particularly in the higher reaches of science, provide an interesting topic for the psychology of research – something, however, to be clearly distinguished from epistemology, and with no direct relevance to our present discussion.) We usually have good reason to think that they can satisfy *some* of the conditions for their truth. But only rarely does this constitute good – much less logically sufficient – reason for thinking that they can satisfy them all. And the history of science effectively illustrates the way in which, even in the case of theories that have satisfied many and exacting conditions, this still has relevance as something more than a general point of logic.

Thus, in important areas of research at least, it is futile to set ourselves to discover The Truth, or even to try to show that a given theory is true. It is not only a matter of a logician tiresomely reminding us that, for all we know, the next crow we encounter may be white, or the next fire we light may freeze the kettle instead of boiling it. There is also the historical evidence that any serious hypothesis, purporting to set out exactly the workings of some part of nature, even if it covers all the data currently available, is unlikely to be more than an approximation to the truth, or to embody some part of it. And thus the task of research is not to seek evidence in favour of the hypothesis; we could after all increase the volume of favourable evidence *ad lib.* simply by repeating the experiments which suggested it in the first place. It is much more valuable to try to get straight to the point where it breaks down, and hence is in need of modification, and for this purpose to devise the most exacting tests, the ones it is least likely to pass – in the case of Einstein's theory, for example, to concentrate on the point where it yielded a prediction clearly at variance with anything that scientific orthodoxy would lead us to expect. The denial of the role traditionally ascribed to induction amounts then to this; what is essential to the development of science (and of our everyday knowledge of the world as well) is the discovery, not of *many* observational data which support a given hypothesis, but of *one* which refutes it.

If we think of *verification* as the primary business of science, then once Hume and his successors have pointed out just how few kinds of statement can be verified in any strict sense, we are driven to despair of science as ordinarily understood. We can only preserve its 'verification' function by allowing it to say less and less – by confining it, like Kant, to the world of phenomena, for example, or, like Schlick and other positivists, denying it the capacity to make general *statements*, and reducing its supposed general laws to prescriptions or instruments for prediction.[13] By contrast, Popper sees it as primarily concerned to *falsify* statements, rather than verify them. As we have already said, we approach all our encounters with the world, even the earliest, ready-equipped with expectations, viewpoints, hypotheses, etc. And the most effective role that science (or any serious enquiry) can perform is that of iconoclast, bring to our attention as quickly and effectively as possible the limitations and defects of this equipment, and hence the ways in which it needs to be improved.

Thus, if we are concerned with the problem of demarcating science (and empirical studies generally) from other fields of interest like pure mathematics, metaphysics or theology, we cannot simply appeal to verification by experience. It will not do to say the all-important difference is that while speculations about, for example, the creation of the world cannot be shown to be true, or even probable, by appeal to observational data, the principle of gravitation can. As Hume showed once and for all, it cannot. The distinguishing mark of a statement belonging to science – or, more generally, an empirical statement, is, according to Popper, its *falsifiability*.

I shall certainly admit a system as empirical or scientific only if it is capable of being *tested* by experience . . . not the *verifiability* but the *falsifiability* of a system is to be taken as a criterion of demarcation . . . *it must be possible for an empirical scientific system to be refuted by experience.*[14]

And, in a later summary of his conclusions about science:

Every 'good' scientific theory is a prohibition: it forbids certain things to happen. The more a theory forbids the better it is . . . A theory which is not refutable by any conceivable event is non-scientific. Irrefutability is not a virtue of a theory (as people often think) but a vice . . . *the criterion of the scientific status of a theory is its falsifiability, or refutability, or testability.*[15]

As it stands, of course, this can scarcely be a sufficient criterion of scientific status – as the term 'science' and its derivatives are ordinarily understood – even if it is a necessary one. For science we should require that to some degree (even if we have no means of specifying to precisely what degree) the theory should be (or contribute to) something of general interest, and the testing should be disciplined and systematic. Thus, the prediction 'It will rain here tomorrow' is, as Popper notes, empirical in the required sense, in contrast to 'It will rain or not rain here tomorrow' which is not,[16] but we should not, in most circumstances at any rate, regard it as a contribution to science. The most immediate advantage, however, of substituting falsifiability for verifiability as part at least of our criterion of science lies in the

*asymmetry* between verifiability and falsifiability; an asymmetry which results from the logical form of universal statements. For these are never derivable from singular statements, but can be contradicted by singular statements. Consequently it is possible by means of purely deductive inferences (with the help of the *modus tollens* of classical logic) to argue from the truth of singular statements to the falsity of universal statements.[17]

Science thus becomes logically respectable, and Hume's famous critique ceases to be relevant.

The price to be paid, as we have seen, is that science has to abandon all claim to tell us general truths about the world. Even if we assume that we *can* establish beyond question of the truth of (some) singular statements − and we shall have to consider later the difficulties involved in this assumption − these still enable us to show only that some of the generalizations which for various reasons have interested scientists are false, never that any of them are true. Science is never in a position to go beyond what is said to have been one of H. A. Prichard's favourite comments on his students' essays − 'Whatever may be the truth, that can't be.' Hence, what is claimed as 'scientific knowledge' depends on the point in history at which the claim is made. For all we can mean by 'scientific knowledge' is that body of theories which have *thus far* survived systematic testing; and the progress of such testing, and the modifications of theory made in response to it mean that our scientific knowledge is in constant process of self-change and self-renewal. There can be no excuse, especially in the light of the recent history of science, for imagining that the scientific knowledge of our generation will fare any better in this respect than that of our predecessors. Indeed, given the ever-increasing volume of scientific research, and the number of workers in the field, the life-expectancy of promising theories has presumably decreased; it seems unlikely that any of them will ever again approach the longevity of, say, Newtonian physics. Even those theories which no scientist is at the moment seeking to refute, and which are ordinarily treated, and taught, in departments of science as though they were established truths, can still, logically, lay claim to no title stronger than that of *conjecture* − conjectures, it may be, that are very well *corroborated*, in the sense of having survived many tests,[18] but conjectures none the less, which future research may well find reason to replace.

A genuinely scientific theory, then, lives dangerously. It puts itself at risk by ruling something out, forbidding something to happen. And the more it forbids the better it is; if, for example, it rules out everything but one quite specific, and *prima facie* unlikely, outcome in a specific set of circumstances, and gets away with it, this is a genuine scientific triumph. As we saw in the previous chapter, this was for Popper the supreme merit of Einstein's theory over those of the other intellectual heroes of his student years, Marx, Freud and Adler. It was not that he thought Einstein had established, or was on the way to establishing, the truth of his theory, while the others had failed. What he found suspect about Marxism and the ideas of the psychologists was precisely what many of his contemporaries seemed to find most admirable about them: their apparently limitless explanatory power.

These theories appeared to be able to explain practically everything that happened within the fields to which they referred. The study of them seemed to have the effect of an intellectual conversion or revelation, opening your eyes to a new truth hidden from those not yet initiated. Once your eyes were thus opened you saw confirming instances everywhere: the world was full of *verifications* of the theory. Whatever happened always confirmed it.[19]

When Einstein, on the other hand, used his novel gravitational theory to predict what would be observed during an eclipse of the sun, by no means everything that could happen would confirm it. Indeed every finding other than precisely the one predicted would refute it. And for Popper

the impressive thing about this case is the *risk* involved in a prediction of this kind. If observation showed that the predicted effect is definitely absent, then the theory is simply refuted. The theory is *incompatible with certain possible results of observation* . . . in fact with results which everybody before Einstein would have expected.[20]

It was this last fact that made the fulfilment of Einstein's prediction a major landmark in the history of science, for it was at the same time the falsification of a body of theory that until then had commanded almost universal assent. But the point to note here is simply that, while getting away with such a risk did not make Einstein necessarily right – there are always further tests to be faced – taking such a risk made him a genuine scientist.

There is, of course, a sense in which *any* genuine, non-tautological statement, whether it belongs to science or not, rules something out. If, for example, I say that this surface is white and rectangular, I rule out all other colours or shapes, everything that is not white or not rectangular. And, in general, we frame our statements by selecting from ranges of possibilities, like the items on a colour chart – and to select is, *ipso facto*, to reject as well. A 'statement' (other than a tautology) which ruled out nothing, which left all possibilities open, would fail to fulfil the essential function of a statement, i.e. to tell us that things are this way rather than any other; and hence it might fairly be called, in the idiom of logical positivism, a 'pseudo-statement', or 'meaningless' or 'nonsensical' in that, even though it may be grammatically impeccable and made up of familiar words, it is only verbal lumber, and serves no purpose in discourse. Falsifiability might then be taken as a criterion of *meaninfulness*, or the distinguishing mark of genuine as opposed to pseudo-statements. And when Popper first put forward his ideas about falsifiability it was in fact widely supposed that he was using it in this way, giving it the same task as contemporary positivists had given to verifiability.

Popper, however, has emphatically denied that he ever intended anything of the kind; he has never offered any general criterion of meaningfulness, or seen any point in attempting to do so, and he has never claimed that statements which were unfalsifiable were therefore pseudo-statements or meaningless.[21] There is an important distinction to be drawn here between saying that any genuine or meaningful non-tautological statement rules out some state-of-affairs, and saying that it rules out some observational result or content of experience. The first of these can scarcely be denied. Indeed it is difficult to imagine what even a pseudo-statement that failed to meet this condition would be like – perhaps one coupled with a rejection of the law of non-contradiction, so that, for example, 'This is white' leaves open the possibility that this is not-white, and so on? (Quite generally, of course, someone who professes to reject the law of non-contradiction cannot tell us anything, not even that he does reject it; for even if he says 'I reject the law of non-contradiction' on his own principles this leaves open the possibility that he does *not* reject it.) But to go on from saying that every genuine statement must meet this condition to saying that it must also meet our second condition, and rule out some *observational* result or content of *experience*, is a very considerable leap, and it is far from clear what justification there could be for making it. A logical positivist, trying to salvage as much as possible of his essential position after being forced to abandon verification might be prepared to make it. But Popper certainly is not.

For him, incompatibility 'with certain possible results of observation' is simply the criterion of being a *scientific* statement, not of being a genuine or meaningful one. Take, for example, the statements 'Every event has a cause' or 'The world was created by God'. As ordinarily used and understood, these are not, I believe, refutable by any observational result or set of such results (though of course they satisfy our weaker condition of ruling out some states of affairs – that *not* every event has a cause, etc.). As we shall see further on, a case might be made for saying that no one could *state that*, say, every event has a cause – as distinct from merely *uttering the sentence* 'Every event . . .' – unless he had, or at least claimed to have, some means of finding out whether or not every event has a cause. That is, a statement as such is essentially a statement of results – the results of some process of enquiry or finding out. And hence presumably there would be some enquiry-results incompatible with any given statement. But, even if this is indeed a general condition of statement-making, we should still be taking a considerable step further – and one in obvious need of justification – if we assumed that such enquiry must always be reducible to observations, or contain observation as an essential part. The history of thought furnishes examples of many different kinds of consideration that have in fact led people to make metaphysical or theological statements; they have rarely been made out of mere perversity. And there are many ways in which specific arguments for or against such statements, can be criticized in detail. (Popper provides some examples of such arguments and criticism in his broadcast talks (1958) on 'The status of science and metaphysics'.[22]) And it may well be that many metaphysical and theological doctrines can be shown to be ill-founded, and many of the traditional ways of arriving at them seriously defective. But Popper's use of the concept of falsifiability – in contrast to the positivist's use of verifiability – does nothing worse to such doctrines than to exclude them from the realm of science, to which few people can ever have thought they belonged.

## 4

We have, then, an attractively simple formula for what makes a given enquiry or piece of research a contribution to science – in effect, a confrontation between imaginative theory and observed fact. The theory is essential but the observations must be allowed the last word; otherwise it is not science.

It is tempting to turn this account of science inwards upon itself – to grant its success as a refutation of an earlier view of science (i.e. that the primary purpose of science is to establish general truths by the systematic use of observation) but to complain that, considered as a positive characterization of science as actually practised, it is seriously over-simplified, and, in its turn, open to refutation and replacement. And certainly the main effects of Popper's work in the development of the philosophy of science have been to turn attention away from the problems raised by the earlier account, in particular the 'problem of induction', and to stimulate a notable variety of attempts to diagnose and correct the over-simplifications of his own. In fairness to Popper, however, it must be pointed out that what was said of philosophy in the previous chapter holds of science also, i.e. that it consists of a whole range of activities and their results, a range with ill-defined and disputed boundaries, and with complex and varied relations between its elements. And while we may identify these elements piecemeal, and trace specific inter-relations, we cannot expect to find an essence of science, any more than an essence of philosophy, which can be summed up in a neat formula. And all that Popper actually claims to do, in putting forward his criterion for the demarcation of science, is to make 'a proposal for an agreement or convention'.[23]

On the other hand, such an 'agreement or convention' is clearly not intended to be wholly arbitrary; to speak of a criterion for the demarcation of *science* is to invite comparison with science as ordinarily understood. And there is no doubt that Popper believed not only that he was calling attention to an important distinction in human discourse – between those statements (doctrines, theories, or whatever) which are falsifiable and those which are not – but that most, at any rate, of what has ordinarily counted as science would also qualify as science according to his criterion. The literature on whether, or to what extent, this belief is justified is too extensive and in many cases too specialized to be discussed in any detail here; but for the remainder of this chapter we may consider briefly some of the major critical points that have been raised.

To begin with, there would seem to be important findings about the world which could *not* be falsified by any observations, but which we should certainly want to classify as science rather than as metaphysics or anything else. Thus William Kneale argues that Popper's criterion of demarcation commits him:

to the paradoxical thesis that all unrestricted existential propositions are metaphysical and non-empirical'.

But

suppose that on some occasion when I have been rashly dogmatic about the behaviour of fish out of water a biologist reminds me, in an unrestricted existential statement, that there are after all lung-fish which can breathe on dry land. I do not dismiss his remark as irrelevant metaphysics, but humbly accept it as good empirical information.

And again,

the discovery of the positron, which we express ... by means of an unrestricted existential statement in the present tense, can properly be said to belong where most people think it does, namely to science, rather than to metaphysics or history.[24]

An 'unrestricted existential statement' is one which asserts, without restriction to any region of space or time, the existence of something, (plant, planet, particle or whatever) with certain specific properties; and obviously while such a statement, in contrast to our unrestricted generalizations, can sometimes be *verified* by observations, it can never be falsified by them. But, as the positron example illustrates, such statements can play an important role in science. Scientific research is concerned to discover the wealth and variety of the furnishings of the world, as well as the laws governing the arrangement and interaction of its elements. And Kneale goes on to point out other things, as well as attempting to formulate general laws, which science characteristically undertakes. For example, in biology, geology, or astronomy, it is often concerned to determine what initial conditions brought about, or might have brought about (in a given framework of general laws), some present situation – the unique flora and fauna of a particular island perhaps, or an unusual rock formation, or the composition of the solar system itself. And here the findings would be given in the form of historical statements about what happened, or might have happened, in a particular spatio-temporal area. In general,

Many studies of different kinds are carried on under the name of 'science' ... In particular we should beware of suggesting ... that the professional assertions of scientists are all about the frame as opposed to the content of nature . . . Of all the sciences, only general physics, or natural philosophy as they still call it in some places, seems to be concerned exclusively with the frame of nature.[25]

In his reply,[26] Popper points out, quite correctly, that he has never said or implied that the only genuine scientific statements are unrestricted generalizations. Many singular statements, for example reports of the results of scientific tests or experiments, are also parts of science; and such statements can, of course, satisfy the falsifiability criterion. (The fact that they may also be, in some circumstances, verifiable in no way prevents this.) But he makes no comment on Kneale's main counter-example – the unrestricted existential statements – which are *not* falsifiable at all. It would seem that it has to be conceded that there *are* some characteristic elements of scientific discourse which do not satisfy his criterion, which are not, strictly speaking, falsifiable. Of course, an entirely arbitrary or random statement of this (or any other) kind would not be a contribution to science as ordinarily understood – for example, if someone simply suggests *in vacuo* that there is somewhere a golden mountain, or a fiery dragon. One condition at least of its being part of science – and arguably, as we saw earlier, of its being a statement at all – is that we have, or at any rate claim to have, some reason for thinking that it is, or might be, the case. We might, for example, in a particular scientific context, offer it as the only, or the best, hypothesis to explain a particular range of observational data. And in such a role our unrestricted existential statement, even if it could never actually be falsified, could in some circumstances be *eliminated* from science, i.e. if the supposed observational data proved to be incorrect, or to be explicable without it. This concept of elimination, as something wider than falsification, which covers rejection on the grounds of superfluity as well as of falsity, has no doubt a use in explaining some elements of the progress of science. But eliminability could not replace falsifiability as a more accommodating criterion of science, since it is a feature of metaphysics as well and indeed of any disciplined study whatsoever. It is in effect simply the application of Occam's razor; wherever we have 'no need of that hypothesis', in any field, it is discarded. Hence a criterion of science as ordinarily understood is still to seek; so far as falsifiability is concerned, there are some falsifiable statements (for example the trivialities and ephemera of everyday discourse) which are not science, and some unfalsifiable statements (our unrestricted existential statements) which are.

To return, however, to our confrontation between theory and observed fact – supposing for the moment that the theory is one which *can* be formulated in an unrestricted generalization. To what extent, or on what grounds, do we in fact give the data of observation the last word? To begin with, if indeed we do allow them such an authoritative role, is it because we are in effect making *inductive* generalizations from them? For unless we think that the tests we have carried out are repeatable, and will continue to yield the same results in the future as they have in the past, why should past unfavourable results affect future confidence in the theory? If we discard a theory on the grounds that it has failed our tests in the past, are we not in effect arguing inductively that, having failed them in the past, it will continue to do so in the future? Granted we should never allow that the *same* test had yielded different results on different occasions; for by 'the same' here we can only mean 'the same in all relevant respects', and our only criterion of relevance is making a difference to the result. Hence, that the same test always yields the same result is not an inductive generalization but an analytic truth. But that some tests at least *are* repeatable, that some set of conditions which have occurred, or been constructed, in the past, will recur or be reconstructed in the future, and that to this extent the future will resemble the past, are not analytical. And yet, it may be argued, a science which did not in effect claim that it could, and did, discover such repeating patterns in its field of study would be deprived of much of its point – is it not a primary function of its programme of theorizing and testing that we should have an increasingly comprehensive and reliable guide as to what we will and will not find in the world? In reply to a similar point raised by Sir Alfred Ayer, Popper comments

there is also a criticism of my theory in the form 'Why should a hypothesis that has failed the test be discarded unless this shows it to be unreliable . . .?' Answer: because if it has failed the test it is false, independently of any pragmatic issue.[27]

This is unassailable as far as it goes. But none the less science as actually practised *does* concern itself with 'pragmatic issues' as well as with truth and falsity, and *does* claim that its systematic sorting out of the false from the true (or possibly true) among theories serves the purposes – even if this is not its only purpose – of providing guidance as to future experience. Test situations will recur and the record of how our various theories fared in them in the past is a guide to how they will fare in the future – otherwise our science would have merely historical interest. And science has always made stronger claims for itself than that.

In an earlier discussion of induction Popper tells us:

Admittedly, it is perfectly reasonable to *act* on the assumption that it [i.e. the future] will, in many respects, be like the past, and that well-tested laws will continue to hold (since we have no better assumptions to act upon); but it is also reasonable to believe that such a course of action will lead us at times into severe trouble, since some of the laws on which we now heavily rely may easily prove unreliable . . . One might even say to judge from past experience, and from our general scientific knowledge, the future will *not* be like the past in perhaps most of the ways which those have in mind who say it will. Water will sometimes not quench thirst, and air will choke those who breathe it.[28]

Again, we may accept this as it stands. But we may still wonder what *makes* it reasonable to act or believe thus. What reasons could we have – or what would make any relevant assumption a good one, or better than another – unless we accept the records of the past as (to some extent) a guide to the future? Like Popper himself at the end of the passage quoted, we should have indeed to 'judge from past experience', i.e. to treat such experience as a ground for looking forward to a certain measure of continuity, punctuated no doubt with novelities and surprises, extending into the future. Hume's argument that it cannot be a logically sufficient ground still holds, of course. But Popper does not seem able to show that science (and our everyday lore about the world) can avoid reliance on it, and still perform the functions they do in human life.

Further, the idea that observational results constitute a final court from which theories have no appeal requires some fairly radical modifications. It has the merit of bringing out one undeniable fact about science, i.e. that the scientist, whatever freedom he may have in the choice of concepts and methods and in the formulation of theories, is still a man under authority; at some point he has to face the question 'But is this how things actually are in the world?', and the answer is not of his own making. But just how this question arises, and how it may be dealt with, are not themselves questions which admit of simple answers.

Consider the various moves open to us in our confrontation situation, where our theory is up against an unfavourable observational result. Clearly there are other possibilities as well as simply withdrawing the theory. To begin with, we might just question whether the observation (experiment, survey, or whatever it may be) has been properly carried out, or its result properly stated. We need not invariably jump to the conclusion that it is our theory which is at fault. If, for example, a student at work in his college laboratory produces a result at variance with some well-attested theory, his teacher does not think of writing to the scientific journals to announce the overthrow of the theory; he tells the student to go back and do the experiment properly, and conformity to the theory in question is here the test of propriety. At the other extreme, a scientist clinging to a pet theory in the face of repeatedly unfavourable results produced by reputable and independent researchers, and who goes on insisting that they are all incompetent, or all conspiring to discredit him, would cease to be taken seriously, and would be demoted in the minds of professional colleagues from scientist to crank. But it is of course logically possible that the student, or the crank, is right; and, very occasionally, he is. And between these extremes, there is often, in many fields of research, an area of doubt and disagreement even among orthodox professional scientists over what should be made of the available experimental evidence and whether it suffices to overthrow a given theory or not.

Testing scientific theories, after all, is very rarely the simple matter suggested by the 'All crows are black' kind of example, where all that is needed is an alert and honest observer. Devising tests is often a very roundabout affair, requiring considerable technical ingenuity as well as familiarity with, and reliance on, a complex of other theories. (The layman may be reminded of, for example, popular scientific programmes on the television screen, where he is triumphantly presented with pictures of barely perceptible scratches on ancient rocks, or indeterminate streaks and blobs on X-ray plates, and simply has to take on trust the accompanying account of what they 'show'.) Hence, checking our theories against the facts of observations, however sound a principle it may be, is only rarely a matter of keeping our eyes open and recording faithfully what we see. And even when it is, the terms we ordinarily use for the recording commit us far beyond the content of any finite set of sense-experiences. The experimenter as well as the theorist has to live with the permanent possibility of falsification; there is no question of simply contrasting speculative theories with infallible observation-statements. Popper is of course well aware of this. As he points out in *The Logic of Scientific Discovery*:

we can utter no scientific statement that does not go far beyond what can be known with certainty 'on the basis of immediate experience'. (This fact may be referred to as the 'transcendence inherent in any description'.) Every description uses *universal* names (or symbols, or ideas); every statement has the character of a theory, of a hypothesis. The statement 'Here is a glass of water' cannot be verified by any observational experience. The reason is that the *universals* which appear in it cannot be correlated with any specific sense-experience.[29]

A few pages further on he says:

I readily admit that only observation can give us 'knowledge concerning facts', and that we can (as Hahn says) become aware of facts only by observation. But this awareness, this knowledge of ours, does not justify or establish the truth of any statement.[30]

Hence, even in the simplest cases, there is no question of reading off from what is presented in sense-experience incontrovertibly true statements to set against our theories. Even our 'basic statements' – by definition 'those asserting that an observable event is occurring in a certain region of space and time'[31] – are, like any others, within the realm of possible error and controversy.

Accordingly we can claim no more than that – Every test of a theory, whether resulting in its corroboration or falsification, must stop at some basic statement or other which we *decide* to *accept* . . . the decision to accept a basic statement, and to be satisfied with it, is causally connected with our experiences – especially with our *perceptual experiences*. But we do not attempt to *justify* basic statements by these experiences. Experiences can *motivate a decision*, and hence an acceptance or a rejection of a statement; but a basic statement cannot be *justified* by them – no more than by thumping the table. Basic statements are accepted as the result of a decision or agreement; and to that extent they are conventions.[32]

Such decisions, etc. are not of course merely arbitrary. There are, in many cases at least, precisely formulated and widely accepted rules for making the required observations, and various checks and supplementary tests to fall back on in cases of dispute. And doubtless agreement within the appropriate group of researchers as to which basic statements should be accepted is normally easy enough to achieve. Indeed the 'motivation' provided by experience is likely to be so well-ingrained that the element of decision goes unnoticed; and, again, consensus might always be ensured by the device of branding as a crank, and excluding from the relevant group, anyone who fails to agree. But the fact remains that our basic statements are inherently fallible for the same reason as our generalizations are, i.e. that we find here again the unbridgeable logical gap between the conventionally appropriate criteria *for* making them and commitments we undertake *in* making them.

But if so, the consequences for Popper's whole theory are extremely serious. Our 'refutation' of any proposed theory can be put only in hypothetical form – '*If* certain basic statements are accepted . . .' etc. But suppose they are not, or that different groups of researchers accept different sets of basic statements? It would seem that the best we can hope for is that everyone who matters in our scientific world will agree on the same set. There can be no final or absolute refutation of any given theory, and hence no absolute scale by which we can measure scientific progress. All we can say is that certain theories and certain basic statements are mutually inconsistent, not that any of them has been shown conclusively to be true – or even false. Towards the end of the original text of *The Logic of Scientific Discovery*, Popper himself makes this point.

In the logic of science here outlined it is possible to avoid using the concepts 'true' and 'false'. Their place may be taken by logical considerations about derivability relations . . . We need not say that the theory is 'false', but we may say instead that it is contradicted by a certain set of accepted basic statements. Nor need we say of basic statements that they are 'true' or 'false', for we may interpret their acceptance as the result of a conventional decision, and the accepted statements as results of that decision.[33]

In a footnote to this passage added to the 1959 English edition, and elsewhere, Popper explains that he had originally hesitated to place too much weight on the concept of truth, and tried to show that it was dispensable, simply because of the lack of any satisfactory account of truth. The discovery of Tarski's theory of truth, which for him supplied this lack, dispelled such hesitations, and made it no longer necessary to play down, as it were, the scientific importance of the concept of truth – but left his 'views on science and its philosophy fundamentally unaffected, although clarified'. There is much more to be said about this in our next chapter, but for present purposes we must note that, whatever Popper's intentions in writing it, it is very difficult to accept the passage just quoted as in fact doing no more than replacing a vague or ill-defined concept with a more precise one. Rather, it sets out an important and unavoidable consequence of Popper's account of basic statements. There is no longer any immovable rock on which to build. And however much he insists on the importance for science of the rigorous and systematic testing of statements, if such tests are never logically sufficient to establish the truth of *any* statement, then they never entitle us to say '*Since* the truth of *a*, *b*, and *c* has been established, *x* must be rejected as false' — but only '*If* we accept *a*, *b*, and *c* as true, then we must reject *x* as false.' No theory can then be conclusively falsified any more than it can be conclusively verified; and scientific progress, *in any absolute sense*, is no more than the illusion of those naive enough to overlook the role of convention in the establishment of our basic statements.

Further, if such an appeal to convention is indeed unavoidable, can we have any objection in principle to the (surely widely adopted) convention which allows us to accept unrestricted generalizations as *true* on grounds which are logically insufficient — for example, an unbroken run of favourable instances? There is no obvious reason why the conventions required for their 'verification' should be any more offensive than the conventions which, as we have just seen, are required for their 'falsification'. So why should we not, after all, licence ourselves to play the inductive language-game according to its own (convention-sanctioned) rules? We might say, as Popper seems inclined to do, that any such licence is only provisional, and that any of our (scientific) statements, whether generalizations or basic statement, can always be tested further, should the need or demand for such testing arise. But if we can claim no more for the result of *any* of our tests than that the appropriate researchers agree to accept it as true, then we are only pitting one convention, or the results of using it, against another. We are still in the realm of decision, rather than where Popper emphatically claims science ought to operate, i.e. in the realm of discovery.

We shall, I think, find that Popper seriously underestimates the strength of the relativism that threatens him here. Indeed, quite generally, this is the main criticism that I have to make of his work, i.e. not that he rejects relativism, about which he may well prove to be right in the end, but that he fails to appreciate the force of the arguments in its favour — even those embodied in his own commendably honest and perceptive remarks, just quoted, about the inherent vulnerability of basic statements. But before we go on to consider the general issue of relativism with respect to truth-claims, we should take note of some further qualifications to our simple 'confrontation' model of scientific enquiry.

5

Theories, obviously, are designed to solve, or to play an essential part in solving, specific *problems*. But, in many cases at least, our theories also *create*, or play an essential part in creating, these problems in the first place. There can be few situations – if indeed any – which in themselves can properly be said to present us with *specific* problems. Doubtless there are some features of our world and our life in it – like 'the starry heavens above, and the moral law within' – which have been a source of wonder and puzzlement to thinkers of many different cultures and generations. But just what questions about them any given thinker sets himself to answer, or what he would accept as satisfactory answers, is determined in essential part by what he himself brings to his subject-matter, by the framework of concepts, assumptions, expectations through which he sees it. There are in this respect no *absolute* problems any more than there are absolute samenesses and similarities. What we find problematic (surprising, puzzling, in need of explication or explanation . . .) in a given field is a function of what our preconceived, though perhaps still unformulated, theories lead us to expect – and so is what solves the problem for us. Without such a framework there would be no reason to ask Why? or How? of one part or aspect of our field rather than another, and no direction in which to look for possible answers. To this extent, then, what we find problematic or unproblematic, soluble or insoluble, difficult or easy, will perforce vary from one such framework to another. We may recall, for example, how the 'problem of evil' has haunted the Christian tradition in religious thought, but would not arise at all for, say, the polytheism of ancient Greece or Rome; or consider the imaginative effort required, for most of us at the present time, to think our way into the position of the eighteenth-century preacher who, when his child was badly injured in an accident, saw as his most pressing problem, 'Why has God thus punished me?' And, again, whether, or how easily, such problems are answerable depends on what theological position one assumes. As in the traditional school textbooks on geometry, where problems were set in the form 'Given that . . ., it is required to prove . . .' what one is required to prove, and how or whether it can be done, is determined (in essential part) by what one is permitted to treat as given.

But is it, we may ask, *simply* a matter of permissions? Do we in effect just decide, or have someone in appropriate authority decide for us, what is to be treated as problematic, and what is to be accepted without question as it stands – as though we were drawing up the rules of a game, and were free to decide how difficult or how easy we should make it for ourselves and other would-be players? Or do we not rather *discover*, when we start to investigate any given field of interest, that there are some features of it which just *are* puzzling, which, as we say, *demand* an explanation, while there are others which it would seem eccentric, or perverse, to call in question? The issue is by no means an easy one to decide. It may be said, for example, that the development of dynamics as we know it depended on a change of mind about what needed explanation with regard to the motion of bodies, i.e. not simply motion as such, but any *change* in a state of rest or uniform motion in a straight line – while such motion is in itself no more in need of explanation than rest is. But, granted that this is so, should we say that it is something that was *seen* or *realized*, or something that was *decided*? Certainly, 'decided' makes the matter seem more arbitrary, and game-like, than is plausible in this case or those of most other subjects of serious scientific investigation. And seeing – perhaps in a sudden flash of inspiration – what the 'real' (or 'essential' or 'fundamental') problems are in a given field, as though it were something that had been there all the time, and only awaiting discovery, is surely a common, and important, phenomenon in the history of original research in any discipline – while inducing pupils to 'see what the problems are' is a major part of any teacher's task.

Often, if not invariably, this seeing, or being induced to see, is a matter of noticing the possibility of *alternatives*. (Generally speaking, theoretical, as opposed to practical, problems trouble only the imaginative.) There *is* x, but there *could be* y or z, so why x? The important point here, however, is just what is involved in this 'noticing' of alternative possibilities. If it were nothing more than the acknowledgement that other things are *logically* possible, we should be in danger of straying into the realm of spurious, or pseudo, problems. An essential element in the setting, and solving, of (genuine) problems is missing. It is, for example, logically possible that the table before me should rise and float in the air, or that it should suddenly vanish. But it would be pointless to look for reasons why it does not – unless, on whatever grounds, we have adopted some theory which *prima facie* leads us to expect that it should or might do so. Again – to oversimplify somewhat – we need a theory, even if only an implicit one, to create expectations, and disappointment of such expectations to set us our problem. This is the missing factor when we raise such 'problems' as 'Why this world rather than any other (logically) possible world?' or 'Why is there any world at all?' Is the existence of this world, or of any world, *surprising*, or not what we should have expected? And, if so, what *should* we have expected, and on what grounds – and what is left unquestioned, or acceptable as it stands to provide a basis for attempted solutions? We can only get a purchase on such 'problems' by, in effect, assimilating the world as a whole to some class of elements within it, like artefacts or complex pieces of mechanism, for example, about which we *have* got theories and expectations. In general, while we can indeed after a fashion come, or be brought, to see that something *is* problematic, or in need of explanation (and certainly do not simply *decide* in every case what is to be treated as a problem, and what taken for granted), we could not do so without our pre-existing framework of theories, etc. It is only when, and because, we have decided on – or perhaps 'adopted' would be a less misleading term – such a framework that certain things *then* present themselves as problems, or demand explanations. As we shall have occasion to mention again in the course of our discussion of relativism, the element of decision or adoption may be too primitive, too deep-rooted in our thinking, to be recognized for what it is. But this does not mean that it is absent or dispensable.

Essentially the same point is made, and developed further, in Thomas Kuhn's famous distinction between the 'normal' and the 'revolutionary' elements in the development of science. As he explains in *The Structure of Scientific Revolutions*:

'normal science' means research firmly based upon one or more past scientific achievements, achievements that some particular scientific community acknowledges for a time as supplying the foundations for its further practice.[35]

Outstanding past achievements can, in suitable circumstances, provide 'paradigms' or models of research, 'from which spring particular coherent traditions of scientific research' – for example 'Ptolemaic' astronomy (or 'Copernican'), 'Aristotelian dynamics' (or 'Newtonian').
And

The study of paradigms ... is what mainly prepares the student for membership in the particular scientific community with which he will later practice ... Men whose research is based on shared paradigms are committed to the same rules and standards for scientific practice. The commitment and the apparent consensus it produces are pre-requisites for normal science

And in a later essay, specifically comparing his own view of science with Popper's, he insists that in normal science — which, as the title implies, covers by far the greater part of what professional scientists spend their working lives on — the tests performed are not 'directed to current theory'.

On the contrary, when engaged with a normal research problem, the scientist must *premise* current theory as the rules of his game. His object is to solve a puzzle, preferably one at which others have failed, and current theory is required to define that puzzle, and to guarantee that, given sufficient brilliance, it can be solved.[36]

This is in effect the point to which our general considerations about the setting and solving of theoretical problems have brought us — that it is our pre-existing framework of theories, etc. that maps our field of interest for us into the puzzling and the expected, the problematic and the unproblematic, what needs explanation and what can be used as material for such explanations. If we abandon the framework, we should find ourselves in unmapped territory where our specific problems, and our recognized means of dealing with them, would alike disappear.

Are our paradigms, or frameworks, then, immovable, protected by their essential role in research from any possible refutation — or alterable only by some 'extraordinary' move (to use Kuhn's term) which is quite distinct from the normal range of scientific activity, and which, in effect, replaces one tradition of research by another, by a kind of 'gestalt-switch' which transforms our whole view of the field, and provides us, not with solutions to existing problems, but with a whole new set of problems? We might perhaps object, following the line Popper himself takes in his reply to Kuhn,[37] that Kuhn's dramatic contrast between the normal and the revolutionary in science is exaggerated and misleading. There may indeed be 'quieter and less quiet, less and more revolutionary periods in science'. But to fall into a 'routine' of puzzle-solving within a framework which we are not prepared to question is something contrary to the whole spirit of science as Popper understands it — though he is prepared to concede that such routine work is no doubt a common enough feature of professional 'science' at the present time. Of course, any theory or group of theories, at any level of generality, may be taken for granted *provisionally* – i.e. for the purposes of a particular research programme. And, as a matter of history, there may well have been theories which, over a long period of time, no serious scientist had occasion to question, and which were treated as incontrovertible truths in much fruitful research. This is quite in accordance with the Popperian conception of science. What is ruled out is the suggestion that, for any of our scientific theories, such immunity from criticism is something more than provisional; that the scientist in the course of his normal work *has to* solve his puzzles without calling them in question, has in effect to treat them somewhat as a priest treats the fundamental dogma of his church, i.e. as something which could only be altered or replaced, if at all, by the desperate expedient of founding a new religion.

Yet, for our orthodox professional scientist who is neither revolutionary genius nor crank – titles which can perhaps be applied safely only with the advantage of hindsight – while there may be no sharp distinction between the unquestionable and the questionable among theories, it is not clear that there are many circumstances in which he would *have to* question the paradigms for which, as Kuhn says, he learnt his discipline in the first place. Nor is it clear how, or from what standpoint, he could do so, even if he wished. To begin with, it can be argued that any practising scientist is aware that it is simply asking too much of any body of theory as far-reaching as, say, Copernican astronomy or Newtonian mechanics, that it should be able to account for all the relevant experimental data available at any given point in history; but that this does not prevent it from surviving, and being accepted by scientific orthodoxy as a basis for further research. It can live indefinitely with the unsolved problems created by apparent exceptions and anomalies. Thus Paul Feyerabend declares roundly[38] – and perhaps with some intentional exaggeration – that '*not a single theory ever agrees with all the known facts in its domain*'.
And he goes on to list examples, among them the following:

Thus the Copernican view at the time of Galileo was inconsistent with facts so plain and obvious that Galileo had to call it 'surely false'. There is no limit to my astonishment', he writes in a later work, 'when I reflect that Aristarchus and Copernicus were able to make reason so conquer sense that, in defiance of the latter, the former became mistress of their belief'. Newton's theory of gravitation was beset, from the very beginning, by a considerable number of difficulties which were serious enough to provide material for refutations.

while Newton's ray theory of colour 'is found to be inconsistent with

the existence of mirror images (as is admitted by Newton himself . . .)'
And even in the present century, the special theory of relativity was
'retained' despite Miller's experimental results, apparently
inconsistent with it, of which no satisfactory account was given for a
quarter of a century. (That such an account was ever given at all is,
interestingly enough, revealed by Feyerabend only in the notes at the
end of his essay.)

   Even allowing, however, that Feyerabend's examples are
historically accurate, we do not necessarily have to accept his
conclusion that

we can change science and make it agree with our wishes. We can turn science
from a stern and demanding mistress into an attractive and yielding
courtesan who tries to anticipate every wish of her lover.[39]

– though again it may have value as a counter-balance to the naive
view of science as the obedient servant and chronicler of fact. There
are various reasons why scientists might indeed 'retain' a theory in the
face of contrary experimental evidence. It is hard to believe that any
scientist worthy of the name would ever say, in effect, 'This theory is at
variance with observed facts. But so what? I still claim that it is true'. If
he intended this seriously and literally it would surely be sufficient
reason for saying he was *not* worthy of the name. But, even setting
aside doubts about the competence of the conduct of the experiments
in question or about what precisely they show, there could be other
grounds for not abandoning the theory immediately. Thus, the
reference to 'reason conquering sense' in Feyerabend's quotation from
Galileo – and a further quotation in the same passage from Newton's
teacher, Barrow, priding himself on not letting mere observational
data 'have so great an influence on me, as to make me renounce what I
know to be manifestly agreeable to reason' – are survivals of a
rationalism rooted far back in Greek thought. According to such
rationalism, reason is, or includes, a source of knowledge of reality
independent of, and superior to, sense-experience – so that science can,
in effect, be developed in essentially the same way as a system of pure
mathematics, and if the result does not accord with our observational
data, then so much the worse for observation. The guiding principle is,
in brief, 'Sit down and think' rather than 'Go out and look'. Whether
rationalism in this sense has ever been strictly *disproved*, or whether it
could be without question-begging, is debatable. But it is at any rate
outmoded. Even a professed empiricist, however, might have sound

reasons for trying to keep alive a theory that was at odds with the experimental evidence. Thus, a theory may well pass through a growing stage in which no one, not even its originator, is quite sure about *exactly* what it is trying to say, or to *exactly* what range of situations it applies, a stage at which it passes through a series of tentative formulations, which may well be recognized as merely tentative even at the time. But although in an admittedly imperfect form – and perfection may take a long time to achieve – it may pass enough tests, enable us to make enough successful predictions, sufficiently outshine its rivals, to leave scientists convinced, or at any rate hopeful, that despite the anomalies and discrepancies it is still substantially correct. It is like an unfinished painting or sculpture which 'still needs working on' but shows sufficient promise not to be discarded out of hand.

We might reply, of course, that as a comment on the history, or psychology, of science this may well be true; but that if this is all that is meant by the claim that scientific theories can be kept alive indefinitely in the face of contrary experimental evidence, then it in no way conflicts with Popper's essential thesis. For, whatever they may have in common, the various tentative formulations are in effect different theories, each in its turn refuted by the experimental results and accordingly modified into, or replaced by, something more in keeping with them. But again, we have to ask whether, or to what extent, our theories – at any rate in the higher reaches of science – are such that they *could*, in fact, ever come into direct conflict with such results. Consider, for example, the claim made by Imre Lakatos, in deliberate contradiction of Popper's criterion of what makes a theory genuinely scientific, that '*exactly the most admired scientific theories simply fail to forbid any observable state of affairs*'.[40] He supports this contention with the tale of an imaginary pre-Einsteinian physicist who, on the basis of the Newtonian mechanics and gravitational theory (plus the appropriate initial conditions) calculates the path of a given planet. The observed path deviates from the calculated one. But, even though our scientist admits the accuracy of the observations in question, there is no question of his regarding Newton's theories as refuted thereby. There is an indefinite number of auxiliary hypotheses – for example a hitherto undiscovered planet exercising an additional gravitational pull – which he can introduce. And even if he runs out of interest or ingenuity before he finds one that will serve the purpose and survive the relevant tests, nothing has been demonstrated but his own limitations as a scientist, and he can still, with a clear conscience, leave the problems to someone else. There is no time-limit on its solution. This, according to Lakatos,

strongly suggests that even a most respected scientific theory, like Newton's dynamics and theory of gravitation, may fail to forbid any observable state of affairs. Indeed, *some scientific theories forbid an event occurring in some specified finite spatio-temporal region . . . only on the condition that no other factor* (possibly hidden in some distant and unspecified spatio-temporal corner of the universe) *has any influence on it . . .*

Another way of putting this is to say that some scientific theories are normally interpreted as containing a *ceteris paribus* clause: in such cases it is always a specific theory *together* with this clause which may be refuted. But such a refutation is inconsequential for the *specific* theory under test because by replacing the *ceteris paribus* clause by a different one the *specific* theory can always be retained whatever the tests say.[41]

For such a theory, it is not a matter of 'If this theory is true, then certain observational results (or all observational results but this one) are ruled out' but rather 'If this theory is true *and* no countervailing conditions are operating, then . . .' – and, in a universe still only very partially explored, we can never say definitely in any given case, that there can be no such conditions. A little later in the passage just quoted, Lakatos suggests that, '*ceteris paribus* clauses are not exceptions but the rule in science', and hence that, *pace* Popper, *irrefutability* may be a hallmark of genuine science.

In a later paper,[42] Lakatos rejects on similar grounds Popper's crucial distinction between genuine science, which is prepared to put itself at risk and specify conditions for its own refutation, and pseudo-science, like Freudian psycho-analysis – and presumably, though Lakatos does not mention it here, Marxism as well – which does not. The Freudians have indeed

refused to specify experimental conditions under which they would give up their basic assumptions. For Popper this is the hallmark of their intellectual dishonesty. But what if we put Popper's question to the Newtonian scientist: What kind of observation would refute to the satisfaction of the Newtonian not merely a particular Newtonian explanation but Newtonian dynamics and gravitational theory itself? And have such criteria ever been discussed or agreed upon by Newtonians? The Newtonian will, alas, scarcely be able to give a positive answer. But then, if psychoanalysts are to be condemned as dishonest by Popper's standards, must not Newtonians be similarly condemned?

Popper, as we might expect, holds his ground in the face of these criticisms. In his reply to Lakatos,[43] he maintains that there are in fact infinitely many possible observations which could refute Newton. The story from which Lakatos generalizes – based presumably on the discovery of Neptune – is a quite exceptional case. But suppose we found a planet that moved in a rectangular orbit; or suppose that the earth, alone among the planets, rotated on its axis or orbited the sun with steadily increasing velocity; or suppose, quite simply, that the cup of tea on the table before us dances in the air, or turns somersaults without spilling. Any such occurrence, according to Popper, would suffice to refute Newton – whereas there are no corresponding examples of oddities in human behaviour which would suffice to refute Freud.

But, even if we were confronted with well-authenticated examples of such un-Newtonian phenomena, we still *could*, strictly speaking, preserve Newtonian theory, without self-contradiction, by introducing some suitable *ad hoc* hypothesis. We might indeed be forced to resort to something scientifically much less respectable than the postulate of a hitherto undetected planet, to an hypothesis that had little to support it beyond its capacity to get us out of the immediate difficulty. At its worst, this would simply amount to the brazen introduction of some unique 'force' or 'power' which had no other manifestation in nature than to counteract the operation of the Newtonian principles precisely to the extent of producing the phenomena in question. (We might claim that this was enough to allow it to satisfy the Popperian criterion of science, since it would be falsified by the *non*-occurrence of the phenomena in question.) The obvious objection is that to place no restrictions on such use of *ad hoc* hypotheses would be to trivialize science. It would be like allowing ourselves to 'explain' puzzling phenomena by postulating ghosts or spirits which, again, manifest themselves only in the production of the phenomena in question. Clearly, with such licence, we could 'explain' anything whatsoever – but our 'explanations' would be theoretically and practically worthless. Yet *some ad hoc* hypotheses *are* indispensable, if only because so many of our theories are designed to indicate what happens, or would happen, under ideally simplified conditions, where we have systems of bodies totally isolated from outside influences, perfectly smooth surfaces, etc. And in dealing with actual situations we have to endeavour to determine the specific deviations from these ideal conditions, which lead them to develop in ways unpredictable from the theories alone.

But how then do we distinguish acceptable from unacceptable uses of such hypotheses? The answer would seem to depend on a number of factors – among them, how important the original theories are to us. Thus the commitment to the Newtonian theories, during their long period of predominance in science, was presumably due in the first place to their outstanding successes in systematizing existing observational data, and, to a remarkable degree of accuracy, anticipating new ones. Feyerabend may well be right in saying that it was never in perfect agreement with them; but at any rate the setbacks were, in comparison with the successes, few and unspectacular. There were no obvious or notorious anomalies. And although even minor ones could not, with a clear scientific conscience, simply be left unexplained, there is a strong incentive to explain them – or explain them away – without disturbance to the theories themselves. No doubt there are sound reasons for wanting our auxiliary hypotheses to meet certain requirements, to be such as to gain some plausibility from current theory, for example, and to be amenable to a range of independent tests. But in the case of a body of theories as well-attested and widely applicable as those in question, we should certainly permit ourselves considerable latitude over both the time we allowed for the finding of an acceptable hypothesis, and what we counted as acceptable. If the kind of un-Newtonian behaviour of planets which Popper envisages were widespread, then of course the Newtonian system would never have got off the ground (if the metaphor is not inappropriate to gravitational theory) in the first place, and the commitment to it by the scientific community would never have existed. But for isolated examples we would obviously be prepared to take seriously hypotheses like that of some unique and otherwise undetectable set of forces operating in a particular situation; and I have no doubt that, as Newtonian scientists, we should prefer to suppose a poltergeist in Popper's study to explain his dancing tea-cup rather than sacrifice our whole system to it.

Another, though related, consideration when the discarding of a given theory, or body of theories, is in question, is whether or not there is a workable *alternative* to which we may turn. Popper himself notes that 'in most cases we have, before falsifying a hypothesis, another one up our sleeves'.[44] And Lakatos insists that we *must* have one; otherwise our business as scientists is to refuse to accept the supposed refutation and continue the search for a 'rescue hypothesis'.[45] To abandon our theories about a given field or topic of research, without a prepared alternative position to go to, would be, in effect, to abandon – temporarily at least – research in that field since, as we have seen, we require the theories to set our problems and direct our observations for us. Thus, for example, whatever difficulties a geocentric view of the solar system may have created for early astronomers, however complicated or far-fetched the hypotheses to which they had to resort, they had really no option but to soldier on with it, until someone had the boldness and originality to demonstrate the feasibility of the heliocentric view. Indeed, it seems likely that we should not even think of the geocentric view *as* a view (picture, theory . . .) and hence as either agreeing with or disagreeing with our observational data, unless we were *already* aware of an alternative. Without this, we should simply think of our problems in terms of such things as finding a regular pattern among the various observed positions of a given planet, or testing hypotheses about what that pattern might be. No doubt we should be taking it for granted that we were observing the actual motions of the planet from the vantage-point of a stationary earth, but, before the alternative had presented itself, we should have no occasion to explicate or take note of this assumption, or consider whether our data agreed with it or not. (Compare the way in which, in epistemology, the naive realism of the plain man only becomes a named and recognized *theory*, when it is contrasted with rival theories. In the absence of these we might have difficulties over explaining what happens in illusions and hallucinations, or over the transmission theories of light, sound, etc. but we should never think of these as difficulties for, or possible refutations of, naive realism.) Once the alternative has been accepted, at any rate tentatively, once we have started using, say, the heliocentric model of the solar system, then obviously the problems change; our hypotheses now concern how for example various possible patterns of movement of the other planets would appear from the moving platform, as it were, of the earth, and we reconsider our existing data, or seek new ones, with a view to testing these. No doubt Feyerabend and others have been right in insisting that this, and comparable scientific innovations are not, and were never thought by their exponents to be, capable of coping immediately with all the relevant data. But presumably one reason for accepting them – at any rate once we have discarded the rationalism which is prepared to over-rule mere observation – is that they are, or show promise of being, less beset by intractable problems in this respect than their rivals or predecessors. (Another reason, of course, might be quite simply that they suggest new and interesting lines of research, and it is part of the business of the scientist to follow such lines and see where they lead, even if he does *not* claim that their starting-point has any decisive advantage over the alternatives.)

A particular field of scientific interest, like astronomy, may, then, have been troubled over a long period, generations or even centuries perhaps, by problems which have proved altogether insoluble, or soluble only by appeal to awkward and implausible hypotheses. With the advantage of hindsight, *we* may trace the difficulties to some fundamental assumption, like that of the geocentric model, and point out that, if this had been abandoned, the problems could have been solved, or need never have arisen. But at the time the difficulties would not, and indeed could not, have been formulated in this way, or seen as putting pressure on the geocentric view or requiring its replacement. And even when promising alternatives are available there is no point where the observational data can *compel* us, on pain of inconsistency, to adopt one rather than the other. Though doubtless the price in dead-ends and implausibilities would in practice often be higher than most scientists would be prepared to pay, once they had the offer of an alternative, they *could* always opt for one of Lakatos's 'rescue hypotheses'. (We may recall how, a century ago, men far from being either stupid or ignorant were prepared to take seriously the hypothesis that rocks had been created with built-in fossils, rather than abandon something as vital to their whole conception of the world as their interpretation of the Genesis account of creation.) Many considerations might indeed influence the decision to make the shift from one alternative to another; but none the less it would appear to remain, strictly, a matter of decision, even where one decision, and its consequences, have grown so familiar to us that it seems the only possible one.

There is an important similarity here between science and what we should ordinarily think of as metaphysical rather than scientific doctrines, theism, for example, or mechanistic materialism. Such doctrines *do* undoubtedly (as commonly understood at any rate) create expectations, even if highly unspecific ones, about what the world should be like. For example, widespread, persistent, and apparently pointless evil and destruction strain the credibility of the doctrine of a world created and controlled by a benevolent, omnipotent and omniscient deity, and certainly give the theist something to explain. Similarly, the intricacy and mutual adaptation, and the sheer beauty, of many parts of nature strain the credibility of the doctrine that it is all produced simply by the workings of the laws of mechanics on a vast concourse of material particles. But there are no facts about nature which either theist or materialist *cannot* accept, without inconsistency, while maintaining his characteristic doctrine. Defensive moves are always available. The theist can postulate that, whatever the appearances to the contrary, all that happens still serves some good purpose, beyond our present comprehension; the materialist that, given time enough, even the most complex patterns could have emerged without the aid of anything beyond what his doctrine allows. A variety of influences – the successes of a science in which mechanics plays a central role, evidence which undermines, or appears to undermine, the Biblical basis of theism – might, as a matter of historical or psychological fact, make one doctrine or the other the more popular or more readily acceptable, at a particular time in a particular culture. But we can never say that either has been definitely refuted, killed by the evidence now available; and both have in fact shown considerable resilience, and capacity for re-establishing themselves after periods of unpopularity.

This conforms very closely to what we have said about science. Some scientific theories (when coupled with suitable statements of initial conditions) no doubt yield expectations about the world which are much more specific than those of metaphysical doctrines – or, for that matter, of Popper's 'pseudo-sciences' like Marxism or psycho-analysis. But this is at best a difference of degree rather than kind, and it is by no means universally true – what, for example, of evolutionary theory? Nor, as we have just seen, can science be distinguished from metaphysics – and pseudo-science – by its willingness to accept risks of refutation without, as it were, a safety-net. It has, and indeed has to have, such a net in the form of *ad hoc* hypotheses, and the other rescue devices we have considered. There may well be striking differences of degree; it may well be that science, or important parts of it, not only takes more specific and more spectacular risks but more often gets away with them without recourse to the safety-net – that the Newtonians and Einsteinians tumble into it less often and less clumsily than the metaphysicians, the Marxists or the Freudians. But we are still unable to draw a demarcation line between science and these other fields of interest by pointing out some technique of self-defence or self-perpetuation which they permit themselves, and science – even in the form of Popper's favourite examples of science at its best – has positively forsworn.

We should notice also how some of these ways of coping with our 'confrontations' in science have already been illustrated in our earlier accounts of the 'crises' which, according to Popper, generate *philosophy*. Take for example the crisis brought about by, on the one hand, Newton's apparent success in establishing general truths about nature, and, on the other, Hume's demonstration that no such truths *could* be established by empirical means. Kant (as Popper portrays him) in effect resorts to a *ceteris paribus* clause. Hume's theory of knowledge is substantially right if, as it assumes, we are dealing with experimental data over which we have no control, data in relation to which the observer is a mere passive recipient. But, granted that our science is about the content of the phenomenal world (rather than things in themselves) and that we *can* to some extent control this content, and impose a certain order on it, then Hume's conclusions no longer apply. Within these limits we *have* sufficient grounds for generalization. Popper himself, in contrast, favours the ploy of claiming that the evidence has been misinterpreted, that it does not show what it is (or was) supposed to show, i.e. Newton's achievements did not show that it is possible to establish general truths about nature, but only that it is possible in favourable circumstances to make brilliantly successful conjectures about it – so there is, after all, no conflict to be resolved . . .

Yet, it may be said, despite the interest of such similarities, and the difficulty, which they illustrate, of drawing any sharp lines of demarcation between what is science and what is not, the differences in *degree* that we have mentioned are not to be dismissed as insignificant. We may grant the continuity between, say, the highly generalized conviction that God is in His Heaven, so all will ultimately be right with the world, or that history is a sequence of struggles between opposing forces, and the very specific, mathematically precise, predictions of physics; and grant also the essential similarity of the moves which can be, and are, made to salvage any of these when there is a *prima facie* conflict with experience. But for many purposes – though not for all – within the economy of our dealings with the world (our attempts to find our way about in it and achieve some measure of mastery over it) the advance from the general to the specific may be all-important. There are obvious incentives for trying to refine what may well have started off as general speculation about the order of the world into something which can be made to yield precise predictions about just what we will find in it under just what circumstances – and for trying to devise techniques and equipment for testing such predictions. Of course, we have still no precise answer to the question 'At what stage in this process of refinement etc. is metaphysics (theology, ideology or whatever) transformed into science?' But we can say, at any rate, that one important characteristic at least of the long process by which science as we know it has disentangled itself from these other interests, and groped towards an identity of its own, has been just this kind of refinement – the shift from the general to the specific, and from the vague to the precise. That is, we pass from asking 'What sort of stuff is the world made of?' or 'What purpose does it serve?' to asking 'What happens when this particular set of conditions is realised?' or 'How does this particular element interact with that?' And it might be said, indeed, that this is nothing more or less than human enquiry about the world coming to know, and accept with due humility, its own limitations – reaching a level of maturity at which it no longer fluctuates between extravagantly optimistic claims to knowledge of the whole scheme of things and despair of the possibility of any knowledge at all, and instead patiently and modestly pursues a succession of strictly limited and carefully defined objectives. And, although all the options and self-defensive moves and excuses we have mentioned are still available to it, its reward is that it can (very often) dispense with them, and create theoretical structures which are impressively simple, durable, and versatile – and highly effective for the limited purposes for which they were designed.

Any such account of science – as simply the practical, down-to-earth offspring of metaphysics or theology, who has prudently resolved to cultivate his own garden and make it pay – would probably smack too much of instrumentalism for Popper's liking.[46] To talk thus of the effectiveness of science for this or that purpose in our dealings with the world is to obscure what is for him its primary commitment, i.e. to the quest for *truth* about the world. And similarly with all that has been said about the scientist's options between holding on to a theory in the face of contrary evidence, shoring it up with supplementary hypotheses, or making a bold revolutionary shift to an entirely new theory. This is the source of Popper's impatience with all such theorizing about science. Granted that, on his own principles, the quest for truth must always be an unended quest (to quote the title of his autobiography) it does not follow that it is a mistaken one; rather, the idea of truth serves as 'the standard of which we may fall short'.[47]

Our astronomer, aware of both the geocentric and heliocentric accounts of the solar system, should, accordingly, be asking, not 'Which account can be reconciled with the observational data with the fewer and simpler supplementary hypotheses?' or 'Which promises to be the more interesting and fruitful to explore?' or 'Which would do more to simplify astronomical calculations and predictions?' but simply 'Which, if either of them, is *true*?' And, even if the issues between them can never be finally settled, he can at least set them every available test which they would fail if they were not true, and thus endeavour to expose and eliminate falsehood. This, as we have said repeatedly, is for Popper the real business of science. And hence he cannot allow that science might properly tolerate indefinitely several mutually inconsistent theories, or leave us free to choose between them on grounds of internal consistency, simplicity, interest, practical utility – or anything else but truth or falsity. The only genuinely scientific reason for discarding a theory is that it is not true; the only one for holding on to it is that it might be.

Undoubtedly, there is much to admire in this Popperian conception of the scientist as someone with plenty of scope indeed for his initiative and imagination, but none the less constrained to submit *all* his creations, however fundamental to his discipline, to the ultimate test of agreement with observed fact. Much to admire also in the idea of truth as something at once all-important and endlessly elusive. But, for the reasons given in this and the previous section – some of the strongest of these reasons, it will be recalled, provided by Popper himself, it seems evident that the simple 'confrontation' model will not do as it stands. There is, and has to be, more to the replacement of an old scientific theory by a new one than it allows. As we have seen, whatever the observational data, there is no point at which, logically, the old theory *must* be abandoned; whether the data are *seen* as conflicting with the old theory, and whether we can abandon that theory without abandoning altogether the relevant field of research, depends on the availability of a feasible alternative; and, to go a stage further, our judgement that a proposed alternative is feasible (promising, better than its rival . . .) must be made by reference to a wider framework of ideas which is left unquestioned. (Because of this last point, when we *do* make the shift to a new theory – even one highly original and far-reaching in its consequences – it is not quite the new birth into a new world that Kuhn sometimes makes it out to be. Our scientific revolutions, however radical – unless we want to say that they are strictly pointless, change merely for the sake of change – have presumably to be justified by an appeal to some still wider framework of ideas which remains constant throughout.) But the fact remains that whatever the role of careful observation and experiment – and the accurate reporting of results – in science, they cannot of themselves suffice to overthrow our theories, or compel their replacement. Thus, as has been already suggested, Popper's insight into the character of science, though profound and original, is still a partial one; and a major part of its influence on subsequent philosophy of science has lain in the attempts it has stimulated to correct and supplement it. Some of the most serious difficulties, as already indicated, arise from what Popper came to call his 'fallibilism',[48] i.e. the thesis that, while as scientists we must always seek truth, we can *never* claim with certainty to have found it – particularly when he attempts to combine this with an uncompromising rejection of relativism. But the issues raised here are complex enough, and important enough in the whole system of Popper's thought, to merit a further chapter.

# 3

## Relativism and truth

### 1

Popper gives his most explicit and forceful condemnation of relativism in his addendum to the fourth (1962) edition of *The Open Society and its Enemies*:

The main philosophical malady of our time is an intellectual and moral relativism, the latter being at least in part based upon the former. By relativism – or, if you like, scepticism – I mean here, briefly, the theory that the choice between competing theories is arbitrary; since either, there is no such thing as objective truth; or, if there is, no such thing as a theory which is true or at any rate (though perhaps not true) nearer to the truth than another theory; or, if there are two or more theories, no ways or means of deciding whether one of them is better than another.

He goes on to prescribe 'a dose of Tarski's theory of truth', which –

stiffened perhaps by my own theory of getting nearer to the truth, may go a long way towards curing this malady, though I admit that some other remedies might also be required, such as the non-authoritarian theory of knowledge which I have described elsewhere.[1]

What we have to consider is whether, or to what extent, this or any other remedy will enable us to ward off relativism, or at any rate the pernicious forms thereof.

We may indeed wonder whether anyone – any of our critics of the Popperian account of science, or indeed any other thinker who merits serious consideration – has ever in fact adopted relativism as Popper defines it, i.e. 'the theory that the choice between competing theories is arbitrary'. Even if there are circumstances where a scientist has, say, to choose between shoring up a well-tried theory with *ad hoc* hypotheses, or venturing on a radically new one, where his training provides no mechanical, rigorously prescribed way of making the choice, and where equally well-qualified colleagues might choose differently ... still, this does not mean that his choice is arbitrary, made on the toss of a coin, as it were, or by closing his eyes and jabbing with a pin. An analogy with backing horses may indeed be appropriate; here also, even though there are certainly no rules obedience to which guarantees success, we should only speak of the rank amateur as making an arbitrary choice. The dedicated student of racing form, whose hunches are the product of long experience, does not. What is really at issue here is not whether the choice between theories might be arbitrary, but whether mutually inconsistent choices, however arrived at, might be *equally right*. This is the essential point of the relativism which Popper and many others have, understandably enough, regarded as potentially disastrous, i.e. the relativism which, in effect, denies that there is any independent standard to determine which of our choices is right and which is wrong – we are all free to set our own standards, and we may set them differently. It is as though our gamblers, having made their selections, are not bound by the decisions of starters or judges; each can decide for himself what is to count as winning the race, and so, as in the Alice in Wonderland story, everyone can win.

Relativism, thus understood, has at least some *prima facie* plausibility in the fields of ethics or aesthetics – where it tells us, for example, that an action is only right or wrong, a picture good or bad, relative to the standards of a particular culture or generation, and that our reluctance to accept some of the applications of this principle is due merely to a deep-rooted prejudice in favour of our own set of standards. (I am not, of course, saying that we will not encounter serious difficulties when we work out the implications of even these manifestations of relativism.) What is hard to swallow is precisely this 'intellectual relativism' (to use Popper's term) which tells us in effect that a statement is only true or false relative to a given standard or criterion of truth, that the same statement may be true relative to one such criterion and false relative to another, and that such criteria have in the last analysis to be adopted without any rational grounds for so doing. Yet it must, I think, be acknowledged that there is a serious case to be made out in favour of such relativism, and one which Popper has never fully examined or answered, even if in the end it does prove to be answerable.

Like other forms of relativism it may be seen as, in the first place, a reaction to the development of self-consciousness about how much we ourselves contribute to our various dealings with the world in the way of concepts, presuppositions, ideals, values, methods, criteria, etc. (Since the systematic cultivation of such self-consciousness is, as we said at the outset, one of the characteristic features of philosophy, it is understandable that relativism has been, since pre-Socratic times, a recurrent temptation to philosophers.) Even the natural sciences, at first sight paradigm examples of subservience to facts beyond our control, have proved on closer scrutiny to be determined, to a remarkable and perhaps startling extent, by what we bring to the search, rather than what is there to be found. Before we can discover anything, there is much that has to be decided or adopted – the concepts in terms of which we frame our questions, what we call in question and what we take for granted, how we set about finding the answers, and what we count as sufficient grounds for accepting a given answer, (all of these, of course, inter-related). To try in the case of any given example of research to explicate these adoptions – a better term than 'choices' or 'decisions' since these suggest a deliberation which is rarely present – is, though difficult, a salutary exercise in itself. But inevitably a further question arises: What if these adoptions were made differently by different individuals, schools, generations or cultures? Is there any neutral and authoritative standpoint from which we can assess them, and decide whether one is in any respect better than, or preferable to another? Or does not any attempt at assessment or arguments for or against, necessarily require in its turn the adoption of the appropriate apparatus, so that at some point adoptions must be made without any arguments, or any rational grounds for making one rather than another? As with Wittgenstein's games, we can assess moves within a particular game as permissible or impermissible, successful or unsuccessful, according to the rules of that game – but from what standpoint, other than that of mere prejudice, can we assess the rules themselves?

Still, it may be said, even if we have to admit that these various sets of concepts, etc., which are, or might be, used in our explorations of the world, are just *different* from each other, and we have no neutral means of determining questions of right or wrong, better or worse, among them, is this so much to be deplored? Suppose there are different views of nature which enquirers of different cultures or generations might arrive at without any of them committing any error at all. Here – as perhaps in ethics or aesthetics as well – might not

relativism provide the theoretical basis for a commendable tolerance
and humility? It appears a good deal less innocuous, however, once we
extend it to cover our criteria of truth and falsity, and think out the
implications of so doing. The concept of a criterion, in general, is a
notoriously elusive one, and one much analysed, especially since
Wittgenstein drew his famous distinction between criteria and
symptoms;[2] and, as we shall discover, the concept of a criterion of
truth (or falsity) raises special difficulties of its own. But for the
moment, despite the questions it leaves unanswered, we may say
simply that a criterion of truth is, in Popper's terms, 'a means of
deciding ... whether a given statement is true or false'.[3] For the
purposes of the relativist argument, we can quite willingly allow the
point Popper makes a couple of pages later, i.e. that there is no *general*
criterion of truth, no all-purpose device for distinguishing true from
false in any field or subject-matter whatsoever. Nor need we suppose,
as J. R. Lucas once suggested,[4] that each discipline, physics,
mathematics, history, etc. has a distinctive criterion of its own. The
relativist starts simply from the apparently commonplace and
uncontroversial point that we do not, ordinarily at least, assign truth-
values at random. In assigning a truth-value to any given statement,
we thus make use of some means – however widely or narrowly it may
otherwise be employed – of deciding which truth-value is appropriate,
i.e. a criterion of truth in Popper's sense of the term. But then how do
we justify the use of any given criterion in any given case; how,
without question-begging can we show it is the right, or the best, one to
use?

The relativist case, reduced to its essentials, is that *any* argument
purporting on *any* grounds to show this, depends for its effectiveness
on the truth of its premises. When we use *any* statements, whatever
they may be, to support this – or indeed any other – conclusion, we are
claiming, at least tacitly, that these statements are true. So, on the
grounds once again that we do not assign truth-values at random, we
must have already adopted some criterion (or criteria) of truth without
any arguments whatsoever in its (or their) favour, since such adoption
is a precondition of constructing any arguments at all (though we may,
of course, fail to recognize that this is what we are doing). Now suppose
these initial adoptions made differently by different groups or
individuals. Obviously, there is no way in which they could argue
about the issue, or try to convince one another by argument; an
essential precondition of such argument, i.e. agreement on a criterion

(or on criteria) of truth, would be absent. They could only hope for quasi-religious conversions, or agree to differ. And all that can be asked of any seeker after truth is that he shall be faithful to the criterion he has adopted; and where two of us have made the initial adoptions differently then we *could* reach opposite conclusions about the truth-value of a given theory (or statement of any kind) without either of us having committed any error, or being able to convict the other of error.

There *is*, then, a case for relativism in the form in which Popper denounces it; and it is a lot easier to feel that there has to be something wrong with it, than to say precisely what is. Understandably, we want to protest that the adoption of criteria of truth cannot be quite such a free-for-all as the relativist makes out; there are some limits or restraints which even he has to acknowledge. Logic, surely, must be in part at least, above the battle – for when we speak of different *possible* criteria (or whatever) any of which we are free to adopt, we can only mean *logically* possible, i.e. consistent with the essential principles of logic. Thus while we may contemplate happily enough different possible systems of morals or aesthetics, or even of physics, we have to draw the line at different possible logics; different logical notations, certainly, or developments of different parts of logic, but what would it mean to postulate, say two different possible systems, one of which accepted the principle of non-contradiction, while the other rejected it? Thus, it would seem, even the most thorough-going relativist must admit the value of consistency; otherwise the whole enterprise of statement-making and truth-evaluation collapses into chaos. Suppose, then, that the application of a given criterion of truth results in our assigning the same truth-value to mutually inconsistent statements. Would this not be a sufficient reason for discarding it? And have we not then one neutral standpoint at any rate from which different possible criteria can be judged, and some of them, at least, eliminated?

The relativist, however, can quite cheerfully accept that we might indeed reject proposed criteria of truth on these grounds, and perhaps on a good many others as well. But he goes on to point out that we are still thinking of a situation in which we are able to argue for a given conclusion, and hence to establish premises for use in such argument – 'The use of criterion *C* leads to this or that inconsistency' – and again we must at least tacitly have adopted some criterion of truth as a condition of doing so. We have simply failed to appreciate the *primitiveness* of the level at which such adoptions are made, *before* (logically if not temporally) we can have any arguments, evidence, reasons, grounds . . . whatsoever.

Similarly if we complain that the relativist is merely creating an artificial problem, that while we encounter many difficulties in the course of formulating, communicating and assessing statements, irreconcilable differences over criteria of truth are not among them. The relativist's answer is that our endeavours to find out about our world, to record our results, communicate them to each other and criticize them, all take place perforce within the framework of a shared culture, or form of life – something which could never have developed in the first place, without, among many other preconditions, a shared criterion (or shared criteria) of truth. To envisage what it would be like to differ over such criteria, we may have to dream up somewhat improbable encounters between members of tribes with radically different cultures. But this does nothing to invalidate the essential relativist argument. After all, a similar need arises in expositions of the theory of Special Relativity in physics; we have to postulate space-travel at speeds far beyond anything currently practicable in order to provide cases where differences in frame of reference would make any appreciable difference to judgements of distance, velocity, etc. But the lack of everyday illustrations does not invalidate the one theory any more than the other.

There is admittedly, at least one important difference between relativism over truth-values and relativity in physics. It may be, as the latter tells us, that statements of the form 'particle $P$ is travelling at velocity $V$', for example, can always be correctly expanded into 'particle $P$ is travelling at velocity $V$ relative to frame of reference $F$', even though in most cases the expansion is superfluous because the frame of reference is not in doubt. But we certainly could not claim that, in the same way, 'statement $S$ is true' is correctly expandable into 'statement $S$ is true relative to criterion $C$'. If we ever do say anything of the latter form (call it $STC$) it fulfils a quite different function from the former ($ST$). We have here something much more like the difference between saying 'action $A$ is wrong according to moral code $M$' and simply 'action $A$ is wrong'. In saying the second of these, we are (among other things, no doubt) condemning $A$, and we stand self-condemned if we thereafter do or encourage $A$. But saying the first would have no such effect of committing the speaker to any attitude towards $A$; it might well occur, for example, in an anthropologist's account of the way of life of a tribe to which he owes no personal allegiance. Similarly, in saying something of the *ST* form, whatever else we may be doing, we commit ourselves to *S*, i.e. we endorse it, accept its logical consequences, sanction its use as a premiss in future discussion, etc. *STC*, on the other hand, carries no such commitment; it merely serves to point out what *would be* the consequences, in a particular case, of adopting *C*. When we actually assign truth-values to statements, as opposed to commenting on their assignment, we simply *give* (or purport to give) the results of applying certain criteria to certain statements; we do not *say* that these criteria, thus applied, yield these results. And to this extent we have to behave like absolutists, i.e. to adopt certain criteria, apply them, and give the results of applying them, without acknowledging that we are so doing, or that any alternatives are open to us. Relativism is essentially the standpoint of the *critic* – in this case of someone standing back from the actual business of statement-making and truth-evaluation and commenting thereon. (Such a critic is, of course, in one respect on the edge of a regress. If he *states* something of the form *STC* he is perforce making an unacknowledged use of some criterion of truth, not necessarily *C*, and similarly if he acknowledges this in a statement of the form $STCC_1$ . . . etc. Relativism, as Ryle said of 'self-commentary, self-ridicule and self-admonition' is logically condemned to eternal penultimacy'.[5]) What the relativist claims to be doing is pointing out some logically inescapable conditions and limitations of making statements and assigning them truth-values; this is something quite distinct from the original statement-making etc., and we get into serious difficulties if we try to assimilate the one enterprise to the other.

Again, however, the relativist can accept all this – and, indeed, use it to explain why his thesis is at first sight implausible, apparently hopelessly at odds with our actual experience of statement-making. He can allow that progress in research, in exploring our world and formulating and assessing our findings, depends on our adopting unequivocally some criterion (or criteria) of truth and ignoring the possibility of alternatives. For as long as we are engaged in such research, we have to act as if there were an absolute or 'objective' truth which can be attained or at least approached. This much we can concede to Popper. Successful research, like successful marriage, depends, once the initial choice is made, on forsaking all others and cleaving only unto this. But when we stand back, as it were, and reflect on the whole process, we may still be quite right in noting that, theoretically at least, there *were* alternatives, and that there is no non-question-begging way in which the adoption of one of these could be shown to be wrong, or worse than the one we actually made. The relativist can, and indeed must, allow that research as such demands that we choose a particular route and follow it; his point is simply that there are alternative routes which might equally well be followed.

Relativism, then, as thus understood, is very far from issuing us all with licenses to say or believe what we please, to alter the rules of the game whenever we feel so inclined. It insists – as indeed it must if it wants to be taken seriously – that the adoptions, or decisions, on which it turns are very rare, and very deeply embedded in the socially shared sub-structure of activities like research. So deeply embedded in fact, that it requires a considerable effort of imagination to envisage what it would be like to alter them, or what the effects of such alteration would be. And failure to appreciate this feature of relativism may account, in part at least, for the fear expressed by Popper and other that it could be made a tool of totalitarianism. The fear is, presumably, that if we once abandon the idea of an absolute, objective truth, of that which is unalterably true whether anyone wants it so or not, then the way is open to the kind of 1984 situation in which history can be systematically rewritten to meet political needs, and whatever the leader, or the party, calls true *is* true, *ipso facto*. Now no doubt totalitarian regimes often have an interest in misleading their subjects about matters of historical fact, and attempt, in effect, to rewrite history. But the point of doing so is surely that they want to give their version the prestige and status of history *as traditionally understood*, to present it as satisfying those criteria of truth which are built in to the whole concept of historiography. To abolish and replace these criteria by official decree, as it were – even supposing that this could be done – would not clear the way for a revised version of history; rather, it would create some novel discipline for which we have no name, and of which the status and effects in society would be quite unpredictable. The regime, then, can draw no comfort from a relativism which says that all that can be asked of the historian (or the researcher in any other discipline) is fidelity to those criteria which, in part, identify that discipline and which he himself has at least tacitly adopted when he identifies himself as a worker within that discipline; for the regime's whole enterprise depends on concealing its *lack* of fidelity to the criteria it professes to satisfy. And, generally, of course, no totalitarian regime could wish to introduce its subjects to the doctrine of relativism; since its stability depends on their acceptance of its

teaching as absolute, unquestionable truth, it can scarcely tolerate the
thesis that there are, after all, different criteria of truth, yielding
different accounts of what is true and what is false, and none of which
can be proved better than another.

## 2

But, it may be said, even if we accept the relativist case, as presented in
the previous section, regarding the functions of criteria of truth, the
resultant necessity of adopting at least one such criterion without
arguments in its favour, and the possibility of alternatives, none of this
meets Popper's main criticism of relativism, that it is 'based on a
logical confusion – between the meaning of a term and the criterion for
its proper application'.[6] This distinction has been set out more
explicitly a few pages earlier:

> it is essential for our present purpose not to mix up questions of actual truth-
> seeking or truth-finding (i.e. epistemological or methodological questions)
> with the question of what we mean, or what we intend to say, when we speak
> of truth or of correspondence with the facts (the logical or ontological
> question of truth).[7]

What is meant by calling a statement true is, according to Popper,
given simply and incontrovertibly in the time-honoured
correspondence theory, as purified or 'rehabilitated' by Tarski.[8] And
every statement is simply and unequivocally true in this sense
(corresponding with fact) or it is not. It is of course quite correct to say
that we do not, ordinarily, *think* or *say* that a given statement is true
without some grounds for so doing. No doubt indefinitely many
criteria might be, and have been, devised and adopted for the tasks of
determining which specific statements, or ranges of statements, are
true, and which are false. And the criteria we adopt no doubt makes a
difference to which statements we *think* are true; and the situation
which our relativist envisages, where the adoption of different criteria
gives rises to irreconcilable differences of *opinion* about truth-values
might well arise. But the crucial point is that they can make no
difference whatsoever to which statements actually *are* true, and
which false.

Popper admits – indeed he insists – that we have no manifestly right
or infallible way of distinguishing true from false in any field of
enquiry. Many errors, philosophical and otherwise, follow from the

thesis that 'truth is manifest';[9] and, according to what he calls his doctrine of 'fallibilism', we have always to acknowledge 'that we may err, and that the quest for certainty (or even the quest for high probability) is a mistaken quest'. Nevertheless,

this does not imply that the quest for truth is mistaken. On the contrary, the idea of error implies that of truth as the standard of which we may fall short. It implies that, though we may seek for truth, and though we may even find truth (as I believe we do in very many cases), we can never be quite certain we have found it. There is always a possibility of error[10]

Thus we are quite right to dwell on the difficulties of discovering or recognizing truths, even the theoretical impossibility of our ever being altogether certain that we have done so, and on the variety of ways of doing or attempting to do so that have been, or might be, adopted. Quite right also to allow the possibility that, where $A$, who adopts criterion $C_1$, judges a certain statement $S$ to be true, and $B$, who adopts $C_2$, judges $S$ to be false or undecidable, each may have applied his own criterion with impeccable skill and care and *to this extent* has made no mistake; and we may have no third criterion, manifestly superior to either of theirs, which we can use to show conclusively which of them was right and which wrong, so that the issue between them remains permanently in doubt. But the fatal error of the relativist, from Popper's standpoint, lies in supposing that if $A$ and $B$ have both used their adopted criteria impeccably then both are equally right – and $S$ is true *relative to $C_1$*, but false or undecidable, *relative to $C_2$*.

Consider the analogy of trying to determine whether a given painting is a genuine Old Master or not. Suppose that $A$ and $B$ are rival art experts, using respectively techniques $T_1$ and $T_2$ for distinguishing the genuine from the skilful copy or fake. $A$, having impeccably applied $T_1$ to the painting in question, judges it to be the work of, say, Botticelli; $B$, having applied $T_2$ equally impeccably, judges that it is not. Now, granted that we have no independent and manifestly superior technique which would enable us to decide authoritatively between them, we may have to remain permanently in doubt about the painting's origin. But what is not in doubt is that either Botticelli painted the picture or he did not, and hence that one of our rival experts is right and the other wrong. We cannot without absurdity suppose that both may be right, that Botticelli may have painted the picture relative to $T_1$, but not relative to $T_2$. Indeed, it might be questioned whether it makes any sense to say that he painted it 'relative to $T_1$', etc. – unless this is just a misleading way of saying that those who rely on $T_1$ and use it correctly will *think* that he did, while those who rely on $T_2$ will not.

Also, is the relativist not tacitly adopting Popper's distinction between the concept of truth in itself (of what it is for a statement to be true) and our criteria of truth, the indefinitely various ways and means by which we try to determine in particular cases whether or not this concept is instantiated? Why else should he speak of these as *criteria of truth*, at all? This title suggests that, in the first place, despite all their diversity they are nevertheless all criteria of the same thing; and, given our ordinary uses of the term 'criteria', that they are simply ways of detecting or recognizing something already there to be detected or recognized, and have no influence over whether it is there or not. The relativist argument started from a premiss that we do not assign truth-values at random. But neither, it may be said, do we subject our statements to a random selection of tests and elect to call 'true' any statement which passes any of these. The whole idea of different, or alternative, criteria of truth is intelligible only if we start from a concept of what it is for a statement to be true, and then present the various criteria as tests of whether or not a given statement, or range of statements, is true in the sense specified. We cannot, as it were, reverse the order, i.e. start with the tests, or criteria, and identify truth as the satisfaction of these, since the whole enterprise would then be pointless; our 'tests' or 'criteria' would be deprived of anything of which to *be* tests or criteria. Indeed, this feature of relativism might be offered as an illustration of Sir Peter Strawson's general criticism of the philosophical sceptic:

his doubts are unreal, not simply because they are logically irresoluble doubts, but because they amount to the rejection of the whole conceptual scheme within which such doubts make sense.[11]

We shall certainly need to enquire more closely into the antecedents of these somewhat mysterious pieces of apparatus which we have been calling criteria or truth; but none the less the relativist may still have serious grounds for questioning the role which Popper assigns to the concept of truth itself, i.e. as 'the standard of which we may fall short'. No doubt common-sense agrees that any genuine statement is either true or not true, quite independently of what anyone thinks about its truth-value, or how he proposes to discover it. And hence someone seeking truth, or truths, in a particular field may well adopt some test or criterion which merely leads him to search diligently and systematically in the wrong direction, so that the more impeccably he applies it, the more certain he is to miss his objective. (The astrologer who makes, or assesses, predictions by appeal to the relative positions of the stars may be a model of astrological orthodoxy, but if the riches or revolutions he has predicted for this year have failed to materialize by the beginning of next, his orthodoxy is of no avail. He is quite simply wrong.) But, then, could not common-sense find parallel 'absurdities' in the implications of relativity-theory in physics — either particle $P$ is moving with velocity $V$ or it is not . . . etc.? And what can it mean to say that someone who applies a given criterion of truth impeccably is (or might be) still wrong, other than that his results fail (or might fail) to conform to those of using some other criterion, (presumably ours rather than his)? The astrologer provides an easy target because we can, in due time, confront his predictions with the records of history. But what we accept as history is determined, in essential part, by the criterion, or criteria, of truth built into our technique of historical investigation. And while we could doubtless produce arguments for preferring the historian's criteria to the astrologer's, such arguments, like any arguments whatsoever, require that we already have some (unargued) criterion of truth, etc. (Compare the challenge of moral relativism to show that, when we want to say, for example, that the primitive tribesman who is entirely faithful to the moral code of his own tribe, may still be acting wrongly, we have any firmer basis than a deep-rooted prejudice in favour of our moral code as opposed to his.)

The crucial question, then, is this. How, on Popper's terms, *can* truth serve as the standard at which we aim, and of which we may fall short, in our various enterprises, however conducted, of research and statement of results? It is not as though he believed that there existed a body of manifest or unquestionable truths against which we could check our efforts — as we might check our measuring-rods against the standard metre. For those who believe in such a body of truths — for example in the Bible or the teaching of the Church as the inspired Word of God, carrying more than human authority and beyond our power to question or correct — then, no doubt this constitutes a standard in Popper's sense. At least, anything inconsistent with it, no matter how it was arrived at, or what other criteria it satisfied, can *ipso facto* be eliminated as false; and it is undeniably an effective barrier against at any rate some manifestations of relativism. Indeed, many who would agree strongly with Popper's statement, quoted at the beginning of this chapter, about relativism as the 'malady of our time' would doubtless trace it to the decline of religion grounded on just such absolute authority. But Popper's fallibilism does not appear to make any allowance for such an authoritative body of truths. Truth is never manifest, but always something elusive, an object of search; and the success or failure of our efforts to find it is always a matter of uncertainty. Hence, we can never confront any proposed criterion of truth, or the results of using it, with The Truth, but only with those relevant statements which we already think to be, or accept as, true. So can taking truth as our standard ever amount to anything more than measuring the results of one human effort of research against those of another?

Here, of course, the relativist goes back to his basic point. We can indeed criticize any given criterion of truth, or the results of applying it, but only at the expense of adopting some other one without criticism. And we can achieve objectivity of a sort, i.e. fidelity to those criteria which are most deeply rooted, most widely and unquestioningly accepted in our culture, and the use of these wherever appropriate to criticize and reject more personal or eccentric criteria. And arguably, whether we realize it or not, this is in effect what we have in mind when we credit some report or description with 'objectivity', and how we distinguish 'objective' from 'subjective' in such situations. But we must not delude ourselves that there is any possibility of assessing *all* such criteria by reference to some standard independent of all of them – though no doubt we are tempted to think so, because some of them are *so* deep-rooted, *so* widely and unquestioningly accepted in our culture, that we fail to recognize them for what they are. So, the relativist argues, all criticism, (checking, assessment . . .) is only theoretically possible given the simple *adoption*, without benefit of these, of some criterion of truth in the first place; and his argument about equally feasible alternatives still holds. And, incidentally, he may add, is the idea of a permanently elusive standard or ideal – one such that we can never be sure whether or not we have attained it – not more liable to promote scepticism than to prevent it? The impulse to ask ourselves 'But is this *the truth*?', even after we have observed to the letter all the standards for the proper conduct of research laid down by our culture or discipline, is in some respects an understandable and salutary one. But what are we worrying about here? That our subject-matter might look differently if seen through the eyes of an omniscient and infallible deity? Or if we adopted some better standards of research? But the 'better' in this context could only mean bringing us closer or oftener to the truth; and if we can never be certain where the truth actually lies, how can we distinguish better standards from worse? We are back again in the realm of the sceptic's 'irresoluble doubts' — since Popper's 'fallibilism' has the effect of ruling out any prospect of our ever resolving them.

## 3

Thus far, then, relativism can hold its own. And the foregoing sections have, I believe, shown that there is a stronger case in its favour than Popper and most of its other critics have acknowledged, and that its essential thesis about the relativity to adopted criterion of any claims to truth, or knowledge, cannot be refuted simply by appealing to the distinction between meaning and criteria. None the less, it cannot be denied that our setting out of the relativist case seems, in important respects, highly artificial and over-abstract. In particular, there is an obvious lack of *examples* of actual criteria of truth and applications thereof — and a difficulty in finding examples to supply this lack that demands explanation. And it is when we start looking for such an explanation that we begin to discover what is really deficient in relativism as thus far expounded.

In the previous section, we noticed that the relativist could be challenged over his right to use the phrase 'criteria of *truth*', i.e. could he, on his own characteristic principles, justify the last word? But in fact the complete phrase, whether used by the relativist, Popper, or anyone else, is suspect. No doubt the assignment of truth-values, in virtually any case likely to be of any interest or importance, is, as we have said, a disciplined and non-random process. But it by no means follows, as the use of the phrase 'criteria of truth' suggests, that such criteria are special devices, or pieces of intellectual equipment, which have somehow at some time to be created or developed, and which we have to choose or adopt. If they were, the devices would obviously be of crucial importance in the development of our knowledge of the world; the emergence of a new one would be a major event in intellectual history, its adoption by any individual a major event in that individual's intellectual biography. But, in fact, such criteria are of (almost) exclusively philosophical concern — always a ground for suspicion — and references to them in the records of research or education are very hard to find. When we consider the equipment we actually need in order to find out about our world, and to formulate, transmit, learn and assess the results, there does not appear to be any place for such special, purpose-built devices. No doubt there is a great deal to be learnt about the various techniques of enquiry appropriate to different subject-matters and circumstances; a great deal to be learnt also about the use of our linguistic equipment (including, of course, such things as mathematical symbolisms as well as words) in formulating our results. (It is not, however, suggested that the two processes, enquiry and formulation of results can be mastered separately or successively.) But once we have learnt thus how to *make* statements, i.e. to use sentences, equations, etc. in order to give our findings, we have all the equipment we need to ascertain their truth-values. Our capacity to make, and recognize, *true* statements – and hence to make and recognize false ones as well – develops *pari passu* with our capacity simply to make statements. If a child has learnt enough to state that the sun is shining or that the cat is on the mat – which involves a great deal more than simply learning to utter the appropriate sentences – then *ipso facto* he has learnt enough to tell whether or not it is true that the sun is shining or the cat is on the mat – even though the *words* 'true', 'false', etc. may be still unlearnt.

Learning these techniques of finding-out and formulation is, obviously, a life-long process, and the number of techniques to be learnt can grow indefinitely. And hence, whatever else may hold of the concept of truth, it is not such that we can learn once and for all how to recognize its instantiations wherever they occur. This also is something that can only be learnt piecemeal over a lifetime – a point which will scarcely be disputed, since, notoriously, anything that can be said correctly about truth in general is totally unhelpful to anyone trying to speak or recognize the truth in a specific instance. The point to be made at present however is simply that all that has to be learnt is statement-making; truth-evaluation is not a separate discipline, but simply a further exercise of the same discipline. (Cf. if you wish to check the accuracy of my arithmetic, you do not need to have mastered two skills, doing such arithmetic and checking it; if you can just do it, then you have in principle all the equipment you need for checking it as well.)

It would appear then that quite simply wherever we have the means of making a statement we have, in principle, also the means of establishing its truth-value. We do not need to go in search of a criterion of truth as an extra piece of apparatus, for a made-to-measure criterion, as it were, is provided by the way in which we arrive at the statement in the first place. It may be said, of course, with some reason, that this is altogether too simple an answer to the relativist's problems; and clearly there are various objections to be met. To begin with, 'criteria of truth', in Popper's wide sense of *any* means of deciding whether a given statement is true or false, covers a lot more than our made-to-measure criteria. And there are surely examples which could have been offered of criteria of truth, in this sense, which are quite independent (or apparently so) of our means of making statements – for example, appeals to hunches or intuitions, to the Cartesian 'clear and distinct apprehension', to various oracles, authorities or sacred texts. And, given these, it is quite easy to envisage the kind of situation with which the relativist is concerned. Suppose, for example, that *A* and *B* both read *C*'s statements of his findings in a given piece of research. *A* in such matters makes a point of relying on his hunches, or intuitive reactions, and since these are unfavourable in this instance, he judges *C*'s statements to be false. *B*, on the other hand, has a childlike faith in *C*'s competence within his chosen field, and the mere fact that it is *C* who has made this statement is enough to make *B* pronounce it true. Now *A*'s appeal to intuition, and *B*'s to authority, are both clearly criteria of truth, in the required sense – and moreover reminiscent, at least, of criteria that have in fact been seriously adopted – but seemingly quite independent of the way in which *C* arrived at his statement in the first place. And it is easy to see how they can, in a particular application, yield different results.

The situation here, however, differs importantly from that of the rival art-experts in our earlier example. For here we should, clearly, want to claim that we *have* a criterion preferable to those of both *A* and *B*, by appeal to which we can, in principle, determine which of them is right, i.e. the careful checking and rechecking of the experiments (observations, surveys, or whatever) through which *C* conducted the original research. And it is preferable simply because what *C*'s statement purported to do, its entire *raison d'être*, was to give the result of such research.

Some important points arise here – though too complex, unfortunately, to be developed beyond their immediate relevance to the topic in hand – regarding, in the first place, conditions for making statements to all (as opposed to merely uttering sentences) and, secondly, the conditions for two of us making or considering, the *same* statement. The question of the conditions for stating, properly so called, was raised briefly in the previous chapter, when we considered the circumstances under which we might actually state, for example, that there is a golden mountain instead of just uttering the sentence 'There is a golden mountain'. It is worth recalling here some of the things said by J. L. Austin about statements and stating. For example, in the famous paper on 'performative utterances':

Of course, philosophers have been wont to talk as though you or I or anybody could just go around stating anything about anything and that would be perfectly in order, only there's just a little question: is it true or false? But besides the little question, is it true or false, there is surely the question: is it in order? Can you go round just making statements about anything? . . . [For example] you can't just make statements about other people's feelings (though you can make guesses if you like); and there are very many things which, having no knowledge of, not being in a position to pronounce about, you can't just state.[12]

The point is not that we *ought* not make statements irresponsibly or at random, where we have no relevant knowledge, or are not in a position to pronounce, but that quite literally we *cannot*. Part of the essential stage-setting for statement-making, properly so called, is missing. As was suggested earlier, one condition at least of actually stating that, say, there is a golden mountain is that we should have, or at any rate think or pretend that we have, some means of finding out whether there is or is not – so that out statement is in effect a statement of the result of some finding-out operation. (We may grant, of course, that statements might anticipate, or guess at, such results, as well as reporting those already achieved.) When someone speaks a sentence (indicative in the grammarian's sense) in circumstances, tone of voice, etc. which suggests that his object is to make a statement, as opposed to telling a story, reciting, or whatever, then it is in principle always appropriate to ask him 'How do you know?' or 'How did you find that out?' And if he admits that he has no means of knowing, or finding out, we should be at a loss to know how to take his utterance; and we might understandably retort 'Then how can you state it?' or, with Austin, 'Then you can't just state it.'

Thus, to make a statement about something, to tell what it is or what it is like, is in effect to claim – rightly or wrongly, sincerely or insincerely – to have found out about, or more generally to be in a position to know about, it – whether through observation, insight, revelation, logical analysis or whatever. To assume the role of statement-maker is *ipso facto* to assume that of discoverer as well. It is, of course, important to remember that there are many different ways of making enquiries, and formulating statements, and giving the results of the one by means of the other. 'Making enquiries', as used here, has to cover simple observations of our surroundings and elaborate research programmes alike, 'making statements' both recording our immediate observations and formulating the most general physical theories. And even in the simplest examples, stating our results is never, as we have already had occasion to note, merely a mechanical foolproof process of 'reading off' the appropriate formula from what is observed. The relationships between words and the world are always complex and elusive; and if we are to seek our criteria of truth in the processes by which we 'arrive at' our statements, or use them to 'give the results' of our enquiries, it is essential not to let our thinking be governed by any single, simple model or paradigm of such processes. But, granted that 'giving the results of enquiries' is a complex business, and a risky one since, as we noted earlier, we are by no means always giving the results of enquiries already safely completed – and perhaps seldom are – the basic point remains. Stating, in contrast with, say, questioning or commanding, or with story-telling or giving examples, is, in essential part at least, committing oneself as to what has been, will be, or might be, discovered in some circumstances. *221659.*

Can we go on, then, to link not only stating but statement-identity with enquiry, to seek here an answer, or one possible answer, to the question of what, in the example given a little earlier, ensures that *A, B* and *C* are all talking about *the same* statement? Obviously, sameness of verbal formula is neither necessary nor sufficient; the same statement can be made by means of different formulae, and the same formula used to make different statements – and, of course, even when the formula *is* a grammatically indicative sentence, used without making any statement at all, e.g. in story-telling. But, given that, for example, *C*'s original statement is *essentially* the statement of the results of a piece of research, that what makes his utterance of this formula on this occasion an example of statement-making at all is his use of it for just this purpose, might we not go on to say that what makes it this *specific* statement is its use to give the result of this *specific* enquiry? The same formula, arrived at in any other way would constitute a different statement. Suppose *A* persists in treating his intuition as the ultimate court of appeal, and refuses to let it be overruled by our careful checking and re-checking of *C*'s work. We take him step by step through the various experiments, observations, measurements, analyses, or whatever, and show him the effects, readings, etc. which *C* claims to have obtained. But he remains unconverted and continues to insist 'My intuitions are against it, and that is all that counts.' We could only suppose that even though he is using (misleadingly) the same verbal formula as *C*, he *takes* it differently, is using it to serve a different purpose in a different field of interest. Hence, despite appearances to the contrary, *A* and *C* are not contradicting each other, since they are not assigning truth-values to the same statement. We are, of course, envisaging a situation in which they differ *irreconcilably* over how the truth-value of the statement(s) in question should be determined. If *A* merely used his appeal to intuition as a convenient shortcut, in the belief that it told him the results of the relevant experiments, etc. without the trouble of actually performing them, and hence took its unfavourable response as grounds for assuming that *C* must have done the experiments badly or dishonestly, there would be no such difference. They would both be agreed that the experimental evidence is the deciding factor, and it would only be a matter of persuading *A* to take a more orthodox and straightforward view of how that evidence is to be obtained.

There would, no doubt, be some awkward problems to be tackled about *A*'s position, if we were concerned seriously to work out its implications. For example, could his eccentricity be confined to a particular statement or range of statements; is it consistent with making and assessing statements as the rest of us do in other fields of interest? And could we communicate with him to the extent of having sufficient grounds for saying that his utterances were in fact intended as statements and were guided by something that could properly be called intuition? . . . Our present purpose is not, however, to establish the tenability of *A*'s position. Rather it is to call in question the assumption underlying the whole relativist case as presented in the foregoing sections, i.e. that it *is* possible for two of us to assess the same statement using (irreconcilably) different criteria of truth. And what the foregoing discussion suggests is that it is *not* possible, that if we apply different criteria of truth, even if the verbal formula is the same for both of us, we are *ipso facto* treating it as making different statements. It would, admittedly, be unwise to use any term stronger than 'suggests'. As already noted the topics of statement-making and statement-identity are too complex for exhaustive treatment here; and, apart from this, it is by no means clear that we have, in fact, as parts of our shared conceptual equipment, ideas of what it is to make a statement, or to make the same statement, such that any single, comprehensive account of them is possible. And hence to give *any* such account may well be to commit the common philosophical sin of professing to discover simplicity and uniformity where none in fact exists.

But if, or in so far as, the making of statements, their identification, and their evaluation as true or false, can be linked in this way, then clearly a decisive advantage is gained in our attempts to avoid the unacceptable face of relativism. We no longer have to allow that, where the initial choices of criteria of truth are different, one man's truth may be another's falsehood, without any error on either side. The relativist has made the mistake of considering statements and criteria of truth in abstraction from each other – of talking as though we might first discover a set of statements, *in vacuo* as it were, and then have to cast around for a criterion of truth by which to assess them. But, given that what makes an utterance a statement at all is its function of giving the result of some enquiry or finding-out process, and that what identifies it as this specific statement is the specific enquiry of which it gives (or purports to give) the result, then no such problem arises. For both the identity of the statement and the criterion of its truth are functions of this process of enquiry by which it was arrived at in the first place. And hence to identify the statement is also, in principle, to identify its criterion of truth; and if we differ irreconcilably about the criterion, then *ipso facto* we differ about the identity of the statement as well.

It may be objected here that the obvious way to identify a statement is surely by appeal to its content, to what it affirms to be the case, rather than to the process of which we arrive at it; and that if two of us affirm the same thing to be the case, then *ipso facto* we are making the same statement, regardless of how we got there. I do not think we need say that this commonsensical account – as no doubt it is – of our criterion of statement-identity is mistaken; we have simply to consider a little further what it entails. All that we can mean by the content of a statement, by what it affirms about its subject-matter, is, perforce, the result of some enquiry as set forth in that statement. For example, the statement that the surface now before us is white, smooth and motionless, even though it *says* nothing about observations, none the less *gives*, or purports to give, the results of certain observations –

made under certain standard conditions of light, eyesight of observer, etc. Of course, as with the physicist's frames of reference, very often the observations or enquiries in question are so familiar and uncontroversial that they can be, and are, ignored without any untoward consequences. But suppose our physicist, having conducted *his* characteristic kind of enquiry, with the appropriate observations made with the help of sophisticated apparatus, states that the surface is a vast concourse of discrete, colourless particles in motion. Superficially his statement flatly contradicts ours. Yet clearly we should have no difficulty in accepting both as true. The content of a statement cannot be detached from the enquiry of which it (purportedly) gives the result; to say how things are is of necessity to say how, *under certain specific circumstances*, we find them. Hence, whether we state the same thing, or contradict each other depends, not simply on the content of our statements, on what they affirm to be the case, taken in isolation, but on the enquiries of which they (purport to) give the results as well. Were the enquiries different then, regardless of what we say, we should not be close enough either to agree or to contradict each other. We shall find similar and related issues arising in subsequent sections; the point to be made at the moment is that it is an insufficient criterion of our making the same statement that we should both say that $x$ is $y$; we have also to agree – tacitly though not explicitly – that $x$ is found to be $y$ under specific circumstances.

This still leaves us with relativism of a kind – but only of an innocuous, and indeed, commonplace kind. This is the relativism which merely points out that there are indefinitely many lines of enquiry about the world and our lives in it, which we might pursue if we were so minded, and hence indefinitely many ways of arriving at and assessing statements – and any enquirer, or school of enquiry, has, in theory, freedom of choice about which line to take. But the result is just difference; and unless we arbitrarily take it for granted that all other enquirers are pursuing our line, and assess their work accordingly – the presumption which it is the self-appointed task of the relativist to warn us against – there are no grounds for conflict or contradiction.

It has already been conceded, of course, that we are far from having shown conclusively that the making, identification, and assessment of statements *are* in fact linked in the way indicated – or that indeed any single, definite answer to the question of how we accomplish such things is there to be discovered in the actual practice of discourse. But if, or in so far as, statements could be identified *independently* of our means of determining their truth-values, then it would seem that the relativist must win his essential point. His basic argument holds, that there is no non-circular way in which any choice or adoption of a criterion of truth can be shown to be the right one, and hence that we might adopt different criteria without error on anyone's part. And, if which criterion we bring to the assessment of a given statement does not determine our identification of that statement, then there is no reason in principle why we should not bring different criteria to the assessment of the same statement and hence, without error, assign different truth-values to it.

In this connection, we may recall what was said in the opening chapter about Popper's philosophy of science, i.e. that it is determined not primarily by what, as a matter of history or sociology, scientists actually do or profess to do, but rather by an analysis of what, as a matter of logic, they can and cannot do. Similarly, we might argue that what is philosophically interesting here is not how phrases like 'making a statement', 'the same statement', etc. are ordinarily used, or what rules, or precedents, for their use can be discovered by a survey of actual discourse. Rather, it is the apparent inconsistency between the claims (whatever our grounds for making them) that statements *can* be identified independently of how we determine their truth-values, and that they *have* absolute truth-values – while, on the other hand, if we are prepared to settle for an account of them as essentially statements of the results of enquiries, and hence with built-in criteria of truth, as it were, which could not be altered without altering the statements themselves, then the inconsistency can be avoided. There is an obvious comparison here with Popper's attempt to show how the claim that there is an empirical basis for the generalizations of science is inconsistent with the claim that these can ever be established truths – while the inconsistency is avoidable if we are prepared to treat them simply as conjectures. In both cases – in the doctrine of statements as statements of results and in that of generalizations as conjectures – the primary concern is to make a point, not about what *is* claimed, but about what consistently *can be* claimed.

## 4

It may be said, however, that even if we have found a way of avoiding the admission that one and the same statement may be true relative to criterion $C_1$ but false relative to $C_2$, we have still made no great inroads on *scepticism*. Granted that statements are, in the way indicated, statements of the results of enquiries, we have already conceded that they by no means always give the results of completed enquiries; and there is an obvious case, on grounds already considered, for doubting whether statements of any scientific or practical interest *ever* do, or could do, so. To put it in these terms, we may well make such statements on the strength of some enquiries which have already been completed and yielded favourable results – doubtless we rarely make them at random – but in making them we commit ourselves as to results of an indefinite range of further, uncompleted enquiries. We have still the gap between the grounds on which we are willing to make a given statement – grounds perhaps sufficient to satisfy the customs or conventions of the relevant discipline – and the commitment we undertake in making it. And so we have still one time-honoured source, at least, of scepticism – including that element of scepticism which, as we have seen, despite any disclaimers, persists throughout Popper's work.

Such scepticism, of course, may be no bad thing; the phrase 'healthy scepticism' has its point. And in so far as Popper reminds us that, no matter how careful and comprehensive our researches in any field, on logical grounds our findings can be wrong, and on historical grounds they are quite likely to be wrong, and hence that we should never regard them as immune from revision, the lesson is a salutary one. But his fallibilism, as already noted, takes us further than this. By denying that we can *ever* establish conclusively the truth of any statement, it deprives us also of the means of showing conclusively that any statement is false. The most we can say is that *if*, for example, certain records of experimental results are accepted as true then a certain generalization must be rejected as false. But it is always, necessarily, a matter of 'if', and hence we can never say unconditionally that a given theory, or whatever, has once and for all been refuted, and that science has advanced beyond it. We are left uncomfortably close to the relativism from which we have been struggling to free ourselves, i.e. with a situation in which different schools of enquiry might each have its own convention as to which 'basic statements' to accept as true, and accordingly, without error on anyone's part reach different conclusions about whether a given theory should, or should not, be deemed falsified.

This does not, of course, in itself show that Popper is mistaken. It may be that, whether we like it or not, there are decisive arguments in favour of a fairly radical form of scepticism, and a resultant relativism which in effect denies that there *is* any absolute sense in which a theory can be said to have been falsified or science to have progressed beyond it. But some of Popper's statements in this connection, already noted, are paradoxical enough to warrant some further scrutiny, i.e. the assertion, in *The Logic of Scientific Discovery*, that 'basic statements' – i.e. the 'statements asserting that an observable event is occurring in a certain individual region of space and time'[13] – 'are accepted as a result of a decision or agreement; and to that extent are conventions'.[14] And, much later, in his addendum to *The Open Society and its Enemies*, 'though we may seek for truth . . . we can never be quite certain that we have found it. There is always a possibility of error'.[15] The first of these makes a group of scientists, agreeing to accept a certain body of experimental evidence as true, seem oddly like a gang of thieves agreeing on the story they are to tell the police or the magistrate if they get caught – where what they say is less important than their all saying the same thing. The second, taken at its face value, requires the admission that we cannot be certain even of the truth of such statements as that the world is furnished with humans and other animals, that the normal human being has two hands and one head, that we have, and have had, various thoughts and experiences, that there is a philosopher named Karl Popper and that he wrote the works we are discussing . . .

Popper does concede, immediately after the last passage quoted, that 'in the case of some logical and mathematical proofs' the possibility of error may be considered slight. And he later (in *Objective Knowledge*) makes a similar point – 'Apart from *valid and simple* proofs in world 3, objective certainty does not exist',[16] (where world 3 has been defined as 'the world of the logical *contents* of books, libraries, computer memories, and such like', i.e. theories, concepts, etc. in contrast with 'world 1', the physical world, and 'world 2', the world of our conscious experiences.[17]) But while logic and mathematics may enjoy immunity from one kind of refutation, i.e. our findings in them cannot be proved wrong by experiment or observations, and this is doubtless one reason for their time-honoured appeal to philosophers, they are certainly not immune from all refutation. For most of us at any rate, logical and mathematical argument offer more, and more serious, possibilities of error than, say, discovering and recording simple facts about our environment.

Popper's conception of world 3 serves – no doubt among other things – to point out that such things as the logical entailments of a given theory or theoretical system, or the logical relationships between concepts, are there to be discovered, as gold-mines or gravitational fields are in world 1. But this simply underlines the fact that world 3, like world 1, is a field for techniques of enquiry – only techniques of logical analysis rather than of observation and experiment – and in the operation of *all* such techniques there is clearly room for errors, even if not the same errors in every case. (Cf. Descartes' question, 'how do I know I am not also deceived each time I add together two and three, or number the sides of a square . . .?'[18]) Thus, there is no reason in principle why scepticism should treat the results of *any* enquiry (scientific, mathematical, or whatever) with special leniency. Doubtless simplicity makes error less likely; but this holds equally of every branch of enquiry – and few have found mathematics and logic to be especially distinguished by their simplicity.

Do we have to accept, then, an unrestricted fallibilism – every statement we make, in whatever field or however arrived at, is inevitably shadowed by the possibility of error, and the best we can do is to agree, in some cases, to ignore this possibility and treat certain statements as true? One response is, of course, that it is merely neurotic to question seriously the truth of a statement solely on the ground of a logical possibility of error, i.e. on the ground that no matter how carefully we observe or count or calculate, and record our results, no matter how often the working has been checked, it is still logically possible that we have mis-observed, mis-counted, mis-calculated or mis-reported. This on a par with compulsive hand-washing, or checking and re-checking that a door has been locked at night without ever being able to rest assured that it has. Again, it is possible that despite careful washing and re-washing, hands are still dirty or get dirty again immediately afterwards, or that our memory is playing us false when we seem to recall locking the door, or that we inadvertently unlock it in the process of testing – and no doubt occasionally such things actually happen. But actually to take account of such possibilities, to allow them to influence our behaviour, would be to show a lack of self-confidence which could be, almost literally, paralysing. Suppose, for example, we are uncertain whether we have learnt or remembered correctly the meanings of everyday words, uncertain whether we have understood correctly the further explanations that are offered – and so on. As Wittgenstein once put it,

'If you are not certain of any fact, you cannot be certain of the meaning of your words either.'[19] (We could, perhaps, imagine such a failure of self-confidence being deliberately induced, as a particularly cruel refinement of torture – say, in a prisoner isolated for a long period from everyone except guards who persistently treat even his simplest judgements, about his own name, past experiences, environment, etc. as absurdly mistaken, or pretend to find even his simplest utterances incomprehensible.) It is a condition of carrying out virtually any task, theoretical or practical, that we have confidence enough to take it for granted that as a general rule, we get things right when we observe, analyse, deduce, record . . . etc. and to demand some stronger and more specific ground than mere logical possibility before we are prepared to consider that we may be mistaken. Otherwise, presumably, we should just go on endlessly and futilely checking and re-checking our first move. Hence, while fallibilism as applied to higher reaches of research, in science or any other discipline, may offer a salutary warning against over-confidence or complacency, fallibilsm applied indiscriminately to *all* statements either seeks to impose impossibly high safety-standards, as it were – or else merely labours the obvious and unhelpful point that such standards cannot be met.

This, in its turn, might be answered by saying that Popper has never implied that we should become neurotic over, or let ourselves be paralysed by, the logical possibility of error. He is well aware that, if we are to make progress in science, or virtually any other field of interest, we have got, in many cases, to ignore such possibilities. He is merely doing for basic statements what he has done for general theories when (in defiance of everyday usage) he classified them as *conjectures*, i.e. pointing out the only status which, as a matter of logic, they *can* have – whatever status may ordinarily be assigned to them. We cannot, once again, bridge the logical gap between the grounds on which we actually make our basic statements, and the commitments we undertake in making them; we can only agree, or license ourselves, in certain cases to take no account of it – the point brought out by saying that their acceptance is a matter of *convention*. And, apart from the inherent value of arriving at a correct version of what we are doing, it is surely practically useful to be reminded, if such indeed is the case, that the 'empirical basis of objective science has thus nothing "absolute" about it',[20] and hence that no part of its structure is immutable, but is liable to change if for any reason we decide to alter our conventions.

However, this term 'convention' suggests a choice between alternative ways of achieving the same end. We impose rules of the road in order to avoid traffic chaos, but whether we elect to drive on the right or on the left is a matter of convention. Our gang of thieves, concerned to give an account, which is consistent, innocuous and difficult to disprove, of their doings on a particular night, might agree upon any of a variety of stories that would suit their purpose equally well – that they were holding a seminar on modern literature, that they were catching up on their hand-weaving, etc. Suppose, however, that the task before us is to count the number of books and pencils on the table before us and report the result. Could we allow that there are alternative answers between which we might, or must, choose, and still retain any clear ideas of what the task was in the first place, of what it is to count and report one's results? We are, it may be, worried by the theoretical possibility that, no matter how much care we exercise, no matter how often we check and re-check, we might still not be counting correctly, but somehow miscounting. But in order to worry about this, we have to know how to distinguish between counting correctly and miscounting. And we know this, presumably, because, as small children, we were taught how to count, and *ipso facto* how to detect and avoid miscounts, and in due course satisfied whatever criteria our mentors imposed for being 'able to count'. And one of the things learnt at this stage is that there is only one way of counting correctly, only one correct answer to a question beginning 'How many'. If we have to appeal to agreement or convention it is because something has gone wrong with the counting operation, some kind of flaw or hitch – the children are still unsure of the number sequence and take a hasty vote before their teacher demands an answer, or the class of things to be counted is ill-defined, or its members hard to detect. But when, say, we carefully and attentively set out the books and pencils on the table one by one, pairing them with the convention and sequence of sounds or marks, 1, 2, 3, . . . etc. this surely could function as a paradigm case of *correct* counting, the sort of thing that might be, and is, used to teach children what it is to count correctly. And granted that the terms 'counting correctly' and 'miscounting' are elements in our common vocabulary, and hence that the only criterion for their proper use is how they are in fact used, to suggest that in such cases we are not counting correctly – even prefaced with 'perhaps' or 'possibly' – is sheer misuse of terms. For the proper, (socially-accepted) use of 'counting correctly' is something exemplified and taught by just such operations. To count correctly *is* simply to act thus; these are the precedents which show us what to do. And to suggest that these may themselves be miscounts is, in effect, to propose new (and as yet unspecified) meanings for our terms. We may recall here two passages in the *Investigations* where Wittgenstein considers the role of examples in thus determining the meanings of terms:

this is just how one might explain to someone what a game is. One gives examples and intends them to be taken in a particular way. I do not, however, mean by this that he is supposed to see in those examples that common thing which I – for some reason – was unable to express; but that he is now to *employ* those examples in a particular way. Here giving examples is not an *indirect* way of explaining – in default of a better. For any general definition can be misunderstood too. The point is that *this* is how we play the game. (I mean the language-game with the word 'game'.)[21]

And, in a later passage:

If language is to be a means of communication there must be agreement not only in definitions but also (queer as this may sound) in judgments . . . It is one thing to describe methods of measurement, and another to obtain and state results of measurement. But what we call measuring is partly determined by a certain constancy in results of measurement.[22]

If so, then it is a condition of our terms meaning what they do mean, that the truth of *some* of the statements in which we use them is not open to question; and hence we do not need conventions to license us to ignore such questions. In general terms, we might say that it is a condition of our having a common language, that most of us are able and willing to speak the truth most of the time. (Imagine, for example, an unfortunate child growing up in a household of pathological liars who, whenever they saw him looking at or touching, say, a table, out of sheer perversity told him 'That's a chair' or 'That's a dog' or anything that occured to them except 'That's a table'. How could he ever learn, in such a situation, the correct use of 'table'?) While it may indeed be very difficult to get at, or to recognize, the truth about a great many things, some of them doubtless of the highest importance to humanity, yet, once again, the indiscriminate scepticism which says we can *never* have the truth, or be sure of having it, is self-destructive.

We have here in effect, a further application of Strawson's criticism of the sceptic, already quoted, i.e. he relies, perforce, on familiar terms and concepts in order to formulate his doubt, but then refuses to abide by the rules for the proper use of these when it comes to resolving that doubt. The counter-strategy is to outflank him, as it were, by focussing attention on the essential conditions for learning and using the concepts he requires. Still, we might wonder, is this altogether a sufficient answer? Even granted that we learn the distinction between counting correctly and miscounting from exemplars or paradigms of the sort indicated; that 'counting correctly' is this systematic pairing-off of the members of the class of things to be counted with our conventional sounds or marks, while 'miscounting' covers such things as overlooking a member of the class, counting one twice, etc.; and that it is socially accepted to regard many operations performed every day as examples of correct counting in this sense – none the less it is not still logically possible that, even in supposed 'paradigm cases', like our books-and-pencils example, we are not counting correctly but miscounting (in precisely the senses of these terms just indicated)? Suppose we were all afflicted with some kind of blind-spot, so that when we tried to count a given class of things, we always overlooked every third one, and where there were in fact nine, the count only reached 'six', and so on. Or suppose we all had permanent double-vision, so that every individual was counted twice over, and the nine appeared as 'eighteen'. In these circumstances, we should always miscount, no matter how carefully we checked and rechecked, and since we all miscounted in the same way, committed the same error, the miscount would go undetected. And it is at least not obvious that there would be resultant practical difficulties or confusions which would alert us to what had gone wrong. If, for example, we tried to distribute the books and pencils among a class of students, we should not be puzzled as to why they went further than, or did not go so far as, we had expected – for we should, of course, similarly miscount the students. It might be said that any such hypothesis is highly unlikely – though it would be more correct to say that, except for philosophical purposes, it is idle or pointless; in the nature of the case we have no means of assessing its likelihood – but *prima facie* it is logically possible. And is this not enough to show that, *pace* Strawson and others, in this instance at least the sceptic's doubts can be formulated *without* misuse of the relevant terms and concepts?

We are now brought back, however, to the issue of statement-identity. Grant that it is possible to envisage two groups of people (or perhaps ourselves at different points in our careers) who could agree on definitions of 'counting correctly' and 'miscounting', in terms of our 'pairing-off' etc. and who set themselves to count the same classes of things, but habitually and systematically arrive at different results.

Thus members of Group *A* regularly overlook some of the things found by members of Group *B*, while members of *B* with corresponding regularity count things to which members of *A* appear oblivious. In this situation, when *A*s affirm that class *X* has six members, and *B*s deny that it has, should we say that they are talking about the same statement, and contradicting each other about its truth-value? If statements are to be identified by reference to the enquiries of which they give, or purport to give, the results, then they are not. Enquiries, after all, are certain exercises of our capacities for observation, analysis, etc. and are identified, in essential part, by reference to the capacities employed in them, i.e. as observations, analyses, or whatever, of such-and-such a subject-matter. Were these capacities different, as between our *A* and *B* groups, then obviously enough the enquiries conducted, even about the same subject-matter (allowing that we can identify *that*) would be different, and hence the statements arrived at different also. But it would simply be a matter of difference; there would be no question of mutual contradiction or the one showing the other to be wrong.

There is an analogous, and somewhat less far-fetched, example (already mentioned above) to be found by considering the effects of the development of scientific apparatus on our enquiries about the world around us. Our scientist, relying on such apparatus, may tell us that the table-top before us is a vast concourse of discrete, colourless particles in motion. But even though we accept this as true, we in no way regard it as contradicting our commonsense view, based on unaided sense-experience, that the table-top is coloured, continuous and at rest. We accept *this* as true also – and so long as we keep in mind the different functions performed by the two statements, the different enquiries of which they (purport to) give the results, no confusion arises. Science can only give rise to scepticism about the reliability of our ordinary sense-experience if we take its statements in abstraction from the functions they are designed to perform, the ways in which the scientist arrives at them. When we are careful to avoid such abstraction then we have, again, merely what we have called the 'innocuous' form of relativism, i.e. the acknowledgment that there are indeed many possible ways of conducting enquiries, and hence many possible ways of making and assessing statements. Our derogatory terms like 'blind-spot', 'afflicted', 'miscount', 'error', etc. become appropriate only where a given statement, or range of statements, fails to do the job which, tacitly at least, it purports to do, i.e. to give the result of some specific enquiry, or range of enquiries. The possibility of other enquiries, (or other ways of, or capacities for, conducting them) is irrelevant. It does nothing to show that, even when we have counted our books and pencils in our everyday, socially-accepted fashion, we might still be wrong; for it is only of such counting that we purport to give the result. And as we have said, the criteria of rightness or wrongness in such counting are determined by what is actually done in countless, commonplace situations, as when we count our books and pencils, when the kindergarten teacher shows her pupils how to count on their fingers or with matchsticks, etc. – situations where due care is taken and the conditions are favourable. Of course, if we are careless or the conditions are unfavourable, in ways like those indicated above, we can miscount. But to suggest that we may still be miscounting no matter what care we take or how favourable the conditions, is simply to destroy the criteria which give point to any such assessment. To any such suggestion we are logically entitled to reply, as doubtless we should, 'Well, if this is not correct counting, then *we don't know what counting is*.' And if we were to encounter, say, beings on other planets who did something recognizable as counting but because of some difference of sensory equipment or whatever, got results systematically different from ours, the worst that could happen would be that we should have to preface our statements of results with something like indications of the appropriate frame of reference – 'by Earthman's counting', etc. Such alternative results would do nothing to cast doubt on the correctness of ours.

Similarly with other distinctions between right and wrong, correct and incorrect – between correctly observing, identifying, measuring, locating . . . and mis-observing, mis-identifying, etc. We cannot suggest that (even possibly) we *always* go wrong, or may go wrong in *any* given case, however favourable the conditions, because to do so would be to deprive ourselves of the means of making such assessments at all. But we can indeed envisage circumstances in which we should still apply these familiar contrasts, but apply them differently from our present practice. Suppose that someone, following the famous Cartesian example, says 'Perhaps what we call our experience of the world is all a dream.' It is undeniably a relevant response to remind him of the essential conditions for learning and using 'dreams' and related terms. But he may go on 'Yes, but can't we envisage an occurrence, perhaps after our physical death, something analogous to waking up and then having perceptions of the world so vivid, coherent etc. that we could only conclude that all the experience of our present lives, viewed in retrospect, were mere dreams.' We may allow, at any rate for the sake of the present argument, that this is possible, and further that, in the situation envisaged, we should not necessarily be misusing the word 'dream' – it might well be the most appropriate term to use. But we should be using it to contrast our present lives with this new mode of experience – to make the point that, *in contrast with such experiences*, it is dream-like (i.e. insubstantial, ephemeral, subjective, etc., in the way that dreams characteristically are). But, from our standpoint *within* these present lives, there is no such contrast to draw, and hence nothing to make the term 'dream' appropriate. The statement made from *this* standpoint, that our present experience is not a dream, and the statement made from the supposed new standpoint that it is, would thus perform quite different functions, characterize our present experience by reference to quite different contexts. And, again, they do not contradict each other, any more than do the different judgements of rest and motion, etc. produced by the different frames of reference of relativity theory.

In general, we may concede to the sceptic that, in examples like those just considered, he is not necessarily misusing terms or conceptions; and that he can present us with possible situations in which we should be constrained to assert a statement made by the use of a given sentence (like 'All the experiences of my life thus far have been dreams') while in our present situation we should unhesitatingly deny one made by the use of that sentence. Where we may, I think, usefully challenge him is on the question of statement identity – is it the *same statement* in both situations, or do the different functions performed not generate two different statements, despite the sameness of the verbal formula?

If statements are indeed to be identified in the way suggested, i.e. by reference to their functions, or more specifically, by reference to the enquiries (in a broad sense) of which they give the results, then none of the arguments we have considered in favour of relativism or scepticism, whatever their merits, would appear sufficient to justify an unqualified fallibilism. There is a substantial body of Popperian basic statements, at least, statements about the specific furnishings of the world, and specific occurrences within it, which can, without qualification, be called true – as we have seen, some of them *must* be, if the whole discussion is to retain its point. No doubt the need to appeal to 'favourable conditions' etc. has the effect of creating a twilight zone of statements whose membership of this body of established truths is open to question. (How favourable do the conditions have to be?) But then we have to remember that the application of virtually *any* concept creates such a zone of questionable cases – which does not in itself cast any suspicion on the value of the concept or the existence of *un*questionable instantiations. And if the truth of some basic statements can be established, then correspondingly there have to be some generalizations which are, quite simply, falsified. What was said in the previous chapter about the defensive moves and delaying tactics open to the theoretician, the *ceteris paribus* clauses, etc., remains valid, of course. But it seems at least unnecessarily pessimistic to say that science has *no* 'solid bedrock' of established truths, which are stronger and more durable than the products of alterable agreements or conventions; and that 'the bold structure of its theories rises, as it were, above a swamp'.[23] There are, surely, *some* humble, commonplace but unalterable truths about ourselves and our environment which *any* theoretical structure has to respect as established once and for all.

5

There may still, however, be a temptation to ask 'But how many members *has* this class of objects, say the books and pencils on the table, actually got?' or 'But *is* this experience actually a dream or not?' – i.e. what are the right or *true* answers to such questions, as distinct from what answers are reached from different standpoints, or by differently equipped enquirers? Again, no doubt, we can return to the analogy with relativity in physics, and reply that this is like insisting on knowing whether a particle is *really* at rest or in motion, or what its velocity *really* is, as distinct from the judgements of observers with various frames of reference. But merely to invoke the prestige of relativity theory may not in itself be sufficient to dispel the temptation to raise such questions. And they are indeed invited by the Popperian conception of truth as a standard independent of what anyone thinks is true, or what any criterion of truth, or any proposed way of seeking or recognizing truth, might lead him to think true. Given this conception of truth, it surely makes good sense to say, 'Yes, I can see that any enquirer, thus equipped, would inevitably reach this conclusion – but, none the less, *is this conclusion true?*'

We have already noted the merits of Popper's distinction between what is true, and what is, for whatever reason, thought to be true, as well as between what is true and what yields practically useful results, simplifies calculations, etc. But we have also noted the scepticism inherent in this conception of truth as a standard which, no matter what we do, we can never be quite certain of having attained even though, paradoxically, in the passage quoted at the outset of this chapter, Popper offers it as a safeguard against scepticism. Doubtless there is an important sense in which truth is independent of our ideas about it, something we seek, and (perhaps) discover rather than something we create; but we need to look more closely at the nature of this independence.

To begin with, our enquiries are never aimed at, and never yield, the truth, *simpliciter*. To would-be researchers in any field, the instruction 'Seek the truth' would be as baffling and unhelpful as Popper's instruction to his Viennese students, 'Observe'. There is always something suspect about attempts to reify or personify Truth as though it were a single, unchanging object of search or veneration. The researcher can only learn, piecemeal, the various techniques of enquiry appropriate to his chosen discipline, how to set up the relevant experiments, carry out the relevant surveys, or whatever, how to observe, measure, count, and report his results to the degree of accuracy required for the task in hand. When he is conscientiously applying such techniques to a particular subject-matter, no doubt it is unobjectionable, if unenlightening, to say in a moment of rhetoric that he is seeking truth – and also, when he has stated a result to the required degree of accuracy that he has found truth (or a truth). But those actually engaged in specific research projects are unlikely to have much use for 'true' and its derivatives as terms of assessment, any more than, say, artists and art-critics have for 'beautiful'; such terms are too general and imprecise for their purposes. The researchers are more likely to be concerned with the degree of accuracy or exhaustiveness achieved by a specific statement of results and with whether, or how adequately, this will serve a specific scientific purpose.

As Austin puts it:

There are numerous other adjectives which are in the same class as 'true' and 'false' which are concerned, that is, with the relations between the words (as uttered with reference to an historic situation) and the world, and which nevertheless no one would dismiss as logically superfluous. We say, for example, that a certain statement is exaggerated or vague or bold, a description somewhat rough or misleading or not very good, an account rather general or too concise. In cases like these it is pointless to insist on deciding in simple terms whether the statement is 'true' or 'false' . . . There are various *degrees and dimensions* of success in making statements; the statements fit the facts always more or less loosely, in different ways on different occasions for different intents and purposes . . .

. . . the truth is a bare minimum or an illusory ideal (the truth, the whole truth and nothing but the truth about, say, the battle of Waterloo or the *Primavera*).[24]

Or, in a later discussion,

It is essential to realize that 'true' and 'false', like 'free' and 'unfree', do not stand for anything simple at all; but only for a general dimension of being a right or proper thing to say as opposed to a wrong thing, in these circumstances, to this audience, for these purposes and with these intentions.[25]

The truth of a statement then, does not consist in any single, simple relationship between what it says and how things are in the world. Granted that the austere, no-nonsense Tarskian position – that, for example, to say that snow is white is true if and only if snow is white – is unexceptionable so far as it goes. But it is still pertinent to ask: 'How white does it have to be?' 'How far could its colour shade off towards grey or yellow, how many specks of black or brown could there be on its surface, before the statement that it is white ceased to be true?' Obviously there can be no single answer – or only a purely arbitrary one. At what point we cast doubt upon its truth would depend on what degree of precise colour-discrimination the occasion required (perhaps also on how pedantic we are disposed to be). Similarly, with statements of, say, the length of time occupied by some event, the size or weight of some body. Do I make a false statement if I say that a certain noise lasted for ten minutes, when a more accurate measurement yields a result of nine minutes, fifty-eight seconds? Well, yes, if the context requires accuracy to the nearest second; no, if accuracy to the nearest minute is good enough. Given the need, no doubt we could go on almost indefinitely devising means of obtaining more and more accurate readings, down to tiny fractions of seconds. But there is no theoretical limit to this progress, no *absolutely* accurate answer which could play the role of *the* truth about how long the event in question took. All we can mean by a true answer is one accurate to the level required by the purpose of the moment. We may compare Austin's example of the statement that France is hexagonal – is this true or false? A high-ranking general, discussing the number of frontiers and coast-lines to be defended might respond to it with 'Yes, that's true'; a geographer, attempting to produce an accurate map of France with 'No that's false'. More likely, they would in effect think of it as Austin does – 'It is a rough description; it is not a true or false one'[26] – and the geographer judge it as too rough for his purposes, the general as close enough for his. And if it is objected 'Never mind speculations about what anyone *would* say; as philosophers we are concerned with what they *should*, are logically entitled to, say. So *is* the statement that France is hexagonal true, or is it false?' the reply is that the objection arises from a misunderstanding of how the concept of truth functions.

There is simply no single way of relating words to the world, so that once a certain form of words has been spoken, or more precisely, used to make a statement, then either a truth has been created (if this relationship holds), or a falsehood (if it does not), regardless of any other facts whatsoever. We may of course agree with Austin's comment on the familiar claim that a statement is true 'when it corresponds to the facts' – that 'as a piece of standard English this can hardly be wrong'.[27] But only if we take the reference to 'standard English' to mean that, in so far as we have a standard use for the phrase 'corresponds to the facts', it is used synonymously with 'true'. This may be so – but it would be a serious mistake (and one against which Austin and others have warned) to suppose that it provides an analysis or explication of what it is to be true, that we start, as it were, with a clearly-defined concept of correspondence and use this to elucidate the comparatively obscure concept of truth. 'Correspond' and its derivatives are used as blanket-terms to cover an indefinite range of relationships, various kinds of copying, picturing, mirroring, fitting, interacting . . . And we very quickly find ourselves in trouble if we seize on any one such relationship, say that of a naturalistic picture to its subject-matter (or a map to a landscape, a translation to its original . . .) and claim that *this* is how a true statement, as such, corresponds to the relevant facts. Any such model, though it may work fairly well while we concentrate on a particular range of examples, comes to grief on the sheer diversity of kinds of statements. So, while it may be acceptable English to use the term 'correspond' to cover the relationship (or relationships) of true statements to the relevant facts, as well as to cover the other relationships mentioned above, it is merely a matter of 'as well as'. There is no question of being *reducible to* any of these.

A 'correspondence theory', like any other general theory of truth, has a choice between being wrong (too limited or restrictive) and being almost totally unhelpful to anyone trying to speak, or recognize, the truth on a specific topic. In the matter of such general theories, it is doubtful indeed if anyone has ever improved on the magnificent Aristotelian formula, 'to say of what is that it is, and of what is not that it is not' — which is incontrovertible so far as it goes, but tells us nothing about what we must do, in any given case, in order to say of what is that it is, etc. As we saw earlier we can only learn *piecemeal* how to fit words to the world and hence how to speak, or recognize, the truth *in particular cases*, i.e. how to conduct this or that particular enquiry and state the result correctly. But if, as philosophers, we seek generality, and ask what is it for *any* statement of the result of *any* enquiry to be true, there is no single quality or relationship which an all-embracing 'theory of truth' can be expected to specify. However disappointingly vague Austin's talk about 'a general dimension of being a right or proper thing to say, etc.' may be, this is as much as any such general theory can properly tell us.

What we have called 'enquiries' and 'statements of results' are, as already indicated, large, complex and indeterminate families. We set ourselves many tasks in the exploration of our world and of our lives within it; we develop physical and conceptual equipment with which to carry out these tasks; and these in turn may suggest further tasks, in a complex pattern of inter-relationships. To pursue the analogy with exploration (in its most familiar, geographical sense) for a moment — for various purposes, including their own inherent interest, we make, or attempt to make, many different maps, covering greater or smaller areas, on larger or smaller scales, showing more or less detail, marking this or that feature or set of features of the area in question, sometimes faithfully reproducing the shapes of coastlines and the courses of rivers, sometimes deliberately simplifying and formalizing for the sake of clarity . . . And if we are asked what constitutes a *good* map, we can only reply that a map is good if, or in so far as, it achieves the specific purpose intended for, or assigned to, it. Beyond this, we can offer no general formula for cartographical merit. It can only be a matter of doing some specific job successfully; and except when we have some such job in mind, we have no means of judging whether it has been successfully done or not.

Similarly with statements. We can only assess a statement as true or false (or apply one of our more specific terms of appraisal) when we know what its function is, or assign some function to it. Does it report a specific fact or summarize a range of facts; what degrees of accuracy, literalness, exhaustiveness, or comprehensiveness, does it aim at; is it offered as a sober, detailed report, an impressionistic word-picture, a rough outline, or a deliberate simplification to highlight certain features of its subject-matter? It is only with answers to these and many other questions in mind, whether we ever make them explicit or not, that we can assess it, i.e. once more, determining first what its job is and then asking how well that job has been done. We may say if we please that in order to discover whether a given statement is true or false we must confront it with the relevant facts and see whether or not it corresponds to them. If we are careful, this is harmless enough, even if unhelpful. But we have to remember that noticing such correspondence cannot be anything like noticing, say, a structural similarity between two diagrams, or two geometrical figures, on the page before us. All we can notice in effect is that some process of enquiry and formulation of result − even if an almost instantaneous one, like counting a small number of objects, or noting the colour or shape of some surface − yields this statement as its end-product.

Do we have to allow then that, after all, the same statement *can* be both true and false, depending on the function assigned to it − so that the statement that the noise lasted for ten minutes is true relative to one standard of accuracy, false relative to another; or the statement that France is hexagonal true relative to the general's standpoint, false relative to the geographer's, and so on? But once again, *is* it the same statement in each case? I have proposed − if that is the most appropriate term − that giving the result of the same enquiry, rather than sameness of verbal formula, should be the criterion of sameness here. But then, once again, what of the criteria of sameness and difference among *enquiries*? Here also there are no firm or obvious guide-lines to be traced in everyday usage; but there is at least no flagrant violation of such usage in the suggestion that timing something to the nearest second is a different enquiry from timing it to the nearest minute or that surveying the outline of France with a view to dividing it into broad sectors with varying defensive needs, is a different enquiry from tracing its intricacies with a view to producing an accurate map. Accordingly, we have no need to relapse into a relativism which says that the same statement can be assigned different truth-values, or that two enquirers can contradict each other, by reason of different standpoints, without any error on anyone's part − but once again only our innocuous kind of relativism which merely reminds us that we can in principle choose between many different lines of enquiry and hence arrive, quite correctly, at many different statements of results.

Given such an account of what it is for a statement to be true, it follows that, if we have for example carried out a piece of counting, measuring or whatever, and formulated the result, to the degree of accuracy required by the enquiry we have undertaken, then it makes no sense to say that, none the less, our statement may not be true. If it satisfies these conditions then *ipso facto* it *is* true. To think of The Truth as being like the buried gold which we may miss no matter how conscientiously we apply our techniques of excavation, unless we are clever or fortunate enough to dig in just the right place, is to misunderstand how the concept of truth functions. As in the old fable, the only gold consists in the harvests reaped by those who conscientiously dig their own fields, and plant and tend appropriate crops. Of course, the crop and the yield may vary greatly from one field or one farmer to another, and even conscientious husbandry may be attended by mistakes and misfortunes, but by and large it does not miss its due reward.

If an enquirer starts out with meagre technical and conceptual equipment, and lacks imagination and incentive enough to improve it, then indeed there are many *specific truths* that must elude him – whole areas and aspects of the world which he is unable to explore, and of which he may be wholly unaware, standard of accuracy in the measurement of distances, times, etc. which he cannot hope to reach, and hence whole branches of science which he cannot begin to develop. The resultant knowledge of the world, the sum-total of findings, will, to the eyes of those better equipped, be variously incomplete, inaccurate, one-sided. And it is doubtless well to reflect that however complex and sophisticated our equipment for enquiry may be, the process of its improvement is never-ending: and hence that there are always truths still to be discovered, new aspects of the world still to be explored, new standards still to be attained. And in this respect at least our science *is* endlessly self-improving. We may claim that we sometimes have the truth (i.e. some truths) but we can never claim to have the whole truth (i.e. all possible truths); and presumably, given human frailty, it would be rash to claim, for any substantial field of interest at least, that our present account of it is nothing but the truth. But there is a crucial difference between the humility that allows that we can never have the whole truth, and can never be entirely happy about the credentials of everything that passes for truth, and the scepticism which says we can never be certain that we have any truth at all.

The development of such equipment for enquiry, both physical and conceptual — with the various leaps forward and breakthroughs, the periods of unspectacular but none the less important sharpening and refinement, the checks and the disappointments — is clearly one of the most important aspects, perhaps indeed *the* most important, of the whole development of science. It is one that has often been ignored, or treated only indirectly by philosophers of science — including Popper himself, and his various critics discussed in the previous chapter. Despite the unquestionable depths of their interest in, and knowledge of, science, they are accustomed, understandably enough, to think primarily of science on the page, as it were, i.e. of science as presented in papers and text-books, rather than on science as practiced in laboratories, research stations and observatories or on research expeditions. And hence their preoccupation with the characteristic *statements* of science, i.e. with the end-products, rather than with the equipment and the operations required to reach them. But we have already noted how the assumption that such statements can be identified and assessed, in abstraction from the enquiries that give rise to them, leaves the way open to relativism — of the pernicious sort — and scepticism. And, apart from this, we may question whether it is not misleading, to say the least, to suppose that major advances in science, of the sort about which Popper shows most concern, consist essentially in the framing of new *statements*, i.e. new theories or hypotheses, which science then sets about trying to verify or falsify. Very often, it would seem, the crucial innovation is the introduction, into a given field of research, of a new, or refurbished, *concept* or a new piece of *technical apparatus*. Such new equipment, as we have said, opens up possibilities for new enquiries, or ranges of enquiries; and the formulation of the results of these generates, in due time, a variety of scientific statements. No doubt, especially at an early stage, when scientists are still refining the new equipment and exploring its potentialities, many of the statements that emerge are in various ways defective — over-hasty, over-simplified, over-confident, or just downright muddled or mistaken — but, given favourable circumstances, there will ultimately be a residue of statements which we can claim, without qualification, are *true*, in the sense that they do adequately the jobs, or some of the jobs, that can be done with the equipment in question. And these are the permanent contribution of that particular innovation to the advancement of science.

A rough analogy might be drawn with the history of painting, where new stages of development are often marked by the emergence, for whatever reason, of new techniques, or new ideas of what painting should aim to achieve (impressionism, cubism, surrealism and the like) rather than by the painting of a masterpiece distinguished not by originality of technique or objective, but simply by the attainment of a beauty absent in lesser works. The emergence of impressionism – or any of our other isms – stimulates a spate of paintings, as artists explore the new ideas and discover their possibilities, with varying degrees of talent and success. And again, granted favourable circumstances, after most of their work has been forgotten, there is left a residue of paintings of permanent interest and value, i.e. those that have taught us something new about what can be achieved with paint and canvas.

In passing we may notice that at least one important contribution to the philosophical study of science *does* concentrate on what we have called the equipment of science, rather than on its theories or its capacities to verify or falsify them – Whitehead's *Science and the Modern World*, published first in 1925. (This is substantially true of Whithead's other works in this area, *The Principles of Natural Knowledge*, *The Concept of Nature*, etc., and is doubtless one reason why he is often neglected in contemporary discussion of the philosophy of science.) Thus, for example, he finds the distinctive development of science in the nineteenth century shaped by 'four great novel *ideas*',[28] (though, as he acknowledges, three of them at least were renovations of ideas with long histories rather than novelties in any strict sense). These, very briefly, were, first, the idea of 'a field of physical activity pervading all space, even where there is an apparent vacuum', in effect the idea of an ether; this provided a basis for the undulatory theory of light which 'demands that there shall be something throughout space which can undulate', and for Clerk Maxwell's theory of electromagnetism which similarly 'demanded that there should be electromagnetic occurrences throughout all space'. Secondly, and at first sight antithetical to these demands for continuity, there was the idea of atomicity, which Whitehead traces not only in the chemistry of the time, but in its biology as well, with the development of cell-theory. Third and fourth were the ideas of the conservation of energy and of evolution.

Nor is he concerned only with the influence of *ideas* on the development of science. In a later chapter, considering the emergence of relativity and quantum theory in the early years of the twentieth century, and consequently the ways in which science has become more remote from commonsense views of the world, he says:

The reason why we are on a higher imaginative level, is not because we have finer imagination, but because we have better instruments. In science, the most important thing that has happened during the last forty years is the advance in instrumental design. This advance is partly due to a few men of genius such as Michelson and the German opticians. It is also due to the progress of technological processes of manufacture, particularly in the region of metallurgy. The designer has at his disposal a variety of materials of differing physical properties. He can thus depend upon obtaining the material he desires; and it can be ground to the shapes he desires within very narrow limits of tolerance. These instruments have put thought onto a new level. A fresh instrument serves the same purpose as foreign travel; it shows things in unusual combinations. The gain is more than a mere addition; it is a transformation.[29]

The half-century or so since Whitehead wrote this has seen the development of a further wealth of equipment, both conceptual and technical. And the unprecedented, and often frightening, speed and volume of modern scientific progress seems indeed to depend, not primarily on the imagination and energy that have gone into the forming and testing of new theories, but rather – as Whitehead suggests just before the first passage quoted[30] – on an altered approach to technology. Technological progress, hitherto 'slow, unconscious and unexpected' became, he tells us, in the nineteenth century, 'quick, conscious and expected'. 'The greatest invention of the nineteenth century was the invention of the method of invention', with the emphasis on *method* – something first explicitly developed in the German technological schools and universities, which 'abolished haphazard methods of scholarship', and freed science from the need to 'wait for the occasional genius, or the occasional lucky thought' – in effect making 'the change from amateurs to professionals'. And the twentieth century has certainly intensified this deliberate and systematic search, *not* initially for new theories or new facts, but for new apparatus and new techniques of enquiry.

Once the equipment for enquiry, both conceptual and technical, has been applied to tasks of setting out and solving actual scientific problems, then, obviously, in due time scientific 'statements' of various kinds, including Popper's 'theories' and 'basic statements', are formulated. And it is of course entirely reasonable to be concerned that such statements should be true, or as close to the truth as possible, and that false statements should be eliminated. But in view of what has been said about the concept of truth, so far as the practising scientist himself is concerned, if he takes care of the enquiry, the truth will take care of itself. (As a simple example, if he undertakes to apply, and give the result of applying, a certain technique of measurement, and observes impeccably the rules of procedure which define that technique, and states his result accordingly, then *ipso facto* his statement is true.) So far as the *reader* of science is concerned, it has to be allowed that he can only understand what is being said, i.e. identify the statement being made, and assess it, to the extent that he knows of what enquiry it purports to give the result. In the lower reaches of science this usually presents no difficulty to the layman since the scientist is merely offering the results of a particularly thorough or systematic application of techniques of enquiry, observing, measuring, counting, etc. which are in principle familiar from everyday affairs. But suppose the layman reads an account of, say, the internal structure of the atom, while under the impression that the scientist is simply recounting what he saw when he looked through a powerful microscope, as one might watch peas in a saucepan of boiling water. Clearly, he can only misunderstand what is being said — a misunderstanding which will quickly become apparent if he tries to draw out the implications of what he has read, or suggest ways in which it might be tested, or in which disagreements about atomic structure might be resolved. He can only, as it were, get onto the same wavelength as the scientist when he is taught something about *how* the scientist conducts his enquiries, as well as about his results; otherwise he will inevitably treat the scientist's statements as giving the results of some enquiry of a kind with which he *is* familiar, and attempt to assess it accordingly. This is, of course, in effect merely to adapt a commonplace about education, i.e. that we learn more about science — or indeed philosophy — as it actually is, by learning, in the case of one major thinker, not just what conclusions he reached but *how* he reached them (what the initial problems were, what equipment was available for solving them, what steps the enquiry followed, etc.) than by having the conclusions of a dozen thinkers summarized for us. (Cf. the analogous commonplace that the nature of art must be learnt in the studio, and not in the art-gallery alone.)

That the technological advances which Whitehead mentions, and other advances since his time, most notably the advent of the computer age, have opened up new fields of enquiry, and new possibilities for the discovery of truths about the world, is too obvious to need elaboration here. The point to be made is that, in any account of the development of science, these have a claim to count as the most important innovations, rather than any of the host of 'statements' – true or otherwise, and variously interesting or important from various points of view – to which they inevitably give rise. And similarly when we turn to conceptual apparatus, to the impact on science of novel, or renovated, concepts such as those of evolution, relativity, quanta, or indeterminacy. What we find is a number of different theories all embodying the concept of, say, evolution, each with its particular explanatory strengths and weaknesses, its advocates and critics. For the reasons set out in the previous chapter, no one of them ever commanded, or deserved, general assent among those qualified to judge – not even for a limited spell as a Popperian thus-far-unrefuted conjecture. But what marked a new era in the history of science, was not the formulation of any specific theory of evolution – Darwin's or anyone else's – or the knock-out victory of such a theory over its predecessors. If we adopt such sporting metaphors, we may say that a whole new game emerged rather than a new champion in a familiar one. What really mattered was that the *concept* of evolution, of a *possible* way in which the elements of the organic world might have developed or might be inter-related, added something new – and as it turned out extremely fruitful – to our equipment for exploring that world, that it prompted new questions, theories, explanations, arguments, lines of research . . . And it has long continued to play this role, prompting and directing enquiry even for enquirers who have ceased to know, or care, precisely what it was that Darwin said about evolution in the first place. Darwin's position as a major figure in the history of science depends not primarily on the truth (or resistance to falsification) of his account of evolution – which few would defend without serious reservations – but rather on the fact that he, more than anyone else, was responsible for introducing the concept of evolution into scientific discussion, at such a time and in such a way that it stimulated a whole new range of enquiries, theories and arguments. (Cf. the reasons why teachers of philosophy continue to recommend, say, Locke to their students as an important figure in the history of their subject, even though they find most of his actual theories embarrassingly easy to refute.) And something similar might be said of the other concepts mentioned. By and large, a new piece of conceptual equipment – like a new piece of technical equipment – in circumstances where it can thus open up new possibilities for enquiry, can have a longer-lasting and more radical effect on the development of science than any specific theory which embodies it.

## 6

This is not, however, the place to try to develop, in any detail, an alternative to Popper's philosophy of science. Our present objective is simply to explicate some of the limitations as well as the merits of that philosophy; and more specifically to show how and why, despite the emphatic rejections of relativism and scepticism, it has no fully effective defences against them.

Clearly, the central issue throughout has been the function assigned to the concept of truth. As I have, I trust, already made clear I am not concerned to question Tarski's version of the correspondence theory, or Popper's estimate of its value. Rather I am concerned with how the concept of truth thus understood can fulfil the function which Popper assigns to it. We can see, readily enough, how this concept supports, and indeed requires, Popper's uncompromising refusal to equate what it is customary or convenient to regard as true with what *is* true, or to postulate any helpful self-manifestations of truth. From any statement about the experiences (from the humblest data of sight and touch to mystical illuminations) which lead us to hold that $S$, it never follows, logically, that $S$ is true. The logical gap remains. But if so, then how can truth play the role of the objective standard by which all our efforts at discovery are to be judged, and which provides a safeguard against relativism and scepticism? If the gap prevents us from ever justifiably claiming, without qualification, that we *have* the truth about something, then how can we actually use the standard to check any given statement? Are we not simply driven back to the relativism which makes it a matter of convention which statements we treat as true, or the scepticism which keeps reminding us that any of them may be false – so that far from abolishing these evils, this use of the concept of truth actually encourages them?

To return to an earlier analogy taken from the field of religious belief, the idea of divine self-revelation, of the Word of God, something beyond all human powers to criticize or correct, has, undoubtedly, in the relevant fields, been a highly effective bulwark against relativism and scepticism. It provides an authoritative way of judging theories and opinions and settling disputes – but only for so long as it is maintained that we actually *have* the Word, embodied in a specific set of statements, for example those of the Bible. But suppose it is allowed that the original Word, as given to the prophets or apostles, had been lost, and that all we have now are transcriptions and translations exposed to human error and interference. Clearly the field is open to rival speculations, all alike fallible, about what it said or might have said; any human effort after knowledge is always haunted with the unanswerable doubt, that whatever its merits it may not be in accordance with the divine Word.

And not only are we barred from knowing when, if ever, we have actually arrived at the truth; it would seem that we cannot even tell when we are getting closer to it. It is, of course, central to Popper's whole account of science that while we can never (justifiably) say of any of our theories, 'Here, at last, is the truth', none the less we can in some circumstances say that theory $t_2$ has the advantage over $t_1$ in that it passes all the tests that $t_1$ passes and some that $t_1$ fails as well. And indeed, according to Popper, scientific progress in general consists in the securing of such advantages. In some of his later writings, he attempted to clarify – but not, he insists, materially alter – this notion by introducing the concept of degrees of *verisimilitude*.[31] This is defined in terms of the 'truth-contents' and 'falsity-contents' of statements. Thus,

Let us consider the *content* of a statement *a*; that is, the class of all the logical consequences of *a*. If *a* is true, then this class can consist only of true statements, because truth is always transmitted from a premiss to all its conclusions. But if *a* is false, then its content will always consist of both true and false conclusions. (Example: 'It always rains on Sundays' is false, but its conclusion that it rained last Sunday happens to be true.) Thus whether a statement is true or false, *there may be more truth, or less truth, in what it says*, according to whether its content consists in a greater or lesser number of true statements.

Then, (simplifying a little) we may call the true logical consequences of a statement its 'truth-content', its false consequences its 'falsity-content', and adopt the following principle:

*Assuming that the truth-content and the falsity-content of two theories $t_1$ and $t_2$ are comparable, we can say that $t_2$ is more closely similar to the truth, or corresponds better to the facts, than $t_1$, if and only if either*
(a) *the truth-content but not the falsity-content of $t_2$ exceeds that of $t_1$, or*
(b) *the falsity-content of $t_1$, but not its truth-content, exceeds that of $t_2$.*[32]

Under these conditions, we can say that $t_2$ has greater (or a greater degree or measure of) verisimilitude than $t_1$.

Doubtless this concept of verisimilitude is potentially valuable. If we have to abandon the hope of scientific theories which are quite simply true, or known to be true, then clearly the next best thing would be theories with the greatest possible verisimilitude; and it would provide a very convenient measure of scientific progress. We need not concern ourselves unduly, in this context, with such detailed points of criticism as that, strictly, any statement taken by itself has few logical consequences. (From 'It always rains on Sundays' alone it does *not* follow logically that it rained last Sunday.) For the most part (and the most interesting part) logical consequences follow from *several* statements taken in conjunction, for example a statement of a scientific theory, plus statements of other relevant theories or initial conditions. The account of verisimilitude could presumably be modified easily enough to cover this point. The real problem over verisimilitude, as over truth itself, is how we are to recognize it in particular cases; how do we know what measure of verisimilitude a given theory has, or whether it has more of it than a rival theory. With commendable consistency, Popper replies 'I do *not* know – I only guess. But I can examine my guess critically, and if it withstands severe criticism, then this fact may be taken as a good critical reason in favour of it.'[33] But again, what is the point of testing our guesses, however severely, if we can do no more than make further guesses about whether they survive the tests or not? It would, of course, be very valuable to know which of two theories (taken in conjunction with the relevant auxiliary theories and statements of initial conditions) yielded the more true consequences or the fewer false ones – but only if we *can* actually know it, i.e. if we are actually able to determine which consequences *are* true and which false. As a mere ideal, such that we can never be certain whether we have realized it or not, the concept of maximum verisimilitude is of no more help to us in avoiding relativism and scepticism than that of truth itself. Once again, indeed, we *invite* relativism and scepticism when we admit that which of our statements realize our ideal can only be a matter of convention, or guesswork.

In the passage just quoted, Popper again draws the distinction which we noted at the beginning of section 2 of this chapter –

we have to distinguish between the question 'What do you intend to say if you say that the theory $t_2$ has a higher degree of verisimilitude than the theory $t_1$'

and the question 'How do you know that the theory $t_2$ has a higher degree of verisimilitude than the theory $t_1$?'[34]

His answer to this second question we have already seen. We don't know; but since presumably we don't make such claims at random, we have some conventionally-approved criteria for making or withholding them. Popper's distinction here is, in effect, once again that between our *criterion* for saying something and the *commitment* we undertake in saying it. We have already identified the gap between the two as a time-honoured source of scepticism in general. And we can see it specifically as the source of this strong and apparently ineradicable element of scepticism (and/or relativism) in Popper's epistemology. In the case of *any* statement the conventionally adequate conditions for making it are never logically adequate, in his view, to cover the commitment we undertake in making it. And hence the unrestricted fallibilism, and its consequences.

But having thus reintroduced our criterion—commitment distinction, we can now see the discussion of the foregoing sections as essentially an exploration of possible ways of bridging the logical gap between the two, and hence avoiding the consequences in question. Thus – to recapitulate briefly – we have considered how the daunting task of discovering and speaking the truth about our world dissolves into an indefinite plurality of specific tasks of enquiry and result-stating, done in various ways and for various ends, and hence with equally various criteria of success or failure. We need have no quarrel with Popper, or Tarski, over the correspondence theory – so long as we realise that 'correspondence' here cannot stand for any single relationship, and all that we can mean by saying that a statement $S$ corresponds to the facts is that $S$ is yielded by the relevant process of enquiry (correctly carried out). Every statement as such gives, or purports to give, the result of some enquiry (in a broad sense of the term), and only an audience with at least a tacit understanding of the nature of the enquiry can identify the statement we are making – and hence assess it appropriately. Thus, when we state that $S$, we are committed to – and only to – a claim that when the appropriate enquiry and formulation of results have been correctly carried out, i.e. when our criteria in the relevant sense have been satisfied, then $S$ is yielded. And thus we may say that the criteria *determine* the commitment – and with it the appropriate method of assessment.

We have seen, further, ways of meeting the obvious sceptical objections – 'But you are committed to much more than this, to a claim that not just the enquiries already completed but *any* enquiries (on the relevant subject-matter, etc.) which satisfy your criteria will yield *S*, i.e. to an unrestricted inductive generalization', or, 'You can never be certain, in any given case, whether your criteria have been satisfied.' That the same enquiry always yields the same result is, as we have noted, *logically* true. By 'same' here we can only mean qualitatively the same, the same in all relevant respects, and we should allow nothing to count as two enquiries thus identical but yielding different results. (If we think that today's experiment is the same in all relevant respects as yesterday's, or yours the same as mine, but it yields a different result, then *ipso facto* some of the differences we thought irrelevant must be relevant after all.) Of course, it is possible that we or our world should change in such a way that we could no longer conduct the same enquiries as we do now. But since our commitment is only to giving correctly the results of *these* enquiries this does nothing to show that we may be wrong. Thus, we do not commit ourselves as to what *any* enquirer will find in a certain situation, but only any enquirer suitably equipped, with normal senses, working under standard conditions, etc., will find. And what determines what is to count as 'suitable', 'normal' or 'standard'? We do not in fact give hostages quite so recklessly as the sceptic suggests.

Regarding his second challenge, the role of particular cases has clearly special importance. For, granted that it is, in essential part at least, by or through such cases that we learn, and teach, what, for example, correct counting is – that we are, as it were, guided by precedents rather than general rules, by case-law rather than statute-law – then to suggest, even as a logical possibility, that these could all be miscounts, is simply a misuse (or at least a proposed new use) of terms. Once more, of course, it is logically possible that in different circumstances we should do things recognizably similar in some respects and get different results. But it does not follow that we may have achieved no truths, merely that we may not have achieved all of them – which is hardly a very startling conclusion.

It would be too much to hope that such considerations will finally silence the hard-line sceptic (unless indeed, as some of his Greek predecessors are said to have done, he regards silent disapproval as the only entirely consistent expression of scepticism). Doubtless he can still find the means to mount, in his turn, yet another out-flanking expedition . . . and so on. And the above discussion has, I hope, shown due respect for the strength and tenacity of scepticism, as of relativism also – qualities effectively demonstrated by the capacity to survive, and even flourish under, criticisms like those of Popper. But it has also brought to light at least some promising ways of avoiding their more pernicious manifestations, and securing that basis of established truths which, however limited, is none the less essential for any serious attack on falsehood or ignorance.

# 4

# *Historicism*

## 1

I mean by 'historicism' an approach to the social sciences which assumes that *historical prediction* is their principal aim, and which assumes that this aim is attainable by discovering the 'rhythms' or the 'patterns', the 'laws' or the 'trends' that underlie the evolution of history . . . I am convinced that such historicist doctrines of method are at bottom responsible for the unsatisfactory state of the theoretical social sciences (other than economic theory).[1]

My intention is to criticise the doctrine that it is the task of the social sciences to propound historical prophecies, and that historical prophecies are needed if we wish to conduct politics in a rational way. I shall call this doctrine 'historicism'. I consider historicism to be the relic of an ancient superstition, even though the people who believe in it are usually convinced that it is a very new, progressive, revolutionary and scientific theory.[2]

When we turn to the discussion of the social sciences in Popper's later writings, we are not entering wholly new or unmapped territory. Many features should be immediately familiar from the foregoing consideration of his philosophy of science and theory of knowledge in general. Thus, for example, we find Popper again adopting his characteristic role as one-man opposition to ideas which he presents as extremely widespread, influential, and pernicious. Again it is his central thesis that claims have been made for the disciplines in question which cannot be substantiated, while their real potentialities have been overlooked. And again he maintains that, on the relevant issues, there are no final or unquestionable authorities, no way of arriving once and for all at the right answers; here also the only course open to research is one of endless self-correction, of trial and error and learning through mistakes.

This is more than just the carrying over of certain distinctive habits of thoughts from one field of interest to another. The essential links between the earlier and later work are not biographical but logical. And it is obvious that, unless Popper were to renounce all his earlier achievements and start afresh, they *must* determine in important respects what he says about social science, and indeed about virtually any other topic. Thus, if *no* generalization can be verified, then *a fortiori* no generalization about human societies, or any aspect of their structure or development, can be verified either; the falsificationist, conjecture-and-refutation, account of general theories must hold of the social as well as the physical sciences. And, given an unrestricted fallibilism, which holds that *no* source of claims to knowledge is authoritative, there are identical implications for our attempts to know the structure and workings of human society, and for our attempts to know those of our physical environment. (Indeed, we might say, quite generally, that a theory of knowledge determines, in essential part, a theory of the whole human situation. And specifically that the Popperian epistemology leads on to something like a Popperian view of man – i.e. as a being forever faced by problems, theoretical or practical, raised by an alien environment and with no guarantees from any source that his solutions are the right ones, and his survival depending on his being able and willing to alter or adapt his solutions in the light of experience.)

So, if we hanker after laws or principles of social development which will enable us to understand what is 'really' happening in society, and to predict, and perhaps influence, its future progress, we must, in the light of what we have already seen of his teaching, expect discouragement from Popper. No general law, however we may arrive at it, can have any status other than that of conjecture. And no method of research, however thorough and systematic, can guarantee the truth of our findings. On his own fundamental principles, Popper has to remain anti-authoritarian, and, despite any disclaimers, essentially sceptical.

Nevertheless, even if we set aside our various reservations and qualifications and allow that Popper is substantially right on these issues, may we not still hope to emulate in the social sciences some of the practical successes of the physical? Though they may be erected 'above a swamp',[3] many of the physical sciences undeniably *have*, by whatever means, managed to create theoretical structures which are notably coherent and well-corroborated, and which (taken in conjunction with appropriate statements of initial conditions) have vastly increased our capacity to control our physical environment – and to predict its future developments. And in our dealing with the physical world, surely the 'rational conduct' of affairs *has* depended largely on this capacity for prediction, however shaky its logical foundations. The primitive hunters or farmers, staking their livelihood on foreknowledge of when the herds will migrate or when the rains will come, and the modern space-technologists aiming a rocket at where they predict a distant planet will be several years hence, are alike exploiting it. And they cannot do their jobs otherwise. The main impact of the physical sciences on human affairs has been the enormous increase in the range and accuracy of this capacity to predict.

Is there anything wrong then, in principle, with hoping for similar results from the systematic development of the social sciences? In their field also, has intelligent planning not always depended on the capacity to predict – to realise in advance that, say, a certain clash of interests or ambitions was inevitable, that a certain policy was doomed to failure, that certain needs would have to be met? As in the physical field, such predictions have often, though of course not invariably, been vindicated by results. So why should we not carry the parallel with physical science a step further and aim – as presumably the historicist does – at a theoretical structure, which will replace whatever rules of thumb, traditions or intuitions the planners of the past relied on, and so vastly increase the range and accuracy of social prediction? Our concern here is to examine Popper's answer to this question. As we shall see, he is quite willing to allow that, in some circumstances, and with some qualifications, we *can* make social predictions and draw up our plans accordingly. What he undertakes to show is, in brief, that any long-term unconditional historical prophecy is in principle impossible and that all attempts at such prophecy, whatever their antecedents, are necessarily misguided. For the field of social science is inherently different from that of physical science in ways which make it impossible for *any* study of society, however conducted, to enable us to predict, say, revolutions as the astronomer predicts eclipses;[4] and we must not be misled by any similarities between the disciplines into supposing that it could.

Understandably, attempts to unravel the plot of the human drama, to show not only how it has unfolded thus far but how it is developing and how it will end, have been a feature of virtually every culture in every age. There have always been seers and prophets credited with the gift of second sight, the power of literally foreseeing the shape of things to come, or with a direct revelation from God, as the original author of the whole drama. Apart from an occasional derogatory reference,[5] Popper has little to say about these. But, as we should at least note in passing, the idea of revelation is scarcely one that can be dismissed out of hand as no more than a historical or anthropological curiosity. It has, after all, been central to the whole Judaeo-Christian tradition, and much more widely influential than any of the examples of historicism Popper actually examines; and, as was mentioned in an earlier chapter, the acceptance, rightly or wrongly, of a body of teaching as having divine authority, and therefore beyond human criticism, has in fact been one of the most effective barriers against relativism and scepticism. For better or for worse, then, it is a manifestation of historicism, in Popper's sense, which has to be taken seriously. For present purposes, however, I propose to concentrate on the examples of historicism which Popper himself is prepared to take seriously, examples drawn from somewhat widely separated phases in the history of western philosophical thought – first Plato, and then Hegel and Marx.

## 2

*Prima facie* at least, Plato seems somewhat oddly cast as an historicist; and, as we shall see presently, Popper has been criticized for giving undue emphasis to certain elements in Plato's thought, and ignoring others, for the sake of forcing it into the historicist mould. Certainly, one of the most striking differences between Plato and, say, Marx, is that while Marx is very much preoccupied with the process by which the classless society of the future will come into being, Plato shows very little interest in how, or whether, the ideal republic might be realized. In the *Republic* itself, Socrates and his friends talk at great length about how they will organize the new state, but have little to say about how or in what circumstances they might find a group of people amenable to such drastic reorganization. And to most readers the immediate impression, at any rate, is of a group of intellectuals exploring an idea for its inherent interest, with little concern to relate it to actual history, and still less to attempt to put it into practice.

This is not to say, of course, that they are doing no more than dreaming up a Utopia, the kind of state that they would merely 'like to see'. Theoretically at least, subjective preferences play no part in their conception of the republic. But neither do they seem to be attempting to discover quasi-scientific laws of social development which would enable them to say: This is how society must develop or this is the limit it must reach, whether anyone wants it so, or not. Rather, their enterprise seems more akin to pure mathematics than to physical science as we now understand it. The whole elaborate discussion of the structure of the state is after all simply part of an attempt to elucidate the essential character of justice – the problem with which the *Republic* starts. It is, or at any rate purports to be, a sustained effort in conceptual analysis. And the obvious analogy is with the geometer explicating the properties of the perfect triangle or circle – i.e. as a condition of doing so, he has to detach himself from empirical considerations and focus on the *concept* of triangle, circle, or whatever; he is well aware that such concepts never are, or could be, instantiated in the world of experience, at best we can have more of less imperfect approximations; but our pure geometry provides us with the standards by which we can distinguish good approximations from bad, or better from worse. All of this holds, substantially, of the treatment of justice in the *Republic*. And indeed we might say that the simplest way to appreciate the role of the Forms or Ideas in Platonic thought generally is to take pure geometry as a paradigm. (Cf. the inscription over the gates of the Academy, which Popper quotes in another context[6] – 'Nobody untrained in geometry may enter my house.')

According to Popper's autobiographical essay,[7] his lengthy critique of Plato, and eventually *The Open Society and its Enemies* in its entirety, grew out of an elaboration of section 10 of *The Poverty of Historicism* – the section entitled 'Essentialism *versus* Nominalism'.[8] Essentialism, briefly, is the thesis – exemplified in the Platonic Theory of Forms – that there are universal objects, or essences, that are designated by our universal terms; and further that these are realities there to be discovered, and explored, rather than our own creations, and that their discovery and exploration is of central importance to science. Hence we have the 'methodological essentialism' – developed explicitly by Aristotle but rooted in Platonism[9] – the exponents of which characteristically formulate

scientific questions in such terms as 'what is matter?' or 'what is force?' or 'what is justice?' and they believe that a penetrating answer to such questions, revealing the real or essential meaning of these terms and thereby the real or true nature of the essences denoted by them, is at least a necessary prerequisite of scientific research, if not its main task.

They are contrasted with the 'methodological nominalists' who

would put their problems in such terms as 'how does this piece of matter behave?' or 'how does it move in the presence of other bodies?' For methodological nominalists hold that the task of science is only to describe how things behave, and suggest that this is to be done by freely introducing new terms wherever necessary, or by re-defining old terms wherever convenient while cheerfully neglecting their original meaning.[10]

As Popper goes on to point out, modern physical science is emphatically nominalistic in this sense. And his characterization of Plato as the original essentialist accords very well with the view that Plato approaches his subject-matter as a mathematician rather than as a scientist. (Our geometer setting out to explicate what necessarily pertains to triangularity as such, rather than to describe the features of this or that particular triangle, is presumably a typical methodological essentialist.) Now doubtless we may criticize essentialism on many grounds; we may argue that the reasons for believing in the reality of Forms or essences are confused and inadequate in the first place; and that the methodological essentialism which stems from such belief has been a serious hindrance to progress in research.[11] We may argue similarly against the long tradition in Western thought – stretching at least from Pythagoras to the seventeenth-century rationalists – which has sought in effect to treat pure mathematics as a paradigm for all systems of knowledge, and generalize its methods indiscriminately. We may say that this tradition has stemmed from a misunderstanding of the nature of mathematics; and that attempts to carry over mathematical methods into other fields of interest – for example into our attempts to understand our physical or social environment – can only lead to futility. But however effective such criticisms may be against Plato, they still amount to saying, in effect, that if he wanted to understand the structure of society or the conditions for social stability and effective government then he was looking in the wrong direction; and they leave us with a picture of Plato, (no doubt a fairly widely accepted one) as the unworldly intellectual, concentrating on an ideal and neglecting historic fact, fondly imagining that he could make statesmen by teaching geometry and philosophy, and, not surprisingly, failing disastrously when he had a chance to put his theories into practice.

Even if we add the often-repeated specific criticisms of the way in which the *Republic* carries out its purported task – the lapses from mathematical rigour in analysis, the sophistries and dubious arguments, the many occasions when Socrates, under the guise of drawing out his companions' ideas, is shamelessly feeding them with his own – it is still not clear that its faults, however serious, are those of *historicism*. To understand why Popper classifies it thus, we have to notice, in the first place, that historicism is not necessarily optimistic, i.e. it does not necessarily present history as an inevitable progress towards the future realization of some ideal state of society. There is another ancient tradition going back to the Biblical account of the Garden of Eden and the fall of man, and the Greek legends of the Golden Age, a tradition no doubt still persisting in various forms, which puts the realization of the ideal somewhere in the remote *past* and sees subsequent history as a record of decline or degeneration – perhaps relieving the pessimism with some hope of a restoration on the further side of catastrophe. Belief in such an inevitable pattern of decline is as much historicism in Popper's sense as belief in an inevitable pattern of progress. And it is to this tradition that, according to his account, Plato belongs.

The Platonic Forms or Ideas are, of course, eternal and unchangeable; in this temporal world we can only have more or less imperfect and mutable copies of them. We may envisage at some point the realization of a nearly, but not quite, perfect copy; but its defects, however slight, are still enough to make it unstable, and liable to change; and change can only be for the worse, since it can only make the copy progressively more unlike the original. Thus,

A sensible or generated thing . . . if it is a good copy, may change only very little at first . . . But every change, however small, must make it different, and thus less perfect, by reducing its resemblance to its Form. In this way, the thing becomes more changeable with every change, and more corruptible, since it becomes further removed from its Form which is its 'cause of immobility and of being at rest'.

And hence, in effect,

Plato teaches *that change is evil, and that rest is divine.*[12]

According to Popper, Plato actually believed that there *had* once been such a realization, that

the *model or original* of his perfect state can be found in the distant past, in a Golden Age which existed in the dawn of history; for if the world decays in time, then we must find increasing perfection the farther back we go into the past, The perfect state is something like the first ancestor, the primogenitor, of the later states, which are, as it were, the degenerate offspring of this perfect, or best, or 'ideal' state.[13]

Plato, in effect, idealized the past. He has a 'romantic love for the tribal form of social life',[14] the simple and stable form of society in which time-honoured beliefs and values were unquestioned, and everyone knew and accepted his place in the scheme of things. And it was this that Plato elaborated in the *Republic* and elsewhere, trying to harden and sharpen its essential features in order to eliminate, so far as possible, those elements which, even in this form of society, made for change — and hence for decay.

Such elements obviously create a problem for any such belief in a past perfection. If it were perfect, how could it contain the origins of its own destruction; how did the serpent get into the divinely-created Garden of Eden? We have already seen a very general Platonic answer to this question, i.e. nothing in the temporal world is ever *entirely* perfect, there can only be varying degrees of approximation to the perfection of the eternal. But Plato has also more specific things to say about how and why societies degenerate; and it is here that Popper finds the specifically historicist elements in his thought. The main source is Book VIII of the *Republic*, where Plato, having described the ideal constitution of the state, goes on to trace the stages of decline from it, and the lines of development between them. In brief,

According to Plato, internal strife, class war, fomented by self-interest and especially material or economic self-interest, is the main force of 'social dynamics'. The Marxian formula 'The history of all hitherto existing societies is a history of class struggle' fits Plato's historicism nearly as well as that of Marx. The four most conspicuous periods or 'landmarks in the history of political degeneration' and at the same time 'the most important . . . varieties of existing states', are decribed by Plato in the following order. First after the perfect state comes 'timarchy' or 'timocracy', the rule of the noble who seek honour and fame; secondly, oligarchy, the rule of the rich families; 'next in order, democracy is born', the rule of liberty which means lawlessness; and last comes 'tyranny . . . the fourth and final sickness of the city'.[15]

This sequence is, effectively, determined by a quite general Platonic 'law of political revolutions', according to which, 'disunion in the ruling class, and their preoccupation with economic affairs, are the origin of all social change.'[16]

Many of the distinctive features of the *Republic* are thus explicable as Plato's efforts to guard, so far as possible, against the operation of this law – for example, the lengths to which he is prepared to go, by way of social reorganization, education and even eugenics, in order to ensure a ruling class free from all interests and preoccupations other than its task of ruling, and his insistence, as the most fundamental principle of the whole constitution, on everyone performing his own function within the system, and interfering with no other. Meddling is the root of all evil, as it were; when the statesman covets military glory or material wealth, or the soldier or the merchant covets political power, then we have the beginnings of a struggle between different classes or factions in society for possession of the same objective, and hence the beginnings of self-destruction.

From such considerations there emerges what Popper calls Plato's 'political programme', which can be distilled into two brief formulae, the 'idealist formula':

*Arrest of all political change!* Change is evil, rest divine. All change can be arrested if the state is made an exact copy of its original, i.e. of the Form or Idea of the city.

And the 'naturalistic formula', which tells how, in principle, this may be accomplished:

*Back to nature!* Back to the original state of our forefathers, the primitive state founded in accordance with human nature, and therefore stable; back to the tribal patriarchy of the time before the Fall, to the natural class rule of the wise few over the ignorant many.[17]

Popper shows due respect for the sincerity of Plato's concern over the ills of Greek society in his time, and of his desire to reform it, and for the immense talent that he brought to his task. But, as we should expect, he has little use either for Plato's theory of social development, as he interprets it, or for the political programme derived therefrom. As we have already noted, he sees the whole theory of Forms and their relationship to the temporal world as nothing more than the product of confusion, and the source of much subsequent confusion. His general arguments against any historicist effort to arrive, by whatever means, at laws of social development we shall consider in a later section. In his specific treatment of Plato, in the first volume of *The Open Society and its Enemies*, much of his space is devoted to an unsparing exposure of the manifest evils which Plato was led, by these initial errors, to advocate or condone. Thus, for example, for the sake of restoring his idealized tribal society, he is prepared to advocate an uncompromising totalitarianism which minimizes individual freedom even to the extent of proposing, in his *Laws*, what amounts to childhood-to-grave military discipline for every citizen; the interests of the state becomes the one ultimate moral standard, and justice consists merely in each element performing its appropriate function within the machinery of the state; education is reduced to indoctrination, the suppression rather than the promotion of independent thought; even religion is pressed into the service of the state, with the sinister Nocturnal Council of Inquisitors prepared to silence all dissent; and the rulers, though supposedly trained as philosophers in devotion to truth, are encouraged to deceive their citizens, and even themselves, when the well-being of the state requires it.

Plato himself, however, emerges not simply as a cold-blooded totalitarian, but as a somewhat tragic figure, torn between what he had learnt from the supreme individualist, Socrates, and his conviction that totalitarianism was the only cure for the sickness of contemporary society – with the latter, unfortunately, becoming increasingly dominant towards the end of his life. Socrates, of course, is a Popperian hero – the tireless questioner of accepted beliefs, humble and clear-headed enough to see himself as merely a seeker after truth and not a possessor of it; the intellectual egalitarian prepared to reason with a slave; the incorruptibly honest man willing to sacrifice his life rather than his integrity. But on all these counts, according to Popper, Plato, the most gifted of Socrates' disciples, betrayed him, abandoning one after another all the essentials of Socrates' teaching while continuing to use him as a mouthpiece for ideas increasingly opposed to his own. (It is, however, allowed that this was not, or not entirely, a deliberate and unscrupulous misuse of Socrates' reputation, that Plato was trying to persuade himself, as well as others, that his own teaching was the logical outcome of that of Socrates.) As Gilbert Ryle put it, according to Popper, Plato

was Socrates' Judas. The very things for which Socrates lived and died are the things which Plato tries to demolish with words put into Socrates' mouth. The 'Laws' justify the silencing and the execution of such people as Socrates, and it is Socrates who is made to give this justification. Socrates had taught Athens that truth knows no authorities but the Socrates of the 'Republic' argues for the Closed Society and an intellectual élite.[18]

The crucial break would appear to be made when truth ceases to be thought of as the object of the Socratic universal quest, and becomes instead something so deeply hidden that only a select few can undertake the long and arduous task of bringing it to light – when we pass, as Popper says Plato did at some point, from an optimistic to a pessimistic epistemology.[19] For, given that the few actually succeed in their quest, as Plato believed they did, then they merit an almost god-like status among their fellows,[20] with the right and duty to demand uncritical obedience and impose on others their vision of truth, and do whatever may be necessary to ensure that it is not lost or contaminated. And thus, while both may still agree that the philosopher as such is distinguished by his devotion to truth, Socrates' philosopher, 'the modest rational individualist' is transformed into Plato's philosopher-king, the 'totalitarian demi-god'.[21]

Doubtless there is much in what Popper quotes from Plato that illustrates very effectively the evils of *dogmatism* and the practical wisdom at any rate – whatever the theoretical difficulties – of the Popperian principle that nothing and nobody should be immune from criticism. (It is well to recall that, in the Biblical story, it was the temptation to 'be as gods' that led to humanity's expulsion from Eden;[22] had they been content to accept their human limitations they might have stayed.) But whether these evils are the outcome of *historicism* is another matter; and it is on this point that Popper's treatment of Plato has been most frequently attacked. He has been widely accused of forcing his preconceived historicist pattern on to Plato's work, and letting it determine his selection of passages for consideration, and his judgements about what Plato 'really' meant and what his 'real' motives were, when he was in earnest and when he was trying to deceive his readers or himself, when he lapsed into inconsistency, etc. In particular, the attribution of historicism rests, as we have seen, on the theses that (*a*) Plato held that the ideal state had actually been realized (or almost so) in the primitive tribal society of the remote past; and (*b*) his account of the stages of degeneration from the ideal was intended as the statement of a general historical law of inevitable decline. And critics have argued that the texts simply do not bear out the interpretation, that there is more and better evidence than Popper produces to show that Plato did *not* believe that primitive tribal society was a (near-) realization of his ideal, that he did *not* intend his speculations about the dangers to the republic, the ways in which it might degenerate, as a statement of a general historical law, that he was *not* such a ruthless totalitarian and enemy of individual freedom as Popper portrays, that his relation to Socrates was *not* such a simple matter of light and darkness.[23] Popper, characteristically, has made some vigorous replies;[24] but, generally speaking, the specialists in the field have remained sceptical.

Obviously, we cannot here enter into detailed textual considerations to determine which is the correct, or the likeliest, interpretation of Plato. But a few general points may usefully be made about the internal coherence of Popper's interpretation. Thus, given the role of the theory of Forms in Plato's epistemology, the attempt to elucidate the essential nature of justice, or the state, or indeed anything else has, as we said at the outset of this discussion, to be an exercise in conceptual, rather than historical, analysis. As in pure mathematics, we have to free ourselves from preoccupation with the spatio-temporal world of sense experience (and indeed this is one of the principal aims of Plato's educational programme). History can do no more than provide (always imperfect) illustrations. And there is certainly nothing in the theory of Forms to require that the first realization of a given form should be better, or more faithful to its original, than any subsequent one, or that there should be any particular order of merit among them. Hence any talk of the perfect state being the 'first ancestor' or 'primogenitor' of subsequent states can be no more than metaphorical. And whether or not Plato did, as a matter of biography, seek an image of his ideal society in the remote past, his general theory of knowledge certainly would not have encouraged him to do so; rather it required him to turn aside from history altogether.

Consider also Popper's version of Plato's 'political programme'. There is a general problem over how historicism, i.e. belief in the working of inexorable laws of historical development, is consistent with *any* kind of political programme, i.e. any proposal for altering or directing such development. According to Popper, for the historicist

Only such activities are reasonable as fit in with, and help along, the impending changes. Social midwifery is the only perfectly reasonable activity open to us, the only activity that can be based upon scientific foresight.[25]

But, even if such activity is reasonable for the *optimistic* historicist, what of the pessimist, like Plato, who wants to stop, or reverse, the operation of the historical law? Is the adoption of his programme not somewhat like trying to legislate against the tides, or marching behind a banner inscribed 'Down with Gravity'? So, if Plato is an historicist, his political programme would seem to show that he is something less than a whole-hearted or consistent one. And Popper is in fact constrained to acknowledge, early in *The Open Society and its*

*Enemies*, that, as well as historicism, there is 'a diametrically opposite approach, also to be found in Plato, which may be called the *attitude of social engineering*.'[26] In effect, then, Plato's belief was that the forces of social degeneration, though powerful, are *not* entirely irresistible; given the requisite knowledge and will the decline can be halted, and even reversed. But if so, he surely lacks the defining characteristic of a Popperian historicist, i.e. a belief in the possibility of social *prophecy*; the practical outcome of his writings is a warning of danger rather than a prediction of disaster. ('Beware of the dogs' rather than 'We are going to the dogs.')

Also, the two elements in the political programme, appear, *prima facie* at least, to be incompatible with each other. Plato, obviously, would only have wanted to 'arrest all change' *if* the ideal state, or something very close to it, had been achieved or restored. And, since he was very far from thinking that this was true of the society of his times, his alleged second principle, 'Back to nature' in the sense of back to the tribal society of our ancestors, amounted to a call for a very radical social revolution. (And given the time-scale which Plato envisaged, the time required for the training of a ruling class for example, it is clear that the adoption of such a principle would have produced an age of revolution extending far beyond the lifetime of Plato or any of his contemporaries.) Hence it is at least misleading to present him as an extreme conservative who thought *change* as such was evil; it would seem that after all he merely deplored what he took to be change for the worse, and advocated change for the better – which, if somewhat unoriginal, is at least unexceptionable.

Plato appears better cast in the role of enemy of the 'open society' than in that of historicist. We shall have more to say later about Popper's famous distinction between the closed and the open society – but, in brief, a closed society is one in which the framework of ideas (values, laws, customs, taboos, etc.) which govern its life and determine its distinctive character, is treated as sacrosanct, beyond its members' power, or right, to criticize or alter. In the open society, by contrast, there is no such unchangeable framework, nothing (except what is imposed by sheer physical necessity) that its members *have* to accept, and therefore nothing outside their responsibility.[27] (Since, however, there is no precise way of defining the framework in question, and since there are many degrees of resistance to change in different societies or at different periods in a society's history, there can be no absolute distinction between closed and open societies; it would be better to say simply that a society is closed *in so far as* it has certain characteristics, open *in so far as* it has certain others.) Popper is, of course, strongly opposed both to historicism and to the closed society, and his *Open Society and its Enemies* is intended as an attack on both. But what precisely is the relationship between the two? An historicist as such presumably holds that every society is in effect closed, in the sense that, whatever its members may imagine, the determining framework is imposed on it by the operation of historical laws, and cannot, in its essentials, be altered at will. He may thus regard any hankering after alternative societies as futile; and, if he accepts the values inherent in the progress of history as the basis of morality, he may also regard it as morally wrong. But, as Popper insists, there is no logical reason why he should make this last move; and hence there is no such reason why an historicist as such should be an *advocate* of the closed society. Nor is there any reason why an advocate of the closed society should be an historicist. Many have resisted change, on the grounds, say, that it would be impious towards gods or ancestors, or simply through fear of the unknown, while remaining wholly innocent of any thoughts whatsoever about historical laws.

Plato clearly advocated a (largely) closed society. But, as suggested earlier, his reasons can more usefully be sought in his general epistemology rather than in his supposed historicism. He believed that the true nature of justice, of the state, of government and of citizenship, could be uncovered and recognized, but only by a supreme effort on the part of the specially gifted. The many who are condemned to live permanently in a world of mere appearance and error, must therefore be discouraged from all speculation and experiment, since these can only bring disaster. And, once the truth has been discovered and put into practice, as in the ideal republic, then the task even of the gifted is to preserve it intact, not to alter or add to it. So, in this sense, Plato wanted a closed society, not as such – since presumably he would have disapproved strongly of most of the closed societies of history – but a closed society of a quite specific kind. But, to leave open the possibility of attaining or approximating to it, he must also have wanted his own, and virtually every other existing, society to remain open.

## 3

While Popper can find at least an element of tragedy, of misdirected greatness, in Plato, when he turns to Hegel he can see very little except moral and intellectual squalor. In a notably angry and contemptuous chapter of polemical writing,[28] he denounces Hegel as a hopelessly confused thinker, whose reputation has depended on obscurity disguised as profundity, and whose influence has been almost entirely pernicious; as an enemy of intellectual and political freedom; as an 'official philosopher' who sold his conscience to the Prussian state; as a forerunner, and one of the creators, of modern racialism, nationalism and totalitarianism. No doubt, the intemperate tone is understandable when we recall the circumstances in which the work was written. It was, as Popper says, part of his 'war work', and it would have been very difficult for him to speak calmly and judiciously of a thinker whose ideas had, he believed, helped to produce the horrors of Nazism and the Second World War. But, as even critics sympathetic to his case against Hegel have noted,[29] he weakens it by overstatement. While we may allow that an almost impenetrable style, and royal patronage, are considerable assets in a philosophical career, it seems inherently unlikely that Hegel's reputation, and his undoubtedly vast influence over subsequent thought, are founded on nothing more than these. And, while Popper quotes extensively from Hegel in support of his accusations, he has again left himself open to the charge that very often his selection of quotations is biased, and his use of them misleading. Thus, for example, Walter Kaufman has been able to match Popper's quotations with others which show Hegel as much less muddled, and much less servile, than Popper makes him out to be; which suggest also that he had considerable, though not unqualified, respect for individual liberty; that he did not regard war as an intrinsic good; was not, at least in his mature years, anti-Semitic; and would have had little sympathy with Nazism.[30]

Fortunately, however, on most of these issues, we are not obliged to adjudicate. Since we are concerned with Hegel primarily as an (alleged) example of historicism, other sins and shortcomings may reasonably be ignored. In respect of historicism, he seems, *prima facie* at least, a more promising example than Plato. When, in tracing the history of post-Renaissance European philosophy, we eventually come to Hegel, probably one of the first things that strikes us about his work, in contrast with that of his major predecessors from Descartes to Kant, is his concern with change and development. For example, his predecessors in general seemed to see their own problems (together with the theories designed to solve them, and the concepts used in the formulation of both) as akin to those of pure mathematics or the more abstract sciences, in the sense of having no *essential* – though no doubt they have an accidental – connection with history. The problems could, in principle, have been posed and solved at any time, by anyone sufficiently able and interested; when and by whom they are tackled is largely a matter of historical accident. A work of philosophy is thus to be understood and assessed simply as an attempted solution to a given problem; its place in an historic sequence is strictly an irrelevance. Hence, in any age, we could hope for final, once-and-for-all solutions, like those supposed to have been achieved in Euclidean geometry or in Newtonian physics; Kant, for example, believed that he had found such solutions to the fundamental problems of epistemology, and, in his preface to the 1787 edition of the *Critique of Pure Reason*, he graciously bequeathed to his successors the tasks of clarifying the details and writing popular expositions. For Hegel, on the other hand, there *is* an essential order among the stages of the development of human thinking – or rather of Thought, as such, manifesting itself in specific thinkers. The emergence of key concepts (and their related problems and theories) is not merely a matter of accident, of luck or unpredictable genius; it has a certain internal momentum, by which each stage requires or necessitates the next. Thus, for example, a history of philosophy which merely tells us that seventeenth-century rationalism was followed in time by the development of empiricism, and points to some extraneous factors, like the increasing success of natural science, or the different talents and temperaments of individual thinkers, to account for the change, misses the essential point. It should seek to show rather that rationalism *gave rise to* expiricism. Hegel extends this idea of an internal momentum, of inherent one-sidedness demanded the complementary element of empiricism. Hegel extends this idea of an internal momemtun, of things thus generating their complements or opposites through their own inherent instability or incompleteness, from intellectual to social, and even physical, developments. He revives in a specific form the old Heraclitean idea of the universal flux. And his work marks the beginning of a period, in nineteenth and twentieth century thought, which is characterized by a preoccupation with change, development, evolution, and the laws governing them – not as an order imposed *ab extra* on essentially changeless material, but as something inherent in the nature of the material itself. It is a preoccupation manifested, in very different ways, by Marx, Darwin, Bergson and Whitehead, and many lesser figures as well.

According to Popper,

> We can say that Hegel's world of flux is in a state of 'emergent' or 'creative evolution'; each of its stages contains the preceding ones, from which it originates, and each stage supersedes all previous stages, approaching nearer and nearer to perfection. The general law of development is thus one of progress; but, as we shall see, not of a simple and straightforward, but of a 'dialectic' progress.[31]

Unlike Plato's, then, Hegel's is an *optimistic* historicism, a belief in inevitable progress towards stability and completeness. There is, however, a price to be paid for progress. For Heraclitus, 'strife is the father of all things'; and for Hegel also progress depends on the engendering of opposition, the movement to overcome it, the engendering thus of still further opposition, and so on. Whence, of course, the famous 'dialectical triad' in which the *thesis*, the original element, calls forth (through its own one-sidedness, or over-abstraction) its opposite or *antithesis*, and the tension between the two requires an effort at *synthesis*, at something which will reconcile, and do justice to, thesis and antithesis alike. (Thus, in the example taken earlier, rationalism and empiricism might be cast as thesis and antithesis respectively. But their rival claims impose on philosophy the task of developing an epistemology which will take account of the valid elements in both of them, i.e. an Hegelian synthesis. And this we may find in Kant's critical philosophy – which, of course, also has its inherent limitations, and these call forth a further critical reaction . . . and so on.[32])

Popper is willing to admit that this concept of dialectic can provide a reasonable enough analysis of at least some historical developments, especially in the history of ideas. In his paper 'What is dialectic?' (which includes a somewhat calmer critique of Hegel, possibly because it was written before the outbreak of the Second World War) he notes the resemblance between the dialectical triad and his own idea of progress through trial and error, conjecture–refutation–more sophisticated conjecture–etc.[33] It is, however, no more than a superficial resemblance. Popper has no use whatsoever for the Hegelian notion of an *internal* momentum, by which the thesis 'produces' its antithesis, and the tension between the two in its turn 'produces' the synthesis. Rather it is left to the *researcher* to find out whether or not there is evidence inconsistent with his original thesis, and, if there is, to decide whether to respond by embodying that thesis in a more complex one, or discarding it altogether and starting afresh. He is not merely the vehicle of progress, but its initiator, and his efforts are checked, and stimulated, by contacts with an independent world. And, according to Popper's account, some of the worst elements in Hegel's thought stem from his attempt to treat thought, or Thought, as a self-generating process, with logical, or quasi-logical, relationships between its stages. If our thesis is not merely to be confronted by an antithesis derived from some external source, but has to produce it from within itself, then it must initially contain that antithesis within itself; in other words it must be inherently *self-contradictory*. So self-contradiction becomes, not an occasional aberration of thought, but an essential element in its progress. And the lesson which Hegel derived from his dialectical triad was, in effect, that

Since contradictions are the means by which science progresses ... contradictions are not only permissible and unavoidable but also highly desirable.

And this, Popper comments,

is a Hegelian doctrine which must destroy all argument and all progress. For if contradictions are unavoidable and desirable, there is no need to eliminate them, and so progress must come to an end.

Since the whole aim of rational argument and discussion is to eliminate contradiction, they become pointless if contradiction is indeed unavoidable. And this, apparently, was Hegel's aim:

By making argument and criticism impossible, he intends to make his own philosophy proof against all criticism, so that it may establish itself as a *reinforced dogmatism*, secure from every attack, and the insurmountable summit of all philosophical development.[34]

He is then free, quite literally, to maintain any doctrine he pleases; for, as Popper points out in the earlier paper, it can be proved formally that, if contradictory statements are admitted as true, any statement whatsoever can follow logically from them.[35] (This proof, it should be noted, shows what happens if we ignore the law of non-contradiction at *one* stage in the argument, i.e. by admitting a pair of mutually contradictory premises, but observe it at every other stage. To abandon it altogether creates even greater havoc. As we have seen, to do this would make it impossible to state anything whatsoever, since all statement is selection among possibilities, and, if we reject the law of non-contradiction, then, no matter what we say, all possibilities remain open.)

Also, given this concept of a self-generative progression from thesis to antithesis, it is a short step from saying that the one contains and produces the other to saying that the one becomes or transforms itself into the other, and so that, despite their opposition, they are in some sense *identical*. And thus things which we should ordinarily think of as mutually opposed, or mutually independent, prove on deeper analysis to be one and the same. According to Popper, this 'philosophy of identity' is virtually a licence to claim that black is white, if we so wish; and Hegel exploits it to identify what is real with what is rational, and therefore good, to find true equality is a rigidly hierarchical system, true freedom in authoritarianism, etc. (We may be reminded here of the party slogans in Orwell's *Nineteen Eighty-Four*: 'Love is Hate', 'Freedom is Slavery', etc.)

Dialectic, thus understood, would doubtless, if taken seriously, open the way to all sorts of excesses of dogmatism and irrationalism. Such excesses have been common enough in modern European history; but Popper's attempts to trace their origins to Hegelianism have produced – as most Hegelian scholars seem to be agreed – something little better than a caricature. Certainly, the use by Hegel and other dialecticians of logical terms like 'contradiction' and 'negation' is often loose and confusing; in their efforts to discover the same triadic pattern in a vast range and variety of developments, 'contradiction' is used to cover many different relationships, not only strictly logical contradictions but many other kinds of opposition, conflict, tension, contrast and complementarity as well. And certainly it is misleading to speak of a 'dialectical logic' as though it were an alternative or rival to our 'ordinary' logic. (Quite generally, of course, as we noticed in an earlier chapter, whatever the scope of relativism elsewhere, we have to be wary of any talk about the possibility of alternative logics; since the criterion of possibility here can presumably only be conformity with the principles of 'ordinary' logic.) But, whatever Hegel had in mind, it was not to propose that we dispense with the law of non-contradiction and feel free to contradict ourselves as often as we please. As we have seen, the whole function of contradiction in the dialectical process is to provide the momentum for change; and it can only do this if contradiction is unacceptable, an unstable or transitory situation in which we cannot rest content but which we must strive to overcome – which is precisely what Popper, very rightly, demands as a condition of rational progress. True enough, as J. N. Findlay has pointed out,[36] Hegel did not regard the contradictions that have emerged in the history of thought as merely superficial or apparent — as confusions that could have been eliminated given a little more precision and clear-headedness. Like Wittgenstein a century later, he appreciated that they can be very deep-seated and intractable, that thought can find itself pushed inexorably towards literally impossible positions ('It can't be like this — and yet it has to be'). But the essential point of the dialectical philosophy is that while such contradictory situations may be unavoidable *at a certain level* of thought, this level can always be transcended, and that at the new, higher level, the contradictions disappear or are reconciled. This is because they are the products of thinking which, however understandably or inevitably, is still in some way one-sided, incomplete or over-abstract; and they are resolved by thinking which has overcome these deficiencies, which takes account of what has hitherto been abstracted from, or omitted. The dialectical process is, essentially, an advance from the abstract to the concrete. In the Hegelian logic, for example, we start from the most abstract concept possible, that of mere indeterminate being, and progress through many stages to the most concrete possible, that of the Absolute Idea. Hegel might well have approved of Whitehead's maxim that the function of philosophy is to be the 'critic of abstractions'.[37]

'Abstract' and 'concrete' in the relevant senses, belong of course primarily to the realm of ideas, and it is not surprising that this realm provides the most convincing examples of dialectical progress. Hegel's attempts to extend it to cover social and physical developments were, in the main, less successful; his philosophy of nature, especially, contains a good deal that his admirers usually pass over in embarrassed silence. But, if we allow for the (no doubt misleadingly) wide use of 'contradictory' and related terms, we can, I think, grant that this concept of dialectical progress has some relevance to these realms also. In its most general terms, it is the concept of a situation unstable because in some way incomplete, incapable of sustaining itself, and hence impelled to seek whatever is required for its completion. Obviously the kinds of situation, of incompleteness, etc., must vary enormously; and it may reasonably be objected that any such formula has to cover so much that it conveys very little. Even granted that it is instantiated in a given situation, almost all the work of discovering the internal dynamics of that situation, why specifically it is unstable and how it is developing, would still be to do. And Hegel and his followers would, I think, have accepted that (almost) everything is in the detail of the system and that, by itself, any attempt at or all-embracing formula tells us very little. But, in the present context, it may at least serve the purpose of placing Hegel's philosophy in a more favourable light, if showing that it is as somewhat less absurd and irrational than Popper makes it out to be.

Again, though a 'philosophy of identity' may indeed tempt us to sophistry and sleight of hand, and Hegel's work has its share of these, he does not misuse it quite so scandalously as Popper claims. Kaufman is probably right in saying that the most notorious example, the identification of the real and the rational, is based on a misunderstanding; for Hegel, the real, or the actual, is the realization, or actualization, of some ideal, and not simply whatever happens to exist.[38] So he was not in fact giving indiscriminate blessings to anything and everything about him. More generally, we can see how an apparently insoluble problem might well arise from treating as two mutually independent entities things which prove, on deeper analysis, to be merely two abstractions, contrasting aspects or elements of the same thing – what Whitehead called 'the fallacy of misplaced concreteness'.[39] For example, since Descartes exposed the difficulties which arise from an uncompromising mind–body dualism, many thinkers from Spinoza to the present time have sought a solution in some form of monism. And, whatever we may think of any specific attempt at such a solution, there is nothing wrong in principle with the approach to a problem which, in effect, says 'Perhaps the distinction, or contrast, giving rise to this problem is not an absolute one; there may be a further level of thought at which it is transcended' – and which then endeavours to establish this further level.

But to return to the issue of Hegel's historicism: however we may understand the dialectic, it clearly embodies the idea of a movement in human history, social as well as intellectual, which has, as we have said, its own internal momentum, and hence is independent of the choices and efforts of individual human beings. History is not reducible to biographies; rather it is what gives biographies their point. The great individuals, in any field of interest, are those who most strikingly manifest, or give expression to, the various stages of its development – the most effective vehicles as it were, but not the initiators. And, as we noted earlier, what is crucial to the understanding of history is to know not merely what *did* happen, but why it *had to* happen. Thus far then, we have a classic example of thorough-going historicism – the belief in a single pattern inexorably working itself in every sphere of history.

As in the example of Plato, however, we find little evidence in Hegel of what is supposed to be the distinguishing feature of the historicist – the urge to historical prophecy. Granted that he had discovered what the pattern was, he might well have used his discovery to make projections into the future, and we should doubtless be much more inclined to believe he *had* discovered it, if he had proved a successful prophet; but he showed no great inclination to do so. One explanation might be that he thought the pattern already complete, that the final, stable position had already been achieved in his own time. And, on many topics, certainly, he often wrote as though he were summing up on the Day of Judgement. This did not mean, of course, that he thought the world was about to end; events might well occur after the completion of the pattern, though they would lack historical significance in the sense that they could contribute nothing essential to it. Thus, for example, Hegel presumably would not have been particularly worried had he known that philosophers later in time than himself would regress, say, to Humean empiricism. It would show merely their failure to appreciate that that moment in the development of thought had already been reached and transcended. This conception of philosophy as a kind of final summing up is embodied in one of the best-known passages in all Hegel's writings:

When philosophy paints its grey on grey, a form of life has become old; and with grey on grey that form of life cannot be made young again, it can only be understood. Only as the twilight begins to fall does the owl of Minerva spread its wings.[40]

We should note also, however, that there are other passages in which he appears to admit the possibility of significant, but *unpredictable*, developments still to come – for example in his *Philosophy of History*, where he speaks of America as 'the land of the future' about which, apparently, nothing can be said except, rather mysteriously, that 'It is for America to abandon the ground on which the History of the World has developed itself',[41] which suggests some new departure that nothing in the past enables us to foresee; and, almost at the end of the same work, 'This is the point which consciousness has attained'[42] – which appears to leave open the prospect of further attainments, but declines to predict their character. Such humility accords very well with what was said earlier of how much the dialectic leaves still to be determined in any specific situation, and to some extent at least accepts the point made by Popper and other critics, that it is too vague to be an instrument for precise forecasting. So, while Hegel may have had some of the makings of an historicist, in Popper's sense, he was not a complete or whole-hearted one. To find that we must turn to Marx.

## 4

Marxism, according to Popper, is 'so far the purest, the most developed and the most dangerous form of historicism'.[43] And indeed, here at last Popper finds a subject that *will* fit into his historicist mould without forcing; Marxism is virtually the paradigm case of historicism in Popper's sense of the term. Here at last, also, he has an opponent whom he genuinely respects. He praises generously the energy and acumen Marx brings to his task, and the sincerity of his desire to alleviate the social ills of his time. Marx, he tells us, has 'forever a place among the liberators of mankind'[44] – a tribute which may startle some of those who have adopted Popper as their champion against Marxism. But, from Popper's standpoint, Marx's qualities, his talent and originality as a social scientist, his genuine desire for justice and freedom, are precisely what makes his errors dangerous, and important to refute.

There is a famous Marxist saying to the effect that, in the writings of Hegel, dialectic stands on its head, and it is necessary to turn it right way up again. Marx took over from Hegel the essential concept of dialectic, of internal contradiction or opposition providing the momentum for change, and made it the basis of his own attempt to formulate laws of historical development. For Marx, as for Hegel, such development is outside the control of the individuals caught up in it; whether they realize it or not, they are inexorably carried along by its progress. It was Marx who actually drew the conclusion that all they could rationally try to do was 'to lessen the birthpangs' of the inevitable – and with this realization, we advance from Utopianism, from dreams or wishful thinking about how we should *like* to see society change, to a scientific grasp of the laws according to which it *must* change. For Popper, of course, to take over the concept of dialectic is also to take over its inherent defects. He has comparatively little to say about these in the discussion of Marx in *The Open Society and its Enemies*; but in the final section of the 'What is dialectic?' paper,[45] he finds in Marxism the faults of dialectical systems in general – the vagueness and elasticity which make it capable of accommodating any situation whatsoever, and (closely related to this) the 'reinforced dogmatism' which makes it immune from all criticism and correction. In addition, Marx's proposed inversion of Hegelianism, his attempt to trace the dialectical progress primarily in the world of material things rather than in that of ideas, robs him of the most plausible examples, which, as we have seen, are those drawn from the history of thought.

We should remember, from what was said in earlier chapters, that to be thus all-accomodating and immune from criticism are *sufficient in themselves* to discredit the claims of Marxism to be science (as Popper understands the term) or to have any scientific basis for its forecasts. In *The Open Society and its Enemies*, however, for the most part Popper is concerned with the specific nature of Marxist dialectics, with the distinctive features and results of the inversion of Hegelianism. As Popper presents him, whatever his theoretical position with regard to materialism, he was in effect a 'practical dualist' who drew a fundamental distinction between the material world on the one hand and the mental or spiritual on the other. His famous materialism consisted not so much in denying or explaining away the latter, but in insisting on the extent to which it was conditioned, inescapably by the material. Thus – 'he recognized in practice (as a practical dualist) that we are spirit *and* flesh, and realistically enough that the flesh is the fundamental of these two'. But, Popper continues,

> although he recognized that the material world and its necessities are fundamental, he did not feel any love for the 'kingdom of necessity', as he called a society which is in bondage to its material needs. He cherished the spiritual world, the 'kingdom of freedom', and the spiritual side of 'human nature', as much as any Christian dualist[46]

Freedom is, indeed, for Marx the ultimate aim of historical development. But it is an aim never fully achieved, since we can inhabit the 'kingdom of freedom' only in so far as we can escape from the necessities of material life; so the practical aim has to be to *minimize and equalize* so far as possible the toil of providing for material needs, so that everyone may have at least some measure of freedom.

There would seem to be two reasons why Marx gave *economics* the central role in his analysis of historical development – in contrast with Hegel for whom history is essentially the self-manifestation of the development of thought, or with Marx's near-contemporary, Mill, who sought the key to history in human psychology. First, as we have just said, there is the obvious fact that man is, in essential part at least, a material being, and whether or to what extent he pursues his other interests, however exalted these may be, depends on his success in simply getting a living from his physical environment. Whatever else an individual is, statesman, soldier, thinker, etc., he is perforce, as a condition of being such, someone who gets, in this or that particular fashion, the wherewithal to survive. Secondly, Marx held, mistakenly in Popper's view, that science as such is deterministic – a point about which we shall have more to say later – and hence that no aspect or element of human life is amenable to scientific study, or scientific prediction, except in so far as it belongs to his 'kingdom of necessity'. If we ever attained genuine freedom, then *ipso facto* no general laws of human behaviour could be discovered and no basis for prediction would exist. Thus,

from the scientific or causal point of view thoughts and ideas must be treated as 'ideological superstructures on the basis of economic conditions'. Marx, in opposition to Hegel, contended that the clue to history, even to the history of ideas, is to be found in the development of the relations between man and his natural environment, the material world; that is to say, in his economic life, and not in his spiritual life. This is why we may describe Marx's brand of historicism as *economism*, as opposed to Hegel's idealism or Mill's psychologism. But it signifies a complete misunderstanding if we identify Marx's economism with the kind of materialism which implies a depreciatory attitude towards man's mental life.[47]

Granted, however, the primacy of economic factors in Marx's actual study of society (even if it is not an instance of dogmatic materialism), a number of its characteristic features become understandable. For example, there is the famous doctrine of the 'class struggle' – the doctrine that the oppositions which provide the momentum for historical development are not, as most earlier historians supposed, those between nations or dynasties, but those between economic classes. Briefly, such classes are distinguished by their sources of income, by the different ways in which they get their living. The interest of a given class is simply everything that furthers its power and its prosperity; and a class struggle arises when such interests are in conflict with each other, when the power and prosperity of one class can increase only at the expense of those of another.

We may note at this point the contrast, which Popper emphasizes, between this account of the class struggle, and the 'Vulgar Marxism' which describes class interest in psychological terms, i.e. greed for material wealth, and class struggle as the outcome of a deliberate conspiracy by a powerful and unscrupulous minority to satisfy their own greed at the cost of the sufferings and privations of others.[48] Conspiracy theories of history – i.e. those which attribute every major historical development to the self-interested machinations of some group or faction, the capitalists, the Trade Unions, the Church, the Jews or whoever it may be – have an obvious appeal. If nothing else, they provide us with simplifications and scapegoats. But, as Popper has argued in various contexts, such theories rarely stand up to scrutiny;[49] and whatever their attraction for Marx's professed followers, he himself did not take them seriously. Faithful to his historicist principles, he held that all elements in society, rich and poor, rulers and ruled, alike were moved by economic forces outside their control:

> the rulers are determined by their class situation; they cannot escape from their social relation to the ruled; they are bound to them, since they are bound to the social metabolism. Thus all, rulers as well as ruled, are caught in the net and forced to fight one another . . . This social net in which the classes are caught, and forced to struggle against one another, is what Marxism calls the economic structure of society, or the social system.[50]

Thus it makes little difference what conscious attitudes or intentions one class has towards the other; whether the rulers are benevolent or oppressive, whether the ruled are submissive or resentful, the system still pushes them, inescapably, into conflict with each other.

It makes little difference, also, what efforts are made to alter or alleviate the effects of the conflict, while the system itself remains intact. A society's legal and political institutions are only superstructures erected upon, and determined by, its underlying economic structure; the state is in effect, even if in no one's intentions, an instrument of class-oppression. Hence, politics as ordinarily understood – the gaining and losing of 'power' by rival parties and politicians, the alternation of conservative and liberal factions, the introduction of reform bills and franchise bills, etc. – only superficially changes a social system, and the lot of those who live under it. (Popper recalls that Marx had before him the example of industrial England in the 1860s when the efforts of liberal politicians, and of many earnest moralists and churchmen as well, over a generation had apparently done little towards ending misery and exploitation; indeed, by creating the illusion of possible reform within the system they had merely, it must have seemed, helped to make the world safe for capitalism.)

Significant changes can come only from changes in the economic reality, in the means of production and hence in the class structure. Political developments will doubtless follow from these, but not vice versa.

According to Marx's economic version of historicism, the significant historical changes occur when a particular social system destroys itself, through the conflict of class interests which is an essential part of its nature, and gives places to another. And the task of social science is to explicate, from the mass of historical detail, the nature of these opposing interests, and of the social upheaval and social transformation they will inevitably produce. Thus, according to Popper's account of it —

A sufficiently penetrating analysis of the feudal system, undertaken shortly before the industrial revolution, might have led to the detection of the forces which were about to destroy feudalism, and to the prediction of the most important characteristics of the coming period, capitalism. Similarly, an analysis of the development of capitalism might enable us to detect the forces which work for its destruction, and to predict the most important characteristics of the new historical period which lies ahead of us.[51]

We may wonder how, in the case of feudalism at least, this squares with Marx's statement, quoted earlier by Popper,[52] to the effect that the hand-mill gives us a society with the feudal lord, the steam-mill a society with the industrial capitalist. *Prima facie*, this would seem to make the transition depend, not on internal conflict, but on an independent technological advance. And, in general, the thesis of a purely internal, self-generating development is difficult to maintain; extraneous, or apparently extraneous, factors keep breaking in, and we have, at least, to put considerable strain on plausibility to present these also as somehow generated by the central conflict. In the case of capitalism (though here again the detailed analysis would seem to introduce a variety of extraneous factors), Marx does make a sustained attempt to exhibit the system as inherently unstable and self-destructive. This is the central theme of *Capital*. Obviously we cannot examine it at any length here, but, as given in Popper's outline, the essential points are these —

capitalist competition . . . forces the capitalist to accumulate capital . . . [and] accumulation of capital means (*a*) increased productivity; increase of wealth; and concentration of wealth in a few hands; (*b*) increase of pauperism and misery.[53]

This ever-widening gap between the only two classes that have any significance in such a society – the capitalist class, which holds the economic and hence the effective political power, growing smaller in numbers and richer, and the wage-earners growing more numerous and poorer – produces inevitably an increasing tension between them. This tension must sooner or later resolve itself in a social revolution, which will sweep away the whole economic system, and with it the legal and political superstructures. Whatever reverses the workers may suffer in the struggle, in the long term their victory is assured. Not only do they have the advantage in numbers, but also, despite the pretensions of their rulers, in any economic, and hence any social, system they are the only indispensable class. A society may survive without its professional managers and advertisers, its teachers and talkers, but not without its farm-labourers, builders and coal-miners. Once these recognize their true importance and their true interests, and learn to organize themselves, they are in the end invincible. And the society which ultimately emerges from their victory is the *classless society*, i.e. one in which the economic interests of all members essentially coincide, and hence there is no basis for class-divisions, or class-struggle, a socialist society based on the principle of common ownership of all means of producing material wealth. With the coming of a classless society, the state as we now know it, being in effect an instrument of class-oppression, ceases to have a function, and 'withers away'. And presumably history, in so far as it is the record of class struggle, comes to an end.

In addition to the general merits mentioned earlier, Popper finds a good deal to commend in this analysis. He is in sympathy with the implicit defence of the autonomy of social science against the attempts of Mill and others to analyse social phenomena into the workings of the principles of individual psychology – and quotes with approval Marx's dictum to the effect that man's social existence determines his consciousness, rather than the other way round. And he accepts that Marx's alternative to such psychologism, what he has called 'economism', focusses attention on something of the highest importance for the understanding of any part of human history. None the less, despite the importance of economic influences on historical developments, they are not the only influences. And, Popper argues, Marx's economism, in so far as it leads us to look to economics for the root cause of every such development and to try to play down or explain away what we have called extraneous factors, inevitably distorts and over-simplifies.

Thus, for example, art and science no doubt have, in a sense, an economic basis. The studio and the laboratory, and the artist's and the scientist's daily bread, have to be provided in some way; they presuppose a society able and willing to support activities not immediately productive of material wealth. If we are trying to understand why art or science flourished at a particular time or place, we may well get further by considering the relevant economic circumstances than by invoking a new stage in the self-development of Thought, or the sudden emergence of unpredictable Genius. And even the *kind* of art or science produced may be determined to some extent by this economic basis; newly-rich patrons may want portraits and ornate mansions rather than ikons or cathedrals, industry may be more willing to sponsor scientific research when it promises useful technological results, etc. But we should be taking a long, and very rash, step further, if we supposed that art and science have, for example, no history of the development of techniques and the accumulation of discoveries, and no standards of success and failure, which are quite independent of economics. And, in the case of science, Popper is surely right in saying that its relationship with the physical means of production is one of *inter*-dependence rather than a one-way dependence. Industry may well encourage science for its own purposes, and to some extent determine the direction of its development, but it is equally true that scientific discovery has, in many instances, determined the direction of industrial development. Popper notes also that the influence of Marx's own social science provides a counter-example to the 'exaggerated economism' it embodies.[54] Thus there is no doubt that Marxist ideas played a very important part in the making of the Russian revolution. But then *after* the revolution drastic measures had to be taken to transform the Russian economy; and Marxist theory had few ideas to offer about how this should be done, since according to that theory, the economic reality should transform itself *before* any significant political change can take place. Hence, there is 'no similarity whatsoever' between the Russian revolution as it actually happened and the kind of social revolution prophesied by Marx; here, at least, the theory helped to falsify itself.

Again, Popper argues,[55] the dictum that 'all history is the history of class struggle', while highly effective in calling attention to an important, and often neglected, facet of history, cannot be taken at face value. Doubtless it is useful as a *policy* – look for the relevant economic factors in any historical situation – but, without making a great deal of havoc with historical evidence, we cannot treat is as a *dogma*. Thus, it seems manifest that there have been many struggles in history which were not waged between classes (in the Marxist sense), for the defence or promotion of their economic interests – for example dynastic wars between families or factions within a ruling class, or religious or racial conflicts within any class. We may well wish that the Marxist formula *was* literally true, and that men did come to blows only for material advantage. The world would undoubtedly be a more peaceful, and more intelligible, place if they did. But one of the wonders of history is the willingness of large numbers of men to kill and be killed in order to determine which of two scoundrels shall occupy a throne – or which of two rival distortions of the Christian gospel of love and peace shall prevail. We can, of course, if we are committed to the dogma, meet such purported exceptions by pointing out, for example, that the real reasons for a conflict are not always the apparent ones, or that differences of religion or race can be used to turn people's attention away from their real interests. And, in some cases, such replies would no doubt be appropriate enough. But it would be very difficult to maintain, seriously, that, say, the first Hundred Years War between England and France, or the Wars of the Roses were 'really' conflicts between exploiters and exploited. And while it may well be true that sectarian divisions among the Irish working class have made them easier victims of exploitation, it still does not follow that Ireland's long-drawn sectarian strife is itself a class-struggle in the Marxist sense.

Examples like this cast doubt on the assumption – again a product of 'exaggerated economism' – that the only serious or intractable grounds for conflict and oppression within a society are economic ones, and hence that unity of economic interests would effectively abolish them. But –

The unity or solidarity of a class, according to Marx's own analysis, is part of their class consciousness, which in turn is very largely a product of the class struggle. There is no earthly reason why the individuals who form the proletariat should retain their class unity once the pressure of the struggle against the common class enemy has ceased. Any latent conflict of interests is now likely to divide the formerly united proletariat into new classes, and to develop into a new class struggle.[56]

More specifically, the leadership of a successful revolution would, in the aftermath of their victory, almost inevitably become a new ruling class, taking over, whether willingly or not, for an indefinite period many of the functions of the rulers they have deposed. And, however sincere their revolutionary idealism to begin with, the requirements of office – the needs for workable administrative machinery, for long-term planning, for national solvency, tolerable relationships with foreign powers, etc. – would, almost inevitably, produce another clash of interests between rulers and ruled, the time-honoured 'them and us', all over again. Hence, the prophecies of a genuinely classless society and the eventual 'withering away' of the state and its traditional functions would appear to be based on false, or at any rate incomplete, premisses.

On a more fundamental issue, Popper challenges the thesis that economic power, in any society, is the source of all other kinds of power. We may say, cynically, and no doubt with a measure of truth, that wealth can buy, and often has bought, the powers of political institutions, of the media of communication, and of sheer physical force. But why, for example, should those with physical power be content merely to be hired to protect the interests of the wealthy? Why should they not simply appropriate the available wealth at the point of the sword or the gun – like the robber-barons or pirate chiefs of more lawless periods of history? And here we have the essential point; wealth is a source of power only in a *law-abiding* society, i.e. one whose *political* institutions are strong enough to guarantee certain basic rights to its citizens, like the protection of life and property. Without governments able and willing to provide such guarantees, wealth in itself would be of little avail; and the wealthy have good reason to be among the most nervous about civil unrest, and among the most fervent supporters of 'law and order'. Hence,

political power and its control is everything. Economic power must never be permitted to dominate political power; if necessary, it must be fought and brought under control by political power.[57]

In effect, then, the Marxist class struggle, the defence and promotion of economic interests, *presupposes* a certain political and legal framework, a set of rules of the game, as it were, which both sides at least tacitly accept. And, whatever cynics may say, there is no reason in principle why political power should not be used to protect citizens from economic exploitation as well as from physical violence. For Popper, the role of the state is indeed essentially a protective one, to protect not only the physically weak from the physically strong, but also the economically weak from the economically strong. To this end the unrestrained capitalism, which Marx rightly denounced, has to give place to an 'economic interventionism', which ensures that, for example, no one is forced by the threat of starvation in accepting inequitable wages or conditions of work. And such state intervention on behalf of the exploited has, according to Popper, already taken place to such effect that the economic system known to Marx and his contemporaries has 'everywhere ceased to exist'. It has been replaced, not by the classless society, but by various 'interventionist systems' in which the state assumes responsibilities for the economic welfare of the citizens, far beyond the protection of property and of 'free contracts'.

The Marxist no doubt will find this, at best, naive. He may, with some reason, direct Popper's attention to some of the dealings of international companies with the 'underdeveloped countries' and ask whether unrestrained capitalism has really ceased to exist there. And he may point out that, even if capitalism could only have developed where a certain political and legal system already existed, it does not follow that it cannot effectively transform that system into an instrument for its own purposes. A system that is time-honoured and widely-accepted is indeed a much more useful instrument that the merely invented *ad hoc*. It is nonsense to expect the state to remain an impartial referee, as it were, ensuring fair play for all, when we consider the pressures, even if only covert and indirect, which wealth can exert; and the pressures can, and often have, become very direct indeed if the state has the temerity to do anything that would seriously alter the economic system.

None the less, even if Popper is somewhat over-optimistic about what may be achieved through the exercise of political power, the fact remains that it *has* had appreciable success in remedying, or alleviating, some of the worst ills of industrial society as Marx knew it. The efforts may often have been slow and inefficient and the results far from perfect, but they are still good enough to lend considerable appeal to Popper's proposed alternative to the Marxist programme. After all, if we hold that significant change can come only with the self-destruction of the present economic system and the emergence of a new one – and hence, presumably, discourage any interim attempts at improvement as merely prolonging the birth-pangs – we may condemn whole generations to unrelieved suffering through a very long-drawn struggle. And, as Popper says, there can be no moral justification for sacrificing the happiness or well-being of one generation for that of another. Also, if the class struggle is allowed, or encouraged, to degenerate to the point of violent revolution, there is the obvious danger that the outcome may be a reign of terror or a military dictatorship rather than a classless society. It is, again, naively optimistic to suppose that, after a swift massacre of the exploiters on the first morning of the revolution, the revolutionary leadership will be gladly accepted by the great majority of the people as the embodiment of their interests, and the need for violence will cease. More likely, once the traditional framework of political and legal institutions has been overthrown, several rival parties and movements will try to fill the vacuum thus created, and since *ex hypothesi* there are no accepted or constitutional means of deciding the issue between them, it can only be resolved by physical force. Popper's alternative is, in effect, a political programme of piecemeal reform, i.e. using existing political means to tackle immediate specific problems, including those created by the workings of the economic system. There are, of course, the familiar Popperian provisos that the carrying out of such a programme is a matter of trial and error, learning by mistakes, achieving improvements but never perfection. But with all its shortcomings it seems at least more promising than merely accepting, or welcoming, the evils of a situation that makes revolution inevitable, or the evils of revolution itself, for the sake of a problematic good beyond it.

We cannot, unfortunately, assume that all politicians who are opposed to Marxism are therefore Popperian 'interventionists' or 'piecemeal reformers'; many of them obviously still hanker after the good old days of unrestrained, or ineffectively restrained, capitalism. And, as we shall see in the next chapter, Popper's programme is vague enough to cover many different degrees of intervention, and many different ideas of what constitutes improvement or reform. But still, there *have* been, and still are, in many industrial societies, sufficient and sufficiently effective political efforts at intervention and reform to ensure that they have not developed, and are unlikely to develop, in the way that Marx, on the basis of pure economism, predicted. Popper (and other critics) have argued that many of Marx's characteristic prophecies have already been falsified – or can be salvaged only by a reinforcement exercise which requires radical reinterpretation of the prophecies themselves and the relevant historical situations. We have already noticed the example of the Russian revolution in which political changes manifestly did *not*, as prophesied, follow upon the appropriate economic changes; and other countries, in which revolutions have produced socialist systems, have, in the main, been likewise economically unready. Also, the predictions of a steadily increasing gap in numbers and wealth between wage-earners and property-owners, and the fading into insignificance of all other social classes, have been largely unfulfilled. Of course, we must beware of generalization (as Popper has taught us) about *all* industrial societies; it is possible that in some of them Marx's most determined enemies may yet do a lot to make his prophecies come true. But Popper has, I believe, established his essential point: Marx's economism, while it has the merit of calling attention to one highly important factor in social development, has the disadvantage of treating it as though it were the only one. (Marx, as Popper presents him, is – like Darwin also, perhaps, or Freud – an example of how immense talent and energy, applied to the working out of a vivid but partial insight, can produce a highly impressive and influential system of thought – all the more striking, but all the more dangerous, because the insight *is* partial.) As a result, Marx was led to his 'one-way-only' account of such development. But there are, and there have to be, other factors as well; and, whether any given society follows them or not, alternative routes of development are possible.

## 5

It is the 'one-way-only' response to political and social problems that characterizes all three of the thinkers criticized in *The Open Society and its Enemies*, rather than historicism as Popper defines it. As we have seen, only Marx meets all the conditions for being an historicist; and Popper has, indeed, left himself open to the charge of ignoring his own definition, and using 'historicism' as a blanket term to cover any political or social doctrine he dislikes. But Plato, Hegel and Marx would seem to have this much at least in common – each offers a single, fixed, once-and-for-all conception of the social ideal, whether as something to which existing societies should aspire, and against which they should be measured, or as something to which the progress of history irresistibly carries them. Such an ideal is not of our own making but something *there to be discovered*; and with its discovery all our individual dreams of Utopias, and attempts to realize them, have to be put away as childish things. So the lesson that we, as members of society, have to learn from these thinkers is, in brief, to conform to what is outside our control. It is a lesson that many people have been grateful enough to learn. One-way-only political creeds have essentially the same appeal to authoritarian religions; whatever obedience they may require, or restrictions they may impose, they offer the satisfaction of knowing that the most fundamental questions have finally been answered, that the ultimate responsibility for the direction of our lives has been lifted from us. And we may readily understand how, for example, intellectuals weary of the operations of the principle suggested in an earlier chapter – to every argument there is an equal and opposite counter-argument – weary of the endlessly shifting sands of debate, may be tempted to seek in some dogmatic, all-embracing system a bedrock on which to build.

To Popper, of course, yielding to any such temptation would be a kind of Sartrean 'bad faith'. For, in his view, there *is* no single ideal, the discovery of which will direct our efforts, no escape from the responsibility of *deciding* what is unacceptable to us in society as we find it, and what steps we should take to bring about the appropriate change. And our decisions determine, in essential part, the subsequent development of our society. Popper's 'open society' is, in effect a society whose members characteristically recognize this responsibility for self-determination, and try to use the opportunities it provides to their own maximum advantage or minimum disadvantage. And in so far as Plato, Hegel and Marx all, from their different standpoints, deny this responsibility, then, whatever their various relationships to historicism, they are at one in being enemies of the open society.

Popper has been criticized, not without reason, for failing to distinguish clearly enough between these two offences – historicism and enmity towards the open society.[58] But the two have at least a common basis, which is precisely this failure to recognize the role, in the historical development of any field, theoretical or practical, of individual ideals and initiatives. We cannot, according to Popper, say in advance, what any individual or group will see as a problem or a demand for action, what action they will take or what means for action they will devise. And here we cannot say in advance how any society will, or must, develop from some point of crisis; where it goes from there depends on how its members respond to the crisis, and there are always in principle several possible responses. We cannot – simply because there *are* no ideals or initiatives other than those of our own making. And Popper's real target is, essentially, any system of thought that denies this – though he may indeed have been guilty of supposing, in effect, that since all historicists deny it, all who deny it are historicists.

His general 'refutation of historicism', as formally set out in the preface to *The Poverty of Historicism*,[59] turns on the theoretical impossibility of predicting our responses to future situations. The argument goes as follows: Social and political developments are strongly influenced by scientific developments, or, if we like, our responses to practical problems are determined, in important part, by our earlier responses to theoretical ones. Thus the growth of knowledge – though we must not forget the basic Popperian doctrine that all claims to 'knowledge' can only be provisional – is a major influence on the course of human history. But 'we cannot predict, by rational or scientific methods, the future growth of our scientific knowledge'; and hence we cannot predict the future course of history. Thus we cannot have a theoretical history, or theoretical social science, which would provide a means of making historical predictions, in the way that our theoretical physics or astronomy provides a means of predicting eclipses. Hence it is in principle impossible to carry out the historicist programme successfully, by any means whatsoever.

The decisive step in the argument, as Popper says, is the assertion that, if there is such a thing as the growth of human knowledge, then *'we cannot anticipate today what we shall only know tomorrow'.*[60] We may be tempted to reply that, while the prediction of future scientific discoveries might be very difficult or indeed impossible in practice, yet on general deterministic grounds, such discoveries should, like all other future occurrences, be theoretically predictable. But, to begin with, how solid are these general deterministic grounds? Take, for example, Laplace's famous postulate that a demon of superhuman intellectual powers, capable of knowing the position, mass and velocity of every elementary particle at a given moment, could, from this initial information together with the principles of Newtonian mechanics, logically predict every future state of the world. It is certainly an intriguing idea. But, given the teaching of modern physics about the nature of elementary particles, and about the theoretical barriers to giving precise, unambiguous answers to questions about masses, velocities, etc. it is by no means clear – as it may well have seemed to be in the eighteenth century – just what the demon is supposed to accomplish, or, in general, just what such determinism entails. And quite apart from this, there were never any sufficient grounds for claiming that such determinism was actually *true*, that from the data in question the future of the world *could*, even in principle, be predicted.

It is not logically necessary that it should be so. No doubt if we reformulated the principle to read 'If we had *sufficiently* accurate and comprehensive data, etc., then we could predict . . .' it would be logically necessary, since 'sufficiently' here could only mean 'sufficing to enable such predictions to be made'; but then this would beg the whole question of whether any identifiable set of data would suffice for this purpose. If, on the other hand, we treat it as an empirical generalization then, obviously, it cannot be verified. And we should note that it fails Popper's test for being a *scientific* generalization, since it cannot be falsified either; for example, no matter how much research is put into trying to isolate the cause of cancer, or some form of it, without success, the determinist as such will never say Perhaps then cancer is an undetermined, or uncaused, phenomenon; he merely says 'We have not found the cause yet.' Determinism is perhaps best described as a methodological principle or a *policy* of research, rather than as a *doctrine* about the nature of reality. As Popper puts it, in *The Logic of Scientific Discovery*:

The belief in causality . . . is nothing but a typical metaphysical hypostatization of a well justified methodological rule – the scientist's decision never to abandon his search for laws.[61]

Undeniably, such a policy – the persistent search for general causal laws which, together with appropriate statements of initial conditions, will enable us to predict, and in suitable cases to control or to forestall, certain phenomena – has proved extremely fruitful in many areas of research. But, granted that is *is* only a policy, we have no obligation to adopt it except where, or in so far, as it proves fruitful or seems likely to do so. As Popper says, in *The Open Society*,[62] in criticizing the Laplacean conception of science accepted by Marx and his contemporaries, no kind of determinism can be considered a necessary assumption of scientific method. And in a later paper – which he recalls in the preface of *The Poverty of Historicism* – he undertakes to show that not only quantum physics (which is often quoted as a paradigm example of scientific indeterminism) but even classical physics as well cannot be strictly deterministic in the sense indicated above.[63]

We may, however, still be inclined to say: 'But none the less this deterministic policy, even if it is nothing more than that, *has* led to remarkable feats of accurate, long-term prediction in some fields, so is there any reason in principle why it should not do as much for the historicist?' Popper gives two, related, answers to this. First, we should note that such prophecies, however striking, are far from being the normal outcome even of the exact sciences; they require a special, and unusual, kind of subject-matter. From the characteristic *conditional* predictions of science – *if* these conditions are satisfied, (and *if* there are no countervailing circumstances) then these results will follow – we can derive long-term, unconditional prophecies

only if they apply to systems which can be described as well-isolated, stationary, and recurrent. These systems are very rare in nature; and modern society is surely not one of them.[64]

We can predict the eclipses, and the succession of the seasons, because our solar system is (almost) isolated from outside interference by vast regions of empty space, and its relevant features are simple and repetitive. Even here, presumably, there are conceivable circumstances – some vast explosion or volcanic eruption in the sun or one of the planets, perhaps, violent enough to alter appreciably its position or velocity in relation to the rest of the system, or some large comet passing sufficiently close – which would falsify such prophecies. We make them unconditionally only because all we know of astronomy suggests that such occurrences are so improbable that they may be safely ignored. But, ordinarily, physical science deals perforce in conditional predictions; the situations with which it deals are too complex and indeterminate, the likelihood of countervailing conditions too high, to permit otherwise. And, manifestly, we can ask no better of social science.

Secondly, in the field of the social sciences there is a specific kind of interference, the effect of which can never fully be taken into account, namely the influence of the social sciences themselves. Stars and planets do not read astronomy, but people, in appreciable numbers, read theories about the nature of society, and prophecies based thereon; and hence such theories and prophecies become a factor influencing their future behaviour. We have only to think of what a powerful force Marxist *theory* has been, and continues to be in twentieth-century politics to realize how important a factor it may be. It can, of course, according to circumstances, work either for or against the fulfilment of its own prophecies. We have already noted, in the previous section, Popper's example of how the influence of Marx on the Russian revolutionaries helped to falsify his theory of the conditions under which a successful revolution could take place. On the other hand, we can readily understand how revolutionaries in many countries have been encouraged to persevere in the face of difficulties, and to overcome them, by the assurance that time and history are on their side, and that they must win in the end.

Referring to the Greek legend in which the prophecy that Oedipus would one day kill his own father, starts a chain of events which ends in his doing so, Popper names this the 'Oedipus effect'.[65] And, clearly, a similar effect would be produced if we devised some means of predicting the future development of science, what lines of research would be followed, and what discoveries made between, say, now and the end of the twentieth century. Suppose that, as historicism requires, we do not simply make random guesses but actually have scientific grounds for saying: This is what will happen. But this would mean, in effect, that we have somehow contrived already to do the research and make the discoveries. And thus our predicted future knowledge would have become *present* knowledge. And since science habitually builds on the foundation of existing knowledge, the effect of predicting development over the next two decades would therefore be a different development from the one predicted. And prediction of *that* development would be similarly self-falsifying . . . and so on. We may, perhaps, suggest that someone might arrive at a prediction and for some reason keep it secret, or, as some seers and oracles are said to have done, publish it only in enigmatic or ambiguous form. And history provides some examples – as in the controversy about the roles of Newton and Leibniz in the discovery of calculus – of discoveries made but left unpublished (and hence largely uninfluential) by one thinker but later published by another. This, however, can scarcely be called prophecy; it is merely the historical accident of the first discoverer's eccentricity, or failure to appreciate the importance of what he has found. And we have to remember, again, that historicism requires that there should be some *scientific* means of making the predictions in question; hence presumably they would be within the competence of many interested researchers – they would not depend on some unique prophetic gift – and concealment would be impracticable.

It may, however, be objected that, despite such arguments, Popper's italicized principle, that '*we cannot anticipate today what we shall only know tomorrow*', is either tautologous or false. If by 'anticipating' knowledge we mean actually possessing it, it is obvious that if we shall only know that $S$ tomorrow (where $S$ is any statement) then, logically, we cannot know that $S$ today. It is obvious also that our supposed 'scientific means of predicting' the future development of science – if, again, this is taken to mean predicting the actual results – would simply be a means of speeding up present research. It would be nonsense to call it a means of *prediction* at all. On the other hand, we *are* often able to anticipate the results of future research in the only sense in which anyone would seriously try to do so, i.e. to anticipate what problems will be solved within a given field of research, and within a given period of time, without attempting to specify what the actual solutions will be. We *can* quite reasonably extrapolate from the history of recent research and predict that certain problems will be solved within a certain period – and make use of this prediction in the relevant planning. For example, if it is known in principle that a guided missile with a certain range and accuracy can be made, and the applied scientists of a technologically advanced nation, with the financial support of their government, are set the task of discovering how to make it, then we can reasonably predict that within, say, two years they will have the requisite knowledge. And politicians and military strategists will take such predictions into account in their long-term planning. In recent history, indeed, such anticipations of future technological progress, both one's own and one's rivals, has become a major factor in determining 'global strategies'. Of course, the 'countervailing conditions' clause applies here also – applies, we might say, with a vengeance, since in this field it is only too easy to envisage a 'development' which will abruptly end the prospect of all others. But, in principle, there would appear to be no difference between such predictions of future knowledge and, say, our prediction, when we see woodmen attack the base of a tree with a chain-saw, that it is shortly about to fall.

We may, however, reply that, as his various references to *long-term* predictions indicate, Popper has never intended to deny that, in suitable circumstances, we might have good grounds for such *short-term* predictions. Also, to give plausibility to the example taken, it has to be specified that, at the time of prediction, we already know in principle that the specific problem can be solved. But the discovery of the principle itself would surely be a very different matter. Adapting Kuhn's famous distinction we may suppose that, while the progress of 'normal science' is, at any rate in some circumstances, predictable to a high degree of accuracy, 'scientific revolutions' must remain unpredictable. Admittedly, Popper has not provided any clear-cut distinction between long and short terms; and, as we saw in an earlier chapter, he has rejected Kuhn's radical contrast between the two kinds of science, normal and revolutionary. But, none the less, there is an all-important difference between the situation where – to simplify somewhat – we know that the answer sought is to be found within a finite range of possibilities, and that these can be sifted through in a certain finite time, and the situation where we do not know that the answer lies within any such range or indeed anywhere at all. In the first kind of situation, we have, obviously, good grounds for predicting that the answer will be found within the time specified, and acting accordingly. In the second, equally obviously, we have no grounds for predicting success within any given time, or at all – except perhaps, for a generalized faith in science as a kind of endlessly resourceful Jeeves who can always be trusted to come up with a scheme to solve any problem, however difficult. It seems clear that, for example, no knowledge however comprehensive of the science available to Marx and his contemporaries could have provided 'good' grounds – even if we allow 'good' to mean something less than 'logically adequate' – for predicting the major scientific advances which have radically affected social and political development in the present century. Consider, say, the medical discoveries that have provided vastly more effective means of controlling and eradicating disease, and hence inadvertently created problems of over-population much sooner, and on a much larger scale, than any nineteenth century Malthusian could have seen reason to predict; or the extent to which technical developments have enabled machines to replace human labour; or the development of communications and 'mass media' and their effects on social and political life; or, above all, the development of weapons of mass destruction which have made, in the second half of the twentieth century, human survival the issue that dwarfs all others. Such examples may indeed dispose us to believe that our future (if any) is likely to be yet further transformed by new scientific discoveries. But this is merely a matter of coming to expect the unexpected, as it were, or, at best, to make more or less informed and inspired guesses as to what those new discoveries may be, guesses that belong to the realm of science fiction rather than serious historical prophecy.

To some degree, the principle that social and political developments are influenced by the growth of knowledge holds of every period of human history. Even from their most primitive beginnings, discoveries in agriculture, shipbuilding, navigation, communications, weapon-making . . ., have made differences, often profound and permanent, to how people organized their lives, what options were open to them, who had the advantage over whom. What distinguishes our present era, as Whitehead points out in a passage quoted in the previous chapter,[66] is not primarily the importance of its scientific discoveries but the speed with which they have crowded one upon another. As Whitehead says —

writing was a greater invention than the steam-engine. But in tracing the continuous history of the growth of writing we find an immense difference from that of the steam-engine . . . the scale of time is so absolutely disparate. For the steam-engine we may give about a hundred years; for writing the time period is of the order of a thousand years.

And, of course, the times taken to develop the jet-engine, the television camera, the computer and the nuclear reactor have been much shorter still. Hence, while Popper's general case against historicism could, in principle, have been made out in any period of history, its force is a lot more apparent now than it would have been, say, to Plato and his contemporaries. We can scarcely fail to agree that, for better or for worse, modern society is about as far as we can imagine from being the kind of 'well-isolated, stationary, and recurrent' system about which long-term prophecies can reasonably be made. And hence, whether it is reducible to a logically rigorous proof or not, the essential case against historicism, in Popper's sense, has been effectively made: the growth of knowledge is a major factor, perhaps the most important factor of all, in determining historical developments, and since we have no rational means of making long-term predictions about the first, we have no rational means of making long-term predictions about the second either.

# 5

## Freedom and values

### 1

Once we begin to rely upon our reason, and to use our powers of criticism, once we feel the call of personal responsibilities and with it, the responsibility of helping to advance knowledge, we cannot return to a state of implicit submission to tribal magic. For those who have eaten of the tree of knowledge, paradise is lost ... *There is no return to a harmonious state of nature. If we turn back, then we must go the whole way — we must return to the beasts* ... if we shrink from the task of carrying our cross, the cross of humaneness, of reason, of responsibility, if we lose courage and flinch from the strain, then we must fortify ourselves with a clear understanding of the simple decision before us. We can return to the beasts. But if we wish to remain human, then there is only one way, the way into the open society.[1]

nothing could be better than living a modest, simple and free life in an egalitarian society. It took some time before I recognized this as no more than a beautiful dream; that freedom is more important than equality; that the attempt to realize equality endangers freedom; and that, if freedom is lost, there will not even be equality among the unfree.[2]

As we saw in the previous chapter, the appeal of both historicism and the closed society — of having the fundamental questions about what we are here for, and how we ought to live, answered for us once and for all — is a powerful and understandable one. What Popper is telling us in these passages, is that, beyond a certain point in human development, the appeal has to be resisted; beyond that point, we are, in Sartre's famous phrase 'condemned to be free'. And whatever the satisfaction of living in a society where people have never questioned and never doubted the established frame of order, and the traditional ways of doing things, once questions and doubts *have* been raised, we can never simply forget them again. We can only suppress them. And there is a world of difference between spontaneous and enforced conformity.

But, even if we are thus, inescapably, responsible for deciding what our mode of life and our values are to be, and what kind of society we are to live in, the decisions are not therefore arbitrary, or irrational. Popper is as firmly opposed to any 'one-way-is-as-good-as-another' form of relativism in matters of practice as in matters of theory (though here, also, we shall have to consider whether he has adequate grounds for his opposition). There are, of course, no indubitably right answers to our practical, any more than to our theoretical, questions, no guarantees against errors. But here also there is an entirely rational programme available to us, i.e. that of progress through self-criticism and self-correction. And, even if it can never fulfil the aspirations of the historicists, there is still an important role for social *science*, i.e. for the systematic, (though not necessarily professional or academic) study of social situations, of the problems to which they give rise, and the possible solutions to such problems.

Despite the obvious differences, there are important parallels to be drawn between physical and social science. In both, the essential method is still that of framing hypotheses and testing them against the data of observation.[3] It may be that in social science there is less scope for controlled experiment, and it is harder to disentangle our theoretical from our practical interests; but this remains the only method of rational enquiry available to us. And in both, the characteristic results are *conditional* predictions – if certain conditions are realized (and if there are no countervailing circumstances) then certain results follow. And in suitable circumstances, these can provide good grounds for short-term categorical predictions – for predicting, say, a rise in the rate of inflation or unemployment over the next quarter, much as the meteorologist predicts a rise in temperature tomorrow. As Popper puts it, physical and social science have alike the function of pointing out to us certain things that *cannot* happen, and hence certain things that we *cannot* achieve. Thus, just as the second law of thermodynamics tells us, in effect, that we cannot construct a machine which is one hundred per cent efficient, social science may show us that, for example, we cannot raise the real income of the working population without increasing productivity, or that we cannot equalize real incomes and at the same time raise productivity.[4] And (granted their correctness) such principles can play an important role in warning us of what we must, or must not, expect when we create, or find ourselves in, the appropriate situations.

It is, of course, notoriously difficult to say in advance what *all* the effects of adopting a given policy of action will be. We may indeed get the effect we wanted; but we may also get side-effects which we did not want. And it is here that Popper locates the distinctive field of the theoretical social sciences. Putting aside the naive conspiracy theories which regard every social phenomenon as intended by someone, they set themselves '*to trace the unintended social repercussions of intentional human actions*'.[5] Popper takes as an example of such repercussions a man seeking to buy a house in a particular area; it is far from his intentions to raise the market value of houses in that area, and yet his appearance as another would-be purchaser will in itself help to push prices upwards. Or to take an example on a larger scale, we may suppose that, at the beginning of the Industrial Revolution, manufacturers had no actual intentions other than to exploit newly-invented machinery to produce more goods and make higher profits. But to this end, they built factories wherever it was cheapest and easiest to obtain their coal and raw materials; large numbers of people, drawn from the rural areas by the prospect of regular work and wages, converged on these sites; vast industrial towns sprang up. And thus, without anyone's specific intention that it should be so, the face of an entire country was permanently altered, and a whole new way of life – and with it a new set of social ills and social problems – emerged.

We may be inclined to object that there is no reason why social science should confine itself to such *un*intended consequences; and that in any case the boundary between intended and unintended is difficult to draw. (How, for example, is the unintended related to the unwanted, and the unforeseen? To a government, presumably, a general lowering of the standard of living of the populace is unwanted; but if, say, in pursuit of a stable economy, it insists that wage-increases must be kept lower than the current rate of inflation, such a lowering is certainly not unforeseen. Is the government then entitled or not to call it unintended?) However, Popper's statement should doubtless be treated as aphorism rather than formal definition; and as such it serves at least to bring out one important point about what social science can and cannot do. When we are confronted with some problem or crisis, it cannot, as historicism supposed, tell us what the solution, the way forward from here, *has* to be. What it can do is point out to us the likely consequences *if* we choose this or that option. Again, the predictions are conditional, and subject to the now-familiar provisos; and clearly no tracing of consequences, however assiduous, can ever claim completion. But none the less it can, in many circumstances, provide a basis – indeed the only conceivable basis – for choosing between our options rationally and responsibly.

It is precisely this possibility of rational and responsible choice that makes the freedom to discuss and criticize essential to Popper's open society. If there were one right answer, and one only, then presumably we had best entrust ourselves without question to a Platonic 'philosopher-king' whose function it is to know that answer; if it is a matter of arbitrary choice, then to a Fascist 'leader' or 'strong man' with the will and the charisma to put his irrational inspirations into effect and thus ensure at least some kind of unity and direction. But, granted that, of society as well as of nature, we have an endlessly developing and self-correcting body of knowledge, and that this is highly relevant to many of the decisions of policy we have to make even though it determines none of them, the importance of such freedom becomes obvious. What Popper said of knowledge in general holds of social policies as well, i.e. they have 'all kinds of sources . . . but *none has authority*'.[6] Our best chance of finding those most effective for our purposes lies in a system of institutions designed to maximize freedom to advocate, and try out, different policies, to criticize those already in operation regardless of their source, and to alter them when we judge that they have failed, or where some alternative seems more promising. Popper's conditions for social progress are essentially the same as his conditions for scientific progress. And hence the constitution of Popper's open society is diametrically opposed to that of, say, Plato's republic; instead of trying to ensure a permanent commitment to a specific set of policies on the grounds that they are the only right ones, its primary purpose is to ensure that no such commitment can ever be made.

Here again we notice, in Popper and Plato alike, how social theory is determined, in essential part, by the theory of knowledge. Granted that it is vain to look for any guaranteed source of right answers to practical questions, (just as it is to theoretical ones) whether in a Platonic aristocracy, in divinely-appointed kings or prophets, or in the people at large, then, as Popper puts it in a famous passage in *The Open Society and its Enemies*, we are forced

to replace the question: *Who should rule?* by the new question: *How can we so organize political institutions that bad or incompetent rulers can be prevented from doing too much damage?*[7]

Since there is no untainted or infallible source of social policies, any more than of scientific theories, the crucial question is not How do we find the right, or the best, policy-makers? but rather How do we ensure that, whoever is entrusted with making and implementing policies, effective means of *criticism* exist; that evidence of failure and the case for alternatives are not suppressed; and that radical changes in policy are, to adapt Kuhn's terms, within the scope of normal, as opposed to revolutionary, politics?

Democracy, as Popper understands the term, is precisely that type of government which ensures that a given policy, and its exponents, can be replaced without violent upheaval. Thus:

> There are only two types of governmental institutions, those which provide for a change of the government without bloodshed, and those which do not . . . We need not quarrel about words, and about such pseudo-problems as the true or essential meaning of the word 'democracy'. You may choose whatever name you like for the two types of government. I personally prefer to call the type of government which can be removed without violence 'democracy' and the other 'tyranny'.[8]

Though we may concede Popper's right to use his terms as he pleases, so long as he defines his use, *prima facie* this appears to be, at least, an eccentric use for a term with the associations of 'democracy'. Suppose, for example, that we had in Britain a franchise restricted to the very wealthy; or suppose we had no elected House of Commons at all, but the hereditary members of the House of Lords elected a government from among their own number, and could at any time force that government's resignation by a vote of no confidence. Either way, it would seem, Popper's condition for democracy – provision for a change of government without bloodshed – would be satisfied, even though we should be very far from democracy as ordinarily understood. Presumably, Popper is well aware of this, but his intention is to highlight what he finds of genuine value in democracy as ordinarily understood. It is not that in a democracy 'the people' achieve freedom from overlords and oppressors and rule themselves; people never rule themselves 'in any concrete, practical sense'.[9] Nor is 'majority rule' (in the sense of universal adult franchise, or almost so) in itself a safeguard of freedom. A majority may vote for the oppression of minorities. It may even vote into power an anti-democratic tyranny which will proceed to dismantle all democratic institutions. This is the 'paradox of democracy', that it may vote itself out of existence – or that an unrestrained tyranny may be democratically elected.[10] Hence, if our paramount value is freedom, we do not *hold* that the will of the majority, as expressed through the ballot-box, must be done at any cost. We value democracy and democratic institutions not for their own sakes, but *only in so far as* they are the most effective means available to us of preserving freedom and restraining tyranny. Thus,

the theory of democracy is not based upon the principle that the majority should rule; rather, the various egalitarian methods of democratic control, such as general elections and representative government, are to be considered as no more than well-tried and, in the presence of a widespread traditional distrust of tyranny, reasonably effective institutional safeguards against tyranny.[11]

The reference to tradition is important. For without a widespread and deeply-rooted respect for freedom within a society, and a general willingness to preserve democratic institutions and use them for the purposes for which they were created, institutions in themselves provide no permanent safeguards.

even the best institutions (such as democratic checks and balances) will always depend, to a considerable degree, on the persons involved. Institutions are like fortresses. They must be well designed *and* manned.[12]

Presumably this is one reason, at least, why democratic institutions, exported from a country which has such a tradition to one which has not, cannot by themselves create a free society. That, once again, is in the hands of its individual citizens; and there is no escaping their ultimate responsibility not only for what institutions they have, but also for how, or whether, these institutions work.

Freedom itself, however, gives rise to paradoxes essentially similar to those of democracy.[13] Total or unrestrained freedom also is inherently self-destructive. If, for example, a society freed itself from all legal restraints by repealing every law on its statute-books, the majority of its members, far from enjoying total freedom, would most probably find themselves totally enslaved to the bullies and exploiters among them. Traditional respect for freedom does not suffice without legal institutions, any more than they suffice without it, if even a minority does not share that respect. And in all likelihood, it would rapidly diminish even among the majority, as more and more people were constrained to counter violence with equal violence. (Only in a community made up entirely of saints could we dispense with the law — and even there it might be well to have some safeguards against excess of zeal.) Hence, since it is vain to expect total freedom, all we can reasonably ask for is the maximum of freedom possible – and accept as its price a minimum of restraint.

For Popper, as we have seen, it is the function of the state and its institutions to protect its citizens against bullying and exploitation, and hence, in effect, to impose this minimum of restraint. But it must not go beyond what is required to maximize the freedom of all its citizens to live their lives as they see fit: 'The state is a necessary evil; its powers are not to be multiplied beyond what is necessary.'[14] Its proper function is a negative one, to prevent evils such as those just mentioned, rather than to try to realize some positive conception of the good life. Any attempt to put into effect the 'greatest happiness' principle of the Utilitarians is liable to provide an excuse for paternalism or benevolent dictatorship. The state, or its embodiments, should concentrate rather on 'lowest misery', and leave the promotion of happiness, in the main, to private initiative.[15]

When he advocates 'minimal government' in these terms, Popper sounds, no doubt, like a champion of the 'get the government off the people's backs' brand of right-wing politics; and he has indeed been welcomed as such. But even the minimum of intervention, required by the tasks which Popper assigns to the state, may still be a great deal. We may recall from our section on Marxism that, according to Popper, the state has the right and the duty to protect, not only the physically weak from the physically strong, but the economically weak from the economically strong – to ensure, for example, that no one is starved into accepting inequitable wages or working conditions. And if it undertakes to do this, and attempts as well to alleviate the miseries caused by disease, ignorance, neglect of children and of the old, etc. (wherever it is the only, or the most effective agency for doing so), then intervention by the state and its institutions must perforce become a major factor in the lives of the citizens. According to Bryan Magee, in his highly enthusiastic exposition of Popper's merits, this is essentially 'a philosophy of social democracy', as plainly anti-conservative as it is anti-totalitarian; and Magee has no difficulty in finding in Popper the philosophical foundations of his own democratic socialism.[16] Popper himself, however, has explicitly renounced socialism. And clearly there is considerable latitude for disagreement over just what the state can do, in any given social or political situation, towards securing the ends in question, and at what point its efforts become counter-productive. Once again, there is no once-and-for-all answer, no all-purposes policy that is right for every situation. But certainly there is nothing in

Popper's teaching to encourage any hankering after a return to unrestrained capitalism or to a society at the mercy of economic forces, and nothing inconsistent in principle with the development of what has come to be called the welfare state. The question to be asked, regarding *any* particular example of state intervention in any particular situation, is whether it is, or is likely to be, in the long term the most effective means of promoting those ends which, as we have said, it is the function of the state to pursue. What is essential to the open society is that this is always an open question, and that we are free to accept, and act upon, a negative answer.

## 2

It is pointless, then, to ask for unqualified freedom. We have just seen one sense in which this claim can be taken – that a demand for totally unrestrained freedom is self-defeating. We should notice here a further sense, i.e. that it is meaningless to ask for freedom unless it is specified (or could be specified on demand) *from what*, and *to do what*, such freedom is sought. Thus, we cannot meaningfully enquire, *in vacuo* as it were, whether or not someone is free. We could, however, meaningfully enquire whether or not he is free, say, to travel abroad – provided it was understood what kind of restriction on his travelling we had in mind. We might, for example, be wondering whether his government will allow him a passport, whether he can get sufficient leave of absence from his work, whether the state of his bank-balance will permit it, whether he has now been released from the moral obligation to stay and care for an ailing parent, whether he has recovered from the agoraphobia that has confined him to his own house . . . Any answer to the original question has to be given with some such restriction in mind; and the answer may of course vary from one to another. He may well be free relative to one possible restriction, but not free relative to another. What he cannot be is free in any absolute sense.

The point is an extremely important one, since the word 'freedom' has such a favourable emotional aura and we rally almost automatically to any call for, or promise of, freedom. But it is well to remember that virtually any policy of action can be presented (correctly enough) as a defence of freedom, since its implementation will almost certainly free us from, or to do, *something*. I can recall one religious polemicist who advocated, in effect, the suppression of all religious opinions except his own, in the name of our right to freedom from religious uncertainties. And dictatorship can be, and doubtless often has been, presented as freedom from political controversy and insecurity. We should remember also that freedom from one restriction will not necessarily bring freedom from others, perhaps equally irksome; it may even increase or multiply them. For example, freedom from foreign domination, however devoutly to be wished for, does not in itself ensure freedom from exploitation or poverty. As Parnell, according to Yeats, told an enthusiastically nationalist road-mender, 'Ireland shall get her freedom and you still break stone.'[17] And in the matter of day-to-day freedom to do and say as he thinks fit, the ordinary citizen of a newly independent state may, unfortunately, find that he is even less free than he was before. Again, exponents of 'minimal government' often talk as though the only restrictions on freedom were those imposed by governments, so that the way to achieve freedom is simply to repeal statutes, and to cut down on the range of governmental powers and agencies. By so doing, of course, we *do* increase freedom, i.e. we give some additional freedoms to some people; and doubtless there are circumstances where these freedoms are of the first importance and the numbers who benefit very substantial. But, on the other hand, they may be gained at the expense of the only effective means of combating what, for a large part of the human race, are and always have been among the greatest restrictions on freedom – poverty, ignorance and exploitation. And it must not be forgotten that while *these* persist, the promise of any other freedoms is, very largely, an irrelevance or an affront.

Freedom, then, is not something one and indivisible. There are, indeed, some time-honoured philosophical contexts in which it has been customary to speak of freedom as though it were either the inalienable birthright of every human being as such, or else forever unattainable, as in the old issue between freedom and determinism, where we are presented with an apparently simple and unambiguous either/or situation – *either* the world accommodates an element of human freedom *or* it is wholly determined – and the problem is to decide which way it is. It would be presumptuous to dismiss all the traditional arguments on this point as merely the products of confusion, without a great deal more consideration than we can give them here. But we may say, at any rate, that their use of 'freedom' and related terms is very different from that of politics and everyday discourse. In these, freedom is emphatically not a single attribute which we all permanently have or lack; rather there are many freedoms, very unevenly distributed throughout the human race, and freedoms are things that are given and withheld, fought for and lost and gained.

In his paper 'A plea for excuses',[18] Austin, after making this point that the traditional philosophical use of 'freedom' is 'only faintly related to the everyday use', goes on to compare this everyday use with that of 'reality' and 'truth'. And we can readily see the kind of similarity he has in mind. For example, taken in abstraction from any specific context, 'reality', 'truth' and 'freedom' are all alike notoriously elusive of enlightening definition. And while we can meaningfully ask 'Is this a real *x* (antique, diamond, Rembrandt, or whatever)?' the question 'Is this real?' *simpliciter* has to be countered with 'It depends on what this is supposed to be'; similarly 'Is this man (or this society) free?' can be answered only when it is understood what actions, and what possible restrictions thereon, are in question. Again, it is as futile to go in search of Freedom as such as it is to go in search of Truth as such. As we have seen, we can only set ourselves this or that specific task of research and formulation of results, and if we accomplish these to the standards of accuracy which the occasion demands, then we can claim that a truth has been established; likewise we can set ourselves to eliminate this or that specific restriction on some proposed course of action, and if we succeed in doing so, then we can claim that a freedom has been secured. But the abstract terms, whatever their emotive force, do not themselves name any specific goals of endeavour, and it is dangerously misleading to employ them as if they did.

With such considerations in mind, we may return then to Popper's concerns about freedom. It is evident to begin with that, *in isolation* a passage like the second of those quoted at the beginning of this chapter – 'freedom is more important than equality . . .' – tells us very little. It could be endorsed by the supporters of vastly different and mutually incompatible freedoms, by the British Liberal Party and the Ku Klux Klan with equal enthusiasm. And to say that Popper is an advocate of freedom, or of a free society, is in itself to say virtually nothing – until we have spelt out the specific freedoms which he claims that we have, or that we should seek, and the scope and limits thereof. To simplify somewhat, the critique of historicism undertakes to demonstrate that we are not constrained by any inexorable laws of historical development, whether imposed by God or nature, whose operation compels us towards a certain kind of future whether we choose to have it so or not. So here is one possible (or at least *prima facie* possible) restriction from which we are free. And presumably one intended effect of the *publication* of such a critique is to confer freedom from another constraint or restriction – that imposed by the delusion that there are such laws, or that some attempt to formulate them is correct. Further, the open society which Popper urges us to seek is characterized essentially by the freedom to judge our rulers, and, if we think fit, to replace them, and to advocate and try to implement alternative policies, i.e. by freedom to criticize any aspect of our society and to try to give effect to our criticisms.

These, very briefly, are what we might call the distinctively Popperian freedoms. And I do not for a moment want to dispute that we do indeed have the freedom the historicists deny, and that we should have the freedoms the exponents of closed societies would deny us. But it is worthwhile to enquire a little into what such freedoms actually entail. For example, granted that the future of our society, or of humanity at large, is not predetermined by the working of historical laws, exactly what freedom do we have in consequence? We may say that we are then free to determine our own future, our destiny is in our own hands, the ultimate responsibility is inescapably ours, and so on. But does this mean that we can envisage alternative long-term futures and decide which of them to realize – or merely that a multitude of decisions on matters of comparative detail combine to determine, in essential part, what kind of future we shall have? If no path is laid down for us, are we therefore free to cut our own path to where we want to go – or merely free to wander? There is always something highly suspect about the kind of rhetoric which tells us that 'we', or 'mankind', can choose, or must choose, between, say, learning to live in peace with each other, or destroying ourselves in another world war. If we were really presented, in these terms, with such a choice, there can be little doubt that the overwhelming majority of the human race would opt for peace. Yet it is only too evident that no such choice ever is, or is ever likely to be, presented, and that even if it were – even supposing, say, a world-wide referendum could be organized, and the result showed that ninety-nine per cent of mankind wanted peace – the prospects for permanent peace would be little improved. So what does it mean to say that we – humanity in general – can, or must, choose?

The point is not simply that the crucial choices are perforce made by a very small number of people, those who hold the key positions in the dominant nations at the moments of crisis; and hence that to speak of mankind choosing peace or war is mistaken in the way that it is to speak, say, of Germany choosing war in 1914, or Russia choosing communism in 1917, when it would be much nearer the mark to say that such choices were made for them. (This is, in effect, the error which Popper calls 'naive collectivism',[19] i.e. treating nations, classes, etc. as though they had a quasi-personal life of their own, and forgetting that decisions can only be made and actions performed by individuals within them.) Certainly, the influence that the decisions of the few can exercise over the lives, and deaths, of the many provides a powerful reason for striving after the freedoms of the open society, the main point of which is, as we have seen, precisely to give the ruled some measure of control, however incomplete or indirect, over the actions of their rulers. But whatever measure of control we may achieve and however beneficial it may be in many respects, we must still question our freedom to choose our long-term future – and question even the freedom of our rulers to choose it for us.

For *anyone* to do so, he would have to be free from many more restrictions than those imposed by the operation of historical laws. And any ruler, even a dictator or an absolute monarch, is, obviously, hedged about by a great variety of restrictions. For example, to say that he does, or proposes to do, this or that is, almost always, no more than convenient abbreviation. He has to work with and through a variety of agencies and institutions, administrative, judicial, military, financial, etc. and he is heavily dependent on their capacities, and always to some extent on their goodwill. Also, however great his political power in his own country, he is still subject to restrictions from things outside his own control, the reactions to his policies of foreign governments or international bankers, for example, or the varying circumstances of international trade. Further, any ruler is restricted by the knowledge and imagination – his own or possibly his advisers' – at his disposal. He can only choose from among the ends he can envisage, and the means thereto that he knows of. And while 'social science' in Popper's broad sense of the term, can, no doubt, help in the short term and in familiar circumstances, it is perforce a very uncertain guide if we seek knowledge of how best to realize some novel or long-term objective. After all, if there are no general laws which enable us to predict our future from the situation in which we find ourselves, then neither are there any which can tell us how to *alter* our present situation so as to achieve the future we desire. In this respect, Popper's demolition of historicism is as fatal to the reformer as it is to the prophet. And when a ruler, however benevolent his intentions, does not know how to obtain the long-term benefits he wants for his subjects, then manifestly he is not free to choose them. An historian, with the advantage of hindsight (and the licence to simplify without which his task would be impossible) may well find reason to single out a particular move by a particular ruler as especially important, as the first step on a road that led to some radical change of state for a whole society or even for the whole world. But almost certainly it was not seen as such at the time in question by the ruler himself. *He* was not standing at a cross-roads with clearly marked paths leading in several directions, helpfully signposted 'War', 'Peace', 'Revolution', etc. Rather he was standing in an unmapped wilderness, and the paths *the historian* now traces are those which he, and his subjects, trod out in their pursuit of a sequence of short-term objectives.

Almost invariably, the important moves have not been made as an effort to realize some single long-term ideal, like peace or prosperity; rather they are made in response to some immediate crisis, where there is a conflict of many influences and interests urgently requiring a solution. And the attempted solution will, in all probability, help to generate a further crisis demanding in its turn another short-term response. (Progress through struggle, indeed, but without the Marxist's guaranteed outcome.) The parallels with what we have said about the progress of philosophy and science are sufficiently obvious. But there is, of course, also the obvious and important difference that, in the theoretical field, a mistaken response to a problem, or one that generates an even more difficult problem, does little harm except perhaps to the reputation or career of a particular researcher; and, usually, little harm comes from admitting that a problem has defeated us, or leaving it to the ingenuity of future researchers. In fact, as Popper says, one of the functions of science is to make our theories 'suffer in our stead',[20] i.e. as physical scientists we deliberately create conditions where we can test our theories about, say, the power of explosives or the strength of metals before we stake our lives on them. But if the theory that we bring to the solution of some economic or political problem is, for example, Monetarism, or Mutually Assured Destruction, then, all too clearly, in the event of failure it is not primarily the theory that will suffer. Practical problems, unlike theoretical ones, do not often allow time or opportunity for several attempts at a solution, or the option of indefinite postponement. We can readily envisage our sequence of crises bringing us to a point when we, or our rulers, have to choose at once and irrevocably, even though the only choice available is a choice of evils. The recurrent nightmare of our time is not of a nuclear war unleashed by some science-fiction figures of perverted genius, who have achieved unprecedented power and cold-bloodedly decided to use it for the destruction of humanity; rather it is of frightened and confused old men in underground shelters, exhausted by days and nights of ever-mounting international crisis, who despairingly conclude that there is no feasible alternative left.

Of course, such nightmares may never be realized; we have no means of knowing whether they will or not. The point to be made is that, granted that historical determinism has been discredited, what we have left is indeterminacy, rather than freedom as ordinarily understood. We cannot predict an inevitable long-term future, but neither can we choose a desired one. We can only exercise such freedoms as we have, and wait to discover what the cumulative effects will be – with a chronic anxiety replacing the pessimism or optimism of the various historicist doctrines.

To return, however, to the characteristic freedoms of the open society, the freedoms to criticize any idea, institution or individual, regardless of status, and to advocate and try out alternative policies of action. The tacit assumption here, we might say, is that what is good for science is equally good for society. The freedoms in question are clearly fundamental to any research institute worthy of the name, necessary, even if not themselves sufficient, conditions for its success. But can such freedoms perform the same function in society at large? The research institute is, obviously enough, a highly specialized element within that larger society. It is, by and large, protected against material want, and, as we have just noted, against any very serious consequences of its errors or failures; in effect, its members are permitted to retain some of the advantages of the schoolroom into adult life, for the sake of the long-term practical benefits, or the inherent interest, of their work. By and large, also, its members are highly intelligent, trained in exact intellectual disciplines, and articulate; their criticisms and suggestions therefore are likely to be well-informed, relevant to the problems in hand, and precisely formulated. And while presumably their detachment is still subject to human limitations, they have at least been schooled to expect criticism of their efforts, and recognize valid criticism when they see it.

Now, when Popper and others expound the merits of the open

society, they appear very often to have in mind a society where these conditions are realized in very substantial measure – a society where the material necessities of survival may be taken for granted, where the problems and policies under discussion are putting no-one's life or livelihood at risk, where the members have sufficient education to put their ideas into words and to recognize and welcome relevant criticisms. And, of course, in comfortable academic suburbs and the like it may often be so, or almost so. But, unfortunately, for most members of most societies it is far from being like this. And, as we noticed earlier, below certain levels of deprivation, many much-lauded freedoms, including those of the open society, lose much – which is not, of course, to say lose all – of their relevance. Thus, for example, where there is persistent overpopulation and malnutrition, and a dearth of capital for investment, there is very little room for trying out various agricultural or industrial policies; many of the theoretically good ideas are simply out of financial reach, and there is too little margin for errors if experiments go wrong. In some circumstances, it is literally impossible to live and learn by our mistakes. Again, the value of the freedom to criticize depends very largely, as we have said, on the criticisms being well-informed and well-formulated, and, of course, on the ability to put them into effect. But, obviously, in many situations the ruled are in these respects at a hopeless disadvantage in relation to their rulers. They may only dimly understand what is going wrong, why, for example, prices are rising or the value of their labour falling; they may simply have to take their rulers word for it that it is necessary to spend vast sums on armaments, or go to war, in order to meet some foreign threat, since they have no way of checking. They may readily be overwhelmed in any verbal confrontation, since they have only a handful of threadbare clichés and slogans with which to express their discontents. Indeed, since their hands are not on the levers of power (since very often, indeed they have little idea where the real levers of power are, or how they operate) their rulers may well feel they can afford to treat the marches and the banners indulgently, and even pay lip-service to their importance; they may, with good reason, see these as providing a useful safety-valve, by creating the illusion of 'doing something' or 'making one's voice heard'. Being free to criticize does not in itself entail being free from all the restrictions on *effective* criticism. And there may be vast differences in the freedom to criticize effectively among the members of a society who are all alike free to criticize as much as they please. Further, even pertinent criticisms and proposals are liable, at any social level, to come up against highly unscientific attitudes of mind. They may encounter, for example, an adherence to particular policies or institutions which is based, not on a rational conviction that these are the best for the task, but on traditions and emotional attachments — so that criticism, far from being welcomed as a step towards improvement, is spurned as a temptation to disloyalty. The 'conjectures-and-refutations' recipe for progress will not work where the response to a refutation is not 'Yes, thank you — I see that I must think again', but rather 'Are you calling me a liar?' or 'Are you asking me to betray my leader (party, church, or whatever)?' Again, the value of the freedom to criticize is, to a large extent, conditional on our first freeing ourselves from other restrictions, in this case those imposed by prejudice and irrationality.

None the less, even if it is granted that in virtually every imaginable kind of society the shaping and reshaping of policy is effectively in the hands of a small élite, it is doubtless still entirely correct to insist on the importance of democracy in Popper's sense — of institutions designed to prevent bad rulers and bad policies from creating too much havoc, and to permit their replacement without bloodshed. After all, whatever unscrupulous cunning or powers of deception we may suspect in a ruling class, the old principle, that you cannot fool all the people all the time, still holds. And if our ruling élite have, say, periodically to justify themselves before an electorate, or if rival groups among them are competing for election, they must perforce take *some* account of the interests and wishes of the electors. And from the electors' standpoint, this can only be an advance on any system which allows their rulers to ignore those interests and wishes altogether. What we are concerned with at the moment is not the value, but the nature and limitations, of these freedoms to judge and to choose.

For this purpose, we have to return to the differences between what happens in the scientific community and what happens in society at large. When we are speaking of the professional activities of qualified scientists, then no doubt we can afford to say, in Popper's somewhat cavalier fashion, that it does not much matter what, or whose, ideas or conjectures are considered, or how they are arrived at; what matters is that the bad are eliminated by experimental tests and observations, and the good survive. But here we are thinking of the ideas and conjectures of people familiar with what has already happened in their field of research, who know what has been already tried, and with what result, and who can make at least a highly informed guess as to what is currently worth trying out – so that, barring accidents and oversights, the most promising ideas, and only those, reach the laboratory for testing. Clearly, the progress of science would be severely hampered, to say the least, if the scientists were constrained to consider seriously, and test, every theory that was put before them, regardless of its source; seriously hampered also if they could only try out those theories which satisfied some condition quite extraneous to their scientific promise, like being approved by some committee of laymen. (Sometimes, of course, such extraneous conditions have to be satisfied – for example, if the proposed experiments are likely to be inhumane, dangerous, or highly expensive, or perhaps, in some settings, if their presuppositions or results are likely to clash with a dominant ideology. And there is obviously a case for saying that the wider society which supports science and has to live with its results, good and bad alike, has a right and a duty to impose conditions on it. However, for the purposes of our present comparison, we may regard science as characteristically having, for better or worse, at any rate a very high degree of autonomy.) Also, despite the reservations mentioned in our second chapter, in the circle of professional scientists we can assume a substantial measure of agreement over what is to count as an adequate test of a theory, or as success or failure in such a test. Such a consensus is more or less guaranteed by the shared discipline of those concerned. But, again, we can imagine the confusion that would arise if there was no such consensus, if those concerned differed radically over the objects of their research and hence over the criteria of success and failure therein.

Presumably the kind of society that would approximate most closely to science in *these* respects (though not in others) would be the Platonic republic, which, of course, makes a virtue of excluding all but a highly-qualified élite from its councils of state. And part of the price of avoiding the drawbacks of the republic – however well worth paying that price may be – is, inescapably, that we forgo some of the advantages enjoyed by science. Thus, there is no longer any guarantee that the policies selected for implementation will be produced or approved by those with the greatest expertise in economics, national defence, or whatever the relevant field may be. Extraneous conditions are liable to predominate here – so that the selected policies are not those which are, by some expert standard, the best, but rather those with the richest, most influential, most energetic or noisiest advocates, or those that have been most skilfully packaged and sold to a largely inexpert public. And, whatever the advantage of institutions which allow the ruled periodically to pass judgement on their rulers, it has perforce to be an inexpert judgement. We cannot reasonably ask the electorate at large to determine precisely the extent to which, say, inflation or unemployment is due to the government's economic policy, or what the effects of any alternative are likely to be; we can ask only for a reaction to the immediate situation as they experience it, and whether or not the result is to preserve beneficial policies, and eliminate harmful ones, is very much a matter of chance. Also, the would-be democratic ruler – unlike the scientist – cannot concentrate exclusively on finding the right, or the best, answers to his problems; if he wants to survive politically, then he has to some extent to court popularity – to seek acceptable packages and compromises, to play many parts and be, if not all things to all men, at least many things to many men. So we must not be surprised to find, in a democracy, an actor taking on the role which Plato assigned to the philosopher.

Popper himself, we should note, has no illusions about the fallibility of public opinion; and clearly any suggestion of '*vox populi, vox dei*' would be contrary to his whole epistemology.[21] But he still shows something of the same uncritical faith in the value of criticism, however fallible the critics may be, as we found earlier in his philosophy of science. And there must, I think, be some reservations about the wisdom of setting aside the question 'Who should rule?' – i.e. 'Who should be given the opportunity to put his policies for society into effect?' – in favour of 'How do we prevent bad rulers (or bad policies) from doing too much harm?' Not only are the consequences of mistakes likely to be much more serious, but the means of detecting and eliminating them are usually much slower and less efficient, in social and political affairs than they are in science. (After we have blundered into a war or a recession, the democratic process may eventually move some senior politicians out of harm's way, to the House of Lords, for example; but almost certainly there will be a long-running and inconclusive debate over whether or not they or their policies were really responsible for the disaster. And, either way, the consolation of its victims will be small.) Also, of course, a system which filters out the bad is effective only if there is some good left; after all, we must presumably have *some* rulers, and *some* policies. So it would seem that institutions which encourage those with moral integrity and intellectual ability to enter politics, and offer them a chance of success, are at least as important as those which restrain the unscrupulous or the incompetent. The progress of science depends not just on the fact that all its theories are amenable to tests designed to eliminate the false among them, but also on the fact that some scientists, by whatever means, have contrived to formulate theories which have survived a great many such tests; and without their capacity to produce a fair number of survivors, science itself could scarcely survive for very long. *Mutatis mutandis*, the same holds of society.

It is, obviously, much easier to point out the need for such institutions, than to say just what kind of institutions would serve the purpose or how they could be created; and nothing more can be done here than to point out the need to supplement Popper's account of his open society in some such way. Something like what we found earlier in his account of science would seem indeed, to hold here also; it embodies a highly valuable insight, but still a partial one, and, for its intended purpose, it will not suffice as it stands. Granted that the aim is to prescribe conditions for a society which is so far as possible, humane, peaceful and rational, which minimizes the occasions for violence between its members and maximizes their freedom to live as they see fit, the conditions which Popper lays down may well be necessary, but they are not in themselves sufficient. What the foregoing considerations about freedom have shown, is that freedoms form an indefinitely numerous and varied set, with a complex of inter-relations, some mutually independent, some incompatible, some dependent on others for their effectiveness. And the characteristic freedoms of the open society would seem to be effective towards the ends in question only where certain other freedoms exist – or, more generally, where certain other conditions are met. We may be tempted to adapt what the New Testament says about the kingdom of God, and say, in effect, Seek ye first the open society and all else (freedom from poverty, ignorance, etc.) will be added unto you. In some situations the freedoms of the open society may well help to promote these others. But there does not appear to be any sufficient basis for the generalization that it must always be so; and, for the most deprived parts of the world, seeking liberation from the host of restrictions and limitations on life therein, it is hard to believe that the establishment of open societies should, or could, be the *first* priority.

In fairness to Popper, it must be remembered that he has never undertaken to give us a blueprint for the perfect society. As we have seen, he has emphatically denied that any set of political or social institutions can in themselves guarantee the good life for anyone. And he might well accept much of what has been said in the present section. Most of it, as I have indicated, has been offered as explication rather than criticism. Understandably, as a whole-hearted advocate of the open society, he dwells on its merits, and tends to contrast it with the closed societies as light with darkness. But appreciation of the light is by no means inconsistent with awareness of the conditions under which it burns brightest, or of the areas which it still leaves in darkness or shadows.

## 3

We come back, finally, to relativism. Granted that we ask of the state and its institutions, if not that they should promote positive goods, at least that they should strive to minimize preventible evils, and of the citizens that they should periodically judge whether their rulers are doing well or ill, we must have some criteria for distinguishing good from evil, and right from wrong. But are there any such criteria which are manifestly or demonstrably the right ones to adopt? Suppose that different groups or individuals adopt different criteria, and hence arrive at different judgements. Is there any authoritative standpoint from which we can settle the issue between them? *Prima facie*, moral relativism is a good deal easier to accept than intellectual relativism (to adopt Popper's terms[22]). It is much harder to persuade ourselves that, because they have adopted different criteria, *A* and *B* may correctly assign different truth values to the same statement, than they might, in such circumstances, correctly assign different moral values to the same action or state of affairs. As we saw in an earlier chapter, actual examples of different criteria of truth, in the required sense of the term, are hard to find; but there would seem to be no difficulty in finding examples of different moral criteria adopted by different cultures and generations, and consequent different assessments of the morality of specific actions. Thus, for example, revenge-killings, judged morally wrong in one culture, may not only be permissible but a moral duty in another. We may say, of course, that although something is right according to the criteria of a given culture, it is none the less actually wrong, or that these criteria are themselves wrong. But then, we can be asked, in accordance with what criteria are we making *these* moral judgements? The answer is, presumably, those of our own culture; and the obvious next question is 'What gives these greater authority than those you undertake to judge? Are you not simply falling into the (quite understandable) error of assigning a uniquely privileged position to your own particular frame of reference?'

If so, then it would seem that there is no absolute sense in which a given society is good or bad, or in which certain features of it are defects, or certain changes would be improvements. If the state and its institutions are set the task of eliminating preventible evils, then what they actually do will depend on what those in power count as evils — and on this point they may well disagree with their subjects or among themselves. Where there *is* agreement about what things are intrinsically good, and about the order of precedence among intrinsic goods, then no doubt we can, in principle, argue about the best means of achieving such goods with some hope of arriving at a right answer. Thus, for example, if we are agreed on the intrinsic value of peace, then, however difficult and fraught with uncertainties and indeterminables the topic may be in practice, we can in principle debate rationally the rightness or wrongness of, say, nuclear disarmament. On the available evidence, is it more or less likely to promote peace than any alternative policy is? But suppose someone denies the intrinsic value of peace; or, more probably, suppose that for some of us peace takes precedence over all other goods, while for others national independence, perhaps, or some individual freedoms rank higher, so that war, however destructive, is preferable to sacrificing these. How, or from what standpoint, can we settle such issues — for example that between those who say Better Dead than Red, and those who say the reverse? And whatever standpoint we might adopt for this purpose, what do we say to those who decline to share *that* standpoint . . . and so on? We seem to have a close parallel to what we found in our earlier discussion of truth, i.e. that some criteria or standards have simply to be chosen, or adopted, without any arguments in their favour, as a precondition of constructing arguments for or against any others. And hence, of course, the possibility of different choices or adoptions without error on anyone's part. No doubt there are in fact societies where this possibility has little practical significance, where, for example, a strong religious tradition ensures that (almost) all the members adopt a single scale of values, or are at any rate constrained to behave as if they did. But it is worth noting that such a society would, almost by definition, be a Popperian closed society. The open society as such, presumably seeks to maximize our freedom to adopt different values if we so wish.

Popper, none the less, is as strongly opposed to moral as he is to intellectual relativism. Doubtless, he is willing to defend our freedom to adopt, and act upon, different moral codes, just as he is to defend our freedom to adopt, and try out, different scientific theories. But, in both cases, the object of inviting all comers to take part in the race, without handicap, is not to declare them all equally swift but to try to discover the swiftest. Even though in both cases different criteria may be adopted – and even though we may have no manifestly authoritative means of choosing between them – we still must not yield to the temptation to say that there is no need to choose since they are all equal, and hence that nothing is true or false, good or bad, in any absolute sense, but merely relative to a given criterion. This, according to Popper, is the most pernicious effect of relativism – that by treating such differences as nothing *more* than differences and denying the necessity or the possibility of discovering right or wrong, better or worse, among them, it is a barrier to any rational progress. There is, indeed, a salutary lesson to be learned from taking note of, say, the moral codes of different cultures; but it is that any such code, even our own, may be wrong, and hence that we ought to adopt a critical approach towards all of them. All the different attempts to formulate such codes that we encounter may be wrong, though they need not be. What they cannot be is all equally right. And

although we have no criterion of absolute rightness, we can certainly make progress in this realm. As in the realm of facts, we can make discoveries. That cruelty is always 'bad'; that it should always be avoided where possible; that the golden rule is a good standard which can perhaps even be improved by doing unto others, wherever possible, as *they* would be done by: these are elementary and extremely important examples of discoveries in the realm of standards.[23]

Again, we should not expect to find any single authoritative source of the relevant knowledge. Philosophers have professed to find such a source of moral knowledge variously in our feelings of pleasure and pain, or in some kind of special moral sense or moral intuition, or in 'practical reason', as a kind of moral analogue of pure reason. But no way of arriving at any moral principle or policy, and no reaction to it – whatever their psychological or historical interest – is a sufficient guarantee of rightness. From the statement, say, that something seems to me, or to any number of people, manifestly and self-evidently right, it does not follow that it *is* right. But, if so –

How do we learn about standards? How, in this realm, do we learn from our mistakes? First, we learn to imitate others (incidentally), we do so by trial and error), and so learn to look upon standards of behaviour as if they consisted of fixed, 'given' rules. Later we find (also by trial and error) that we are making mistakes – for example that we may hurt people. We may thus learn the golden rule; but soon we find that we may misjudge a man's attitude, his background knowledge, his aims, his standards; and we may learn from our mistakes to take care even beyond the golden rule.

We must never forget, however, that –

whatever we accept we should trust only tentatively . . . we are in possession, at best, of partial truth (or rightness) . . . we are bound to make at least some mistake or misjudgement somewhere – not only with respect to facts but also with respect to the adopted standards.[24]

Certainly there is much to admire in this resolve neither to assume that the standards most familiar to us are necessarily the right ones and beyond criticism, nor to concede that no standard is better or more defensible than another, but rather to keep up an endless quest for moral improvement. Here again, however, we encounter the problems created by Popper's unrestricted fallibilism. We have never, it would seem, logically sufficient grounds for saying, without reservation or qualification, that any specific action is right or wrong, any specific state of affairs good or bad, any change in moral standards an improvement or a retrograde step. And the ideal of an absolute or objective standard of rightness or goodness does not provide us with a yardstick with which to measure our efforts, or a standard of which we may fall short – any more than that of truth does – unless we have access to *some specific instantiations* of it. Our quest, however earnest and well-intentioned, is ultimately pointless unless we have some fixed signposts or landmarks telling us in which direction to look, and some means of recognizing the object of our search if we ever stumble upon it. Otherwise, we are like prospectors who admit that they cannot recognize gold. And we are, in effect, driven back to relativism; we can say no more than that *if* certain things are accepted as right, *then* certain standards should be adopted. But if different groups or individuals make different moral judgements, we have, again, no authoritative standpoint from which to arbitrate; and even if we refuse to allow that they all may be equally right, we have to allow that the question of *which* is right remains permanently open – which in practice at least comes to much the same thing. Our actual moral lives will have to rest on decisions, or adoptions, rather than discoveries.

Popper indeed claims, as we have seen, that in the realm of moral standards we *can* make discoveries, and learn by our mistakes, just as we can in the realm of facts. But in both realms, we have to question the appropriateness of terms like 'discover' or 'learn', which imply that we have achieved a success or got something right. On Popperian principles, whatever may prompt us to say that something is the case or that something is right or wrong, or whatever may provide *conventionally* sufficient grounds for saying so, it never provides *logically* sufficient grounds. Thus, for example, we are said to 'discover' the badness of cruelty, or to 'learn' the inadequacy of a traditional morality by discovering that we can obey its rules and still hurt people. But no matter what feelings of revulsion we have when we encounter cruelty, or how immediately and unshakeably we are convinced of its badness – or how many people share these reactions – none of this, in Popper's own showing, is logically sufficient ground for saying that it is bad. And if we discover that behaviour traditionally regarded as moral can still be hurtful, this again is logically insufficient to show that it is morally wrong. We may *elect* to renounce all cruel and hurtful behaviour, and frame our code of conduct accordingly; but we cannot claim to have discovered, or learnt, that we should do so. Nor can we justify our code by any appeal to facts about the social or evolutionary effects of cruelty, hurtfulness or their opposites. There is an irreducible dualism between facts and standards,[25] and whatever influence the observance of a given code of conduct may have on progress towards a new kind of society, or even on the survival of the human species, nothing follows about its goodness or badness. So, it would seem, with a moral code as with a scientific theory, we are never (logically) entitled to say that we have discovered something which discredits it, but only that we have decided on, or adopted, something inconsistent with it; and all progress is relative to such decisions or adoptions.

As we have already noted, such relativism is at least plausible where morality is concerned. We can readily imagine – indeed cite from experience – examples of changes which to some have seemed improvements (say, towards a more caring and compassionate society) but to others seemed retrogressions (towards a less hardy and self-reliant one). Sometimes, of course, such disagreements prove to be about the right, or the best, means to an end which is not in dispute, and hence – if we may set aside for a moment the Popperian fallibilism even over matters of fact – can in principle be settled; but it seems clear that there could be disagreement also over *intrinsic* goods, or the order of precedence among them – and hence irreconcilable differences over what specific actions or states of affairs are right or wrong, good or evil.

So here also, as in the case of truth and falsity, Popper is unable to justify his rejection of relativism; it can survive, and even flourish, on his characteristic epistemology. But it is worthwhile to consider briefly the extent to which the additional counter-moves which we tried earlier against intellectual relativism might be effective against moral relativism as well. It will be recalled that two main theses were put forward: (*a*) That statement-identification is so linked to criteria of truth that it is not possible for those who adopt different criteria to assign different truth-values to the same statement; if they differ irreconcilably over criteria then *ipso facto*, even though they may use the same form of words, they are concerned with different statements. (*b*) That the unrestricted fallibilism, which effectively spoils Popper's case against relativism, is untenable; it cannot, for example, be allowed even as a logical possibility, that any or every example of counting may in fact be a miscount, without depriving the distinction between the two of its points. Could similar theses be argued in the case of actions or states of affairs and their moral values?

Consider how the first of them might apply to the example mentioned earlier, that of different moral values assigned to a revenge-killing by the upholders of different moral codes. Is there any relevant sense in which we might say that, despite appearances, they are not talking about *the same* action? We may grant that they are, at any rate, talking about the same *occurrence*, or sequence of occurrences – *A* shooting or stabbing *B*, at a particular time and place, and *B*'s subsequent death. But, then, much more than the occurrence itself is taken into account when we identify it as a revenge-killing, or a murder, or an execution, or an act of war, or whatever and judge it accordingly. To do so is to link it in a specific fashion to a background of values, embodied in laws and customs, social institutions and patterns of behaviour. Thus, for example, in some societies there may be a powerful tradition of 'defending the honour' of one's family, and reacting violently to any insult or injury to it. And members of such a society, who are otherwise law-abiding and who would never think of killing, say, for the sake of gain, may feel constrained to kill for this reason. For them, there is an important distinction between revenge-killing, which is thus sanctioned, and murder, which is not; and to call a revenge-killing murder is simply to misidentify it. Our own ancestors, presumably, drew a similar distinction between killing in a duel and killing in other circumstances. And we still discriminate sharply between killings done at the behest of a government, and those done as a matter of private enterprise – a distinction gratefully taken over by many varieties of political rebel, who pride themselves on committing, not murder, but acts of war.

It is obvious that such distinctions, and the traditions, institutions, etc. which embody or give expression to them, are of central importance in the morality of the societies and individuals concerned. They do not merely provide a means of differentiating the morally acceptable from the morally unacceptable among the various – independently identifiable – kinds of killing. They provide also the means of identifying the actions, or kinds of action, on which moral judgement is passed, i.e. we do not pass judgement simply on *A*'s shooting or stabbing *B*, but on his doing so, say, in defence of his family's honour, or of his country's freedom, or, alternatively, for the sake of gain, or in a fit of rage or jealousy. And such identifications are (very often) the essential part of moral judgement. Once we have identified the action to be judged as killing for the sake of honour or freedom, or as simply murder, we have in effect already passed our moral judgement. It follows from the identification itself. ('Murder is wrong', for example, is an analytic truth.) Thus, we do not have two, logically independent, sets of equipment – one for identifying the actions to be judged, the other a scale of values against which we check them to decide their moral rightness or wrongness. Our scale of values determines, in essential part, both the means by which we identify actions, and the means by which we judge them.

If, or in so far as, such a connection holds, then to have different scales of values is not merely to have different means of judging actions, but different means of identifying them also. Suppose, for example, that in our scale of values respect for human life takes absolute precedence over family honour or national freedom, so that in no circumstances, can they over-ride it. When we come to identify *A*'s action for the purpose of moral assessment, we simply do not take them into account. We may be aware that others, with different scales of value, do so, but to us they are morally irrelevant. All that is relevant is that it violates the principle of respect for human life, and whether *A* acted as revenger, duellist, executioner, soldier, pirate or gangster makes no difference to the morality of his act. Killings by all of these are on a moral par, as it were; and most probably we call them all by a single, explicitly condemnatory, title – such as 'murder'. Between us, then, and the upholders of a different scale of values, there is disagreement, not only about the morality of what *A* did, but also about *what* he did. In a sense, of course, we are talking about the same person, and the same episode in his career; but, *as subjects for moral assessment*, we are picking out, from the whole complex of the episode itself and the social and cultural environment within which it occurred, *different* elements or patterns – and it is of these different elements or patterns that we make our different moral assessments. And hence, it might be argued, we may say of moral evaluation something similar to what we said earlier of truth evaluation – i.e. that we can replace the disquieting relativism which says that one person's right may be another's wrong, with a more innocuous variety, which says merely that, out of the complex web of human affairs, there are different ways of selecting subjects for moral assessment, and hence, not surprisingly, different assessments to be made. (And, again, if, or in so far as, such a logical connection between identification and assessment does *not* hold, then, however much we may dislike the consequences, the original relativist thesis is substantially correct.)

We may notice here Roger Trigg's comment[26] on a statement once made by D. Z. Phillips[27] to the effect that it would be a mistake to condemn child-sacrifice among some remote tribe as murder, since child-sacrifice has a very different relationship to their form of life from that which murder has to ours, and hence it cannot properly be identified as such. Trigg remarks

This is relativism with a vengeance. It suggests that nineteenth-century missionaries had no right to tell Fijians that cannibalism was wrong, on the ground that no one outside the society could possibly know how they regarded eating people . . . no practice can be condemned from outside the culture of which it is a part . . . the repugnance we feel might be said to be merely a sign of our personal commitment to the standards of our own society.

However, this may not be quite so effective a *reductio ad absurdum* as it appears at first sight. For it would indeed have been pointless for the missionaries to go to heathen tribes and merely contradict their characteristic moral judgements – just tell them that eating people is wrong (or child-sacrifice, or whatever). It would be rather as if a missionary from some strange religious cult came to tell us, without preamble, that honesty is wrong or that murder is right. We should simply find such claims bewildering, and even, as we noted earlier, self-contradictory. Of course, the Christian missionaries wanted to convert their tribespeople to a new code of morals, but only as part of a much more radical conversion from heathenism to Christianity. They never supposed that they could let the tribespeople retain their own traditional concepts of human life, and of its place in the scheme of things, and superimpose on these the moral outlook of an Anglican vicar. They taught Christian morality *within* the framework of Christian teaching about nature, man and God. And clearly this was the only way in which it could be done.

We may, with sound reason, insist on the dualism of facts and standards, i.e. that no moral evaluations are logically determined by statements of fact. But, at the same time, we should notice at least one important link between the two – namely that facts, or what we take to be facts, determine for us the range of the *possible* values we may hold. For example, we cannot value the well-being of an immaterial soul, or one-ness with a personal God, as such terms are ordinarily understood, unless we believe that such a soul, or such a God, actually exists. We cannot think it a duty to offer service or sacrifice to bloodthirsty tribal deities unless we believe that there are such things. We cannot think it a duty to strive towards the fulfilment of the manifest destiny of the master race, or lessen the birth-pangs of the inevitable revolution, unless we believe in the master race or in historical inevitability. We cannot feel guilty about treating members of another race or nation as our inferiors unless we believe that, in the relevant respects, they are not inferior. And so on. What the missionaries offered their prospective converts was, in the first place, a new conception of reality, and of man's place within it, one which opened up a new, and much wider, range of possibilities for human life, of things to which people might aspire. The converted as such took their new values from this range, and in due course embodied these, in new customs, loyalties, institutions, etc. As a result they now identified, say, the killing of a child before an altar very differently from the way in which they identified it in their heathen days. They no longer saw it as a sacrifice owed to some tribal deity, or a means of protecting the tribe against his wrath; rather they saw it as a violation of the laws of their new God who cared for mercy and not sacrifice, and in whose sight the child was infinitely precious. When they reached this stage, then indeed they would have understood what the missionaries meant by saying that such treatment of children was wrong. But at this stage they would scarcely have needed to be told.

We may recall here a further point made in our discussion of science, i.e. that often important stages in its development were marked, not by the formulation of new truths, or purported truths, but by the opening up of a new range of possibilities – in the way that, for example, the idea of evolution offers a new way of looking at a whole range of phenomena, and hence new problems to consider, new hypotheses to test, etc. Something similar might be said of morality, i.e. that important moral progress is made, not only or primarily when someone 'discovers', by some means, that something is right which was previously thought wrong, or *vice versa*, but rather with the opening up of a new range of possible values. Thus, for example, our tribespeople encountering Christianity for the first time may glimpse the possibility of seeking something more in life than physical survival, or success in struggles with tribal enemies, or gaining the favours of arbitrary deities or spirits, of aspiring to nothing less than living in this world and beyond in unity with, and under the fatherhood of, God. (Cf. the saying of Jesus about his mission – I am come that they should have life, and have it more abundantly.[28]) Or, on a more limited scale, consider the impact of the idea of a universal brotherhood of mankind, living in peace and mutual cooperation, on people who have hitherto had no aspirations or ideals beyond success in national or factional struggles. Whether or not the kingdom of Heaven, or the brotherhood of man can ever be realized does not, of course, concern us here. The point is simply that, once the *ideas* of such things have been presented as possibilities, they can be – and have been – accepted as values, and specific actions and situations can be – and are – identified and evaluated in the light of them. And the introduction of ideas, or sets of ideas, which play such a role in the life of an individual, or of a whole society, is, at any rate, one essential element in moral development.

None the less, it may be said – and indeed with some reason – this will not do as it stands. Granted, if only for the sake of argument, that we do thus choose or adopt our basic values from the range of possibilities known to us; and also that these choices or adoptions determine not only our specific evaluations but our identification of subjects for evaluation as well, and hence never lead us into mutual contradiction. Still, while we might say that one range of possibilities was richer or fuller than another, can we have any grounds for calling it morally superior? We can see, for example, how acceptance of Christianity leads the formerly heathen tribespeople to adopt a *different* moral code but can we have any reason, apart from mere prejudice, for calling it a *better* one? We may trace the conditions under which people may come to treat $X$ as a value, or a good – but surely it can still reasonably be asked 'But are they right about it' '*Is X* in fact good?' And if we have to admit that there is no authoritative way of answering such questions, are we not still left with the scepticism which says that we can never be sure that the values we have adopted are the right ones or not – and the relativism which adds that in practice, at least, different and mutually inconsistent codes of values must be treated as equally good?

There is an obvious parallel here with our problem about truth; even granted all that was said about the conditions for ascribing truth-values to statements, could we not still reasonably be asked 'But are your evaluations correct?' 'Whatever may lead you to claim that a statement $S$ is true, *is S* in fact true?' Our proposed line of reply was that a statement which is the outcome of a correctly conducted process of enquiry (and formulation of results) is *ipso facto* true, that there is no additional criterion it has to satisfy; and further than an indiscriminate scepticism about the correctness of *all* processes of enquiry is not even logically tenable, since we cannot make sense of, for example, the notions of correct and incorrect counting unless we allow that some specific counts *are* correct and known to be such. Could we now adopt a similar approach to moral evaluation? Certainly, we might argue it is pointless to keep on obstinately asking 'But is *that* good?' or 'Is *that* right?' of whatever grounds are offered for an evaluation, if we are not prepared to accept anything as a sufficient answer. In a sense, of course, we *can* always ask such questions regarding anything whatsoever – they do not violate any rules of syntax or semantics – but to persist in asking them, after we have rejected all the means by which we ordinarily arrive at answers, and put no others in their place, shows, not a laudably critical cast of mind, but merely a failure to think through the conditions for asking them *usefully*. And, to go back to Popper's own examples, where he spoke – somewhat unguardedly it would seem, in view of his fallibilist principles – of discovering that cruelty is wrong, or that some things approved by conventional standards are wrong because they are hurtful, here we should surely want to say that further questioning is pointless. Just as we said earlier of our example of counting a small group of things under ideal conditions – 'If this is, or even could be, a miscount, then we do not know what counting is' – so we might say 'If gratuitous cruelty, or the infliction of unnecessary suffering, is not wrong, then we do not know what rightness or wrongness is.' If we are told that we must remain critical even of judgements such as these, are we not at a loss to know *how* to be critical; what other judgements *could* we frame, more certain than these, which might serve as evidence for or against them? These, after all, were the sort of paradigms or examples from which we learnt our conceptions of right and wrong in the first place, and which still effectively guide our moral thinking. If these are called in question, then we lose our way; we no longer have any idea of what we are looking for.

It would seem then that there have to be some humble, everyday moral judgements which are, quite literally, beyond reasonable doubt. To question them is, in effect, to destroy our apparatus for dealing with such questions. And these judgements, however commonplace they may be, and however wide a field of doubts and alternatives they still leave open, have clearly a highly important function. Just as any proposed theory has to square with certain humble, everyday, but incontrovertible truths, so any proposed policy or course of action has to square with these. And, as we have just said, they serve as the paradigms without which moral criticism, and moral discourse in general, would not be feasible.

Again, however, it may be objected that this by itself is insufficient. If our moral thinking is thus governed by an apparently indefinite and mutually independent set of paradigms, then (*a*) there may be many areas in which these provide us with contradictory guide-lines, or with none at all, and (*b*) we may find that other individuals or other cultures give a similar role to other paradigms. So, either we allow that there may be different concepts of, say, rightness – somewhat confusingly, since it is not clear what would make them all, despite their differences, concepts of *rightness* – or else that these other people do not have the concept of rightness, as we understand it, at all. (Compare the problems of our missionaries trying to learn the local language as a preliminary to teaching the tribespeople; how would they determine whether it contained an equivalent for 'right' or not?) In respect of truth and falsity, it will be recalled, our paradigm cases of incontrovertible truths were not simply a random collection of successes drawn from any field of activity; they were, specifically, successful outcomes of *enquiry*. The concepts of truth and falsity were essentially linked to that of enquiry; our efforts to find out about our world, and to formulate our findings, provided, as it were, the field in which they operated. Could we now find some analogue for enquiry, something which would relate to rightness and wrongness, good and evil, as enquiry does to truth and falsity – and thus determine for us the field or morality properly so called, more definitely and comprehensively than an apparently random collection of paradigms can?

The question, obviously, is much too complex to be discussed at all adequately in the present context. But we may find, perhaps, the beginnings of an answer in the reflection that, whatever else may hold of it, the field of moral evaluation is, at any rate, that of *rational* activity. We make such evaluations about the characteristic activities and creations of rational beings, i.e. of beings capable of envisaging alternative courses of action and weighting up their possible consequences, of placing themselves under the discipline of general laws, of suppressing instinctive reactions for the sake of long-term advantage, of achieving a certain detachment from immediate concerns, a certain capacity to see things, as it were, 'in the light of eternity' ... And one element, at least, of moral progress in the individual, or in society at large, is surely the development of rationality thus understood, the growth of its influence in determining our behaviour. It may be objected, of course, that it could not be the *only* element, even on the fairly generous interpretation of rationality we have just given. We should have to add, for example, that our 'detachment' from our own immediate concerns, must be extended to cover, not only being aware of the needs and desires of others, but *caring* about them as well. We should, in effect, take account of St Paul's famous warning to the Corinthians, that even 'to understand all mysteries and all knowledge' is in vain, if we 'have not charity' as well. But even without such amendments, the appeal to the development of rationality – though it may not by itself tell us what we ought to do – can still provide us with a filter to eliminate things that we ought *not* to do (somewhat in the manner of Kant's famous categorical imperative – the relevance of which to our present topic might indeed repay exploration). Thus, for example, it would lead us to condemn as retrograde steps any action done on mere impulse without thinking of consequences, where such thinking was possible, any preference for force over argument as a means of settling disputes, and, of course, any explicit glorification of irrationalism as a mode of life. And we could now give as grounds for our moral condemnation of war as a means of settling international disputes, or the glorification of physical force for its own sake, that such things are defeats for rationality or betrayals thereof. There is still, once again, plenty of room for doubt over what rationality sanctions or forbids in many individual cases; and still plenty of room for innocuous differences between the fields in which different individuals or societies characteristically seek to express and develop their rationality. (As we have just seen, to give such a role to rationality does not by itself commit us to any specific policies of action.) But, again, there are some cases, like those just noted, where there can be no reasonable doubt about what rationality sanctions or forbids. Also, granted that rationality and morality are thus essentially linked, there can be no question of an alternative morality, properly so called, which is *not* so linked to rationality; and there can be no standpoint from which we can call in question the moral value of rationality itself. To attempt to do so is simply to put oneself outside the pale of moral discourse altogether.

It is evident that for Popper himself rationality plays an essential part in morality, and rational development an essential part in our moral progress. We have only to recall the examples quoted a few pages back, or his earlier account of social progress towards the open society, or indeed the many specific moral judgements scattered throughout his writings. Thus, it is a moral advance when we pass from the childhood stage of simply obeying the rules laid down for us by parents and mentors, either through fear of superior force or because it has simply never occurred to us to do otherwise, to the critical stage of *judging* such rules by their effects on human well-being. And our arrival at the traditional golden rule, or Popper's improved version of it, is presumably due in part at least to our now seeing the arbitrariness of treating our own well-being as uniquely important, and hence extending our concern to others as well. At the social level, also, Popper presents the archetypal closed society as being, like the child, subservient to a host of arbitrary rules, customs and taboos. Its members conform because they fear the wrath of tribal chiefs or tribal deities, or because they can envisage no alternative. But progress towards the open society is, in contrast, progress towards a society whose members are free, and encouraged, to question all such rules and customs, to demand justifications for them and explore alternatives – in short towards a society fit for rational beings to live in. Popper has often and emphatically identified himself as a rationalist; and he would certainly have no quarrel with the theses that, in essential part, to act morally is to act rationally, that our moral progress, both individual and social, is a function of our self-fulfilment as rational beings, and, conversely, that any denial or betrayal of our rationality is morally a retrograde step. What the foregoing discussion has done, in effect, is to point out some necessary conditions for adopting such rationalism – and for preventing its self-destruction through excess of rationalistic zeal.

## 4

When we reflect back on the various elements of Popper's work we have dealt with in this book, we might indeed say that such excess of rationalistic zeal is the most – perhaps the only – serious flaw that we have found. And, if so, then it is the defect of a considerable merit. As we have, I trust, sufficiently emphasized, throughout his long career Popper has brought outstanding energy and acumen to the defence of the values of truth, self-consistency and freedom. And these we may fairly call the essential rationalistic virtues, not merely in the sense that they have been upheld by a particular school of thought, but that they must be upheld by any rational being as such. If someone repudiates other values, however widely adopted, and tells us, for example, 'I do not care about the general happiness', or '. . . about peace', this may be shocking or distasteful, but at least rational discourse with him remains possible. But, if he says 'I do not care about truth' or '. . . about consistency' then all such discourse loses its point, which is after all precisely the realization of these values; and similarly, though perhaps less obviously, if he says 'I do not care about freedom', since rational discourse also loses its point if we are not free to follow where the argument leads and accept its consequences without constraint from tradition, taboo, or arbitrary violence. If we are to take him at his word, then he has renounced the whole realm of rationality for one dominated, presumably, by brute force or brute instinct.

Clearly, it would be hard to overestimate the importance of such values for any recognizably civilized society – or the merits of a philosophy which notably defends them at a time when, in many quarters, they are endangered by neglect and denigration. But to uphold any values we must, perforce, be mindful of the inescapable conditions for so doing. Thus, if a given theory is commended for its practical utility, its mathematical simplicity, or whatever, we may very properly insist, as Popper does, that the crucial question remains: 'But is it true?' – and that truth must be clearly distinguished from utility, etc. as well as from the various criteria by which we try to identify it in particular instances. But at the same time, we have to remember that the ideal of truth can only guide our researches, or provide a standard by which we can judge the results, if there are some identifiable statements which actually realize this ideal, which *are*, without qualification, true. To treat *every* statement as permanently open to criticism, and to keep on demanding evidence for its truth or falsity, have, as we saw at length in our third chapter, merely the effect of dismantling the essential apparatus for acquiring such evidence. We may say of the search for truth what a saint once said of the search for God – that we cannot seek unless we have already, in some measure, found. And a rationalism which is reluctant to admit that the search for truth ever ends anywhere, effectively prevents it from ever beginning; and thus drives us back into the relativism and scepticism which it tries so strenuously to avoid.

Again we may well share Popper's intolerance of inconsistency, his contempt for any claim that *p* and not-*p* may both be true. But then, again, we have to take account of the means and the methods whereby we actually construct our statements, and realize that, since our conceptual equipment for making them is always liable to be in some degree inadequate or inappropriate to our subject-matter, our statements, especially in the higher reaches of theory, are also liable to be variously over-abstract, over-simplified or one-sided. And hence we may arrive at mutually contradictory statements neither of which is the product of mere carelessness or incompetence in the use of our statement-making equipment, so that it is pointless to say sternly: 'One of them must be true and the other false, and our business is to determine which is which.' It may be that only a radical shift in standpoint, a shift to more adequate or less abstract conceptual equipment, will enable us to resolve the conflict between them, and do justice to the partial insights that both endeavoured to convey. This is the kind of situation with which dialectical philosophy has characteristically been concerned. And it is primarily a failure to give due weight to such situations and the role of contradiction within them – and hence to the crucial difference between saying 'Self-contradiction is inevitable at this level of abstraction and can only be overcome by an advance beyond it', and saying 'Self-contradiction is inevitable', full stop – that has produced Popper's notorious blind-spot about dialectic in general, and Hegel in particular. (It may also have a share in producing some of the over-simplification about scientific method discussed in our second chapter.)

Or take the third value mentioned, that of freedom. Here again, we cannot do other than praise the force and sincerity of Popper's defence. Our reservations are about his apparent neglect of some of the conditions for its realization, of the way in which freedom perforce resolves itself into an indefinite variety of freedoms from ... and freedoms to ..., many of which can be enjoyed only in specific circumstances, and many of which are mutually incompatible. Often Popper has seemed unaware of how little terms like 'freedom' or 'a free society', despite their emotive force, actually convey, unless we go into detail about just what freedoms we have in mind, who could enjoy them and under what conditions, and what price, measured perhaps in other freedoms, they might exact.

In general terms, Popper's zeal for his rationalistic values becomes, as we have said, excessive and self-destructive when he attempts to pursue them in abstraction from the conditions under which we can meaningfully ask for their realization. And most of the critical passages in this book have been concerned, quite simply, to reconstruct the concrete situation from which these abstractions have been made. Thus we have examined what is involved in seeking, and finding, not the truth as such, but a specific truth about some humble, everyday matter like the number of things on the table before us; we have considered situations in which a philosopher or a scientist might, with good reasons, want to affirm two mutually contradictory statements, and the lines of response to such situations open to him; and considered the difficulties facing a statesman or a citizen trying to establish or exercise this or that particular freedom. And in the course of these reconstructions we have, I believe, found good grounds for claiming that the realization of these values can be, and is sometimes, actually achieved.

# Notes

### Chapter One  The philosophy of philosophy

1  *Conjectures and Refutations* (Routledge and Kegan Paul, London, fifth edition, 1974; hereinafter *CR*) p. 66f.
2  *CR, loc. cit.*
3  Such views exemplify the doctrine of *essentialism*, a favourite target for criticism, as we shall see, throughout the range of Popper's work. See, for example, *CR* p. 103ff; *The Open Society and its Enemies* (Routledge and Kegan Paul, London, fourth edition, 1962; hereinafter *OSE*) Vol. II, p. 10ff; *Objective Knowledge* (Oxford University Press, 1972; hereinafter *OK*) p. 194ff.
4  *The Logic of Scientific Discovery* (Hutchinson, London, English edition, 1959; hereinafter *LSD*) p. 19.
5  *CR* p. 71f.
6  For Popper's own account of his early studies in Vienna, see his autobiographical essay in *The Philosophy of Karl Popper*, edited by P. A. Schilpp (Open Court Publishing Co. Illinois, 1973; hereinafter *PKP*) Vol. I, esp. p. 29ff. (This essay was published separately by Fontana, 1976, under the title *Unended Quest*.)
7  R. G. Collingwood *An Autobiography* (Pelican edition, London, 1944) p. 26.
8  *CR* p. 73.
9  *Inquiry*, (Summer, 1958), p. 102.
10  *Individuals* (Methuen, London, 1964 edition) p. 10.
11  *Philosophical Investigations*, translated by G. E. M. Anscombe (Blackwell, Oxford, second edition, 1958) Pt I, 109.
12  *op. cit.*, Pt I, 126, 127.
13  *Remarks on the Foundations of Mathematics*, edited by G. H. von Wright, R. Rhees, and G. E. M. Anscombe, translated by G. E. M. Anscombe (Blackwell, Oxford, 1956) Pt I, 141.
14  *CR* p. 75. Cf. the development of the same thesis in *OSE* Vol. 1, p. 250ff.
15  *CR* p. 87.
16  *CR* p. 87f.
17  *OSE* Vol. I, p. 18ff.

18  *CR* p. 93.
19  *loc. cit.*
20  *PKP*, Vol. I, p. 65.
21  *PKP*, Vol. I, p. 24.
22  *CR* p. 34.
23  *PKP*, Vol. I, p. 27.
24  *CR* p. 37.
25  *PKP*, p. 91.
26  *CR* p. 71.
27  *CR* p. 89f.
28  Edited by P. A. Schilpp, Open Court Publishing Co., Illinois, 1949.
29  *op.cit.*, p. 9.
30  *CR* p. 94f.
31  *PKP*, Vol. I, p. 97f.
32  R. B. Braithwaite, 'An empiricist's view of the nature of religious belief', Eddington Memorial Lecture, 1955; reprinted in *The Philosophy of Religion*, ed. B. Mitchell (Oxford University Press, 1971) p. 72ff.
33  See, for example, 'Religious beliefs and language-games', *Ratio*, Vol. XII, 1970, p. 26ff (also reprinted in the Mitchell collection, p. 121ff).
34  *Lectures and Conversations on Aesthetics, Psychology and Religious Belief* (Blackwell, Oxford, 1970) p. 53ff.
35  See *Philosophical Investigations*, Pt I, 133.
36  *CR* p. 115.
37  Cf., for example, K. Nielsen, *Scepticism* (Macmillan, London, 1973) esp. p. 31f.
38  Cf. B. Magee, *Popper* (Fontana, London, 1973) p. 9f.
39  *Philosophical Investigations*, Pt I, 109.

## Chapter Two  The philosophy of science

1  *LSD*, p. 278.
2  *CR*, p. 114.
3  *OK*, p. 319.
4  *A Treatise of Human Nature*, edited by L. A. Selby-Bigge (Oxford University Press, 1888) p. 139.
5  *CR*, p. 53. See also *LSD*, p. 40.
6  *PKP*, p. 87.
7  *OK*, p. 1.
8  *CR*, p. 46f.
9  *OK*, p. 259.
10  *CR*, p. 47.
11  *CR*, p. 44f. See also *LSD*, p. 420ff.
12  *OK*, p. 261.
13  See *LSD*, p. 37 and n.
14  *LSD*, p. 40.
15  *CR*, p. 36f.
16  *LSD*, p. 41.

17  *LSD*, p. 41.
18  See, for example, *LSD*, p. 251ff.
19  *CR*, p. 34f.
20  *CR*, p. 36.
21  See *LSD*, p. 35ff and p. 278; also *CR*, 39ff and 250ff.
22  Reprinted in *CR*, p. 184ff.
23  *LSD*, p. 27.
24  *PKP*, p. 206ff.
25  *PKP*, p. 212.
26  *PKP*, p. 987ff.
27  *PKP*, p. 1110.
28  *CR*, p. 56.
29  *LSD*, p. 94f.
30  *LSD*, p. 98.
31  *LSD*, p. 103.
32  *LSD*, p. 104ff.
33  *LSD*, p. 273f.
34  See, for example, *PKP*, p. 1103f.
35  Second edition (University of Chicago Press, 1970) p. 10f.
36  *PKP*, p. 801.
37  *PKP*, p. 1145f.
38  'Against method', *Minnesota Studies in the Philosophy of Science* (University of Minnesota Press, 1970) p. 36ff.
39  *op. cit.*, p. 92.
40  *The Methodology of Scientific Research Programmes. Philosophical Papers*, Vol. I, edited by J. Worrall and G. Currie (Cambridge University Press, 1978) p. 16.
41  *op. cit.*, p. 17f.
42  *PKP*, p. 241ff, reprinted also in *The Methodology of Scientific Research Programmes*, pp. 46f.
43  *PKP*, p. 1004ff.
44  *LSD*, p. 37n.
45  *The Methodology of Scientific Research Programmes*, p. 35n.
46  For his criticisms of instrumentalism, see *CR* p. 97ff.
47  *OSE*, Vol. II, p. 375.
48  See, *OSE, loc. cit.*

### Chapter Three  Relativism and truth

1  *OSE*, Vol. 2, p. 369. The 'elsewhere', according to a footnote, refers especially to *CR*, Introduction and Ch.X.
2  *The Blue and Brown Books* (Blackwell, Oxford, 1969) p. 24f.
3  *OSE*, Vol. 2, p. 371.
4  'True', *Philosophy*, Vol. 44 (1969), p. 184.
5  *The Concept of Mind* (Hutchinson, London, 1959) p. 195.
6  *OSE*, Vol. 2, p. 374.
7  *OSE*, Vol. 2, p. 371.

8  Among Popper's many references to the significance of Tarski's work in this field, see especially *CR* p. 223ff. and *PKP*, Vol. 1, p. 112ff.
9  *CR*, p. 7ff.
10 *OSE*, Vol. 2, p. 275.
11 *Individuals* (Methuen, London, 1959) p. 35.
12 *Philosophical Papers* (Oxford University Press, 1970) p. 249.
13 *LSD*, p. 103.
14 *LSD*, p. 106.
15 *OSE*, Vol. 2, p. 275.
16 *OK*, p. 79.
17 *OK*, p. 74.
18 *Meditation I*, translated by J. Veitch (Everyman's Library, London, 1912) p. 82.
19 *On Certainty* (Blackwell, Oxford, 1969) para. 114.
20 *LSD*, p. 111.
21 *Philosophical Investigations*, Pt. I. 71.
22 *op cit.*, Pt. I. 242.
23 *LSD*, p. 111.
24 'Truth'. *Philosophical Papers* (Oxford University Press, 1970 edn) p. 129f.)
25 *How to do Things with Words* (Oxford University Press, 1971 edn) p. 144.
26 *op. cit.*, p. 142.
27 *Philosophical Papers*, p. 121.
28 *Science and the Modern World*, (Cambridge University Press, 1926 edn) p. 122ff. (Italics mine.)
29 *op cit.*, p. 143f.
30 *op. cit.*, p. 120ff.
31 See his paper 'Truth, rationality and the growth of knowledge', *CR*. esp. p. 228ff; also A. J. Ayer's paper 'Truth, verification and verisimilitude', *PKP*, Bk II, p. 684f and Popper's reply, *op. cit.*, p. 1100ff.
32 *CR*, p. 233.
33 *CR*, p. 234.
34 *loc. cit.*

### Chapter Four  Historicism

1  *The Poverty of Historicism* (Routledge and Kegan Paul, London, 1961, edn; hereinafter *PH*) p. 3.
2  *CR*, p. 336.
3  *LSD*, p. 111.
4  See *PH*, p. 36ff.
5  For example, *CR*, p. 337f.
6  *CR*, p. 87.
7  *PKP*, Vol. I, p. 90f.
8  *PH*, p. 26ff.
9  *PH*, p. 28ff; also *OSE*, Vol. I, p. 31ff.

10   *PH*, loc. cit.
11   On this last point, see, for example, *CR*, p. 103ff.
12   *OSE*, Vol. I, p. 36f (italics in original).
13   *op. cit.*, p. 25 (italics in original).
14   *op. cit.*, p. 84.
15   *op. cit.*, p. 39f.
16   *op. cit.*, p. 55.
17   *op. cit.*, p. 86 (italics in original).
18   Critical Notice of *OSE*, *Mind* (Vol. LVI, 1947), p. 169.
19   *CR*, p. 10f.
20   See the *Republic*, 540.
21   *OSE*, Vol. I, p. 130.
22   Genesis, III, 5.
23   See, for example, G. C. Field, *Plato Today* (Oxford University Press, 1949) and review of *OSE* in *Philosophy* (Vol. XXI, 1946), p. 271ff; J. Wild, *Plato's Modern Enemies and the Theory of Modern Law* (University of Chicago Press, 1953) and article on 'Popper's interpretation of Plato', *PKP*, Vol. II, p. 859ff; and, the most detailed critique, R. B. Levinson, *In Defence of Plato*, (Harvard University Press, 1953).
24   See his 'Reply to a critic' added to the Fourth Edition of *OSE* (*OSE*, Vol. I, p. 323ff) and his reply to Wild's article in *PKP*, Vol. II, p. 1159ff.
25   *PH*, p. 49.
26   *OSE*, Vol. I, p. 22.
27   See, for example, *OSE*, Vol. I, pp. 57, 173, 202.
28   *OSE*, 12, Vol. II, p. 27ff.
29   For example, Ryle, *loc. cit.*, p. 170f.
30   W. Kaufman, ed., *Hegel's Political Philosophy* (Atherton Press, New York, 1970), p. 139ff.
31   *OSE*, Vol. II, p. 37.
32   For Popper's comment on this example, see *CR*, p. 324f.
33   *CR*, p. 314.
34   *OSE*, Vol. II, p. 39f.
35   *CR*, p. 35.
36   *Hegel: A Re-examination* (Allen and Unwin, London, 1958) p. 64.
37   *Science and the Modern World* (Cambridge University Press, 1953 edn) p. 73.
38   *op. cit.*, p. 151f.
39   *op. cit.*, p. 64f.
40   *The Philosophy of Right* (see, for example, Meiner edn, Hamburg, 1955), p. 17.
41   *The Philosophy of History* (trans. by J. Sibree, Willey Book Co., New York, 1944) p. 57f.
42   *op. cit.*, p. 456.
43   *OSE*, Vol. II, p. 81.
44   *op. cit.*, p. 122.
45   *CR*, p. 333ff.
46   *OSE*, Vol. II, p. 103.

47   *op. cit.*, p. 104.
48   *op. cit.*, p. 100f; 111f.
49   In addition to the passages mentioned in *OSE*, see, for example, *CR*, p. 341f.
50   *OSE*, Vol. II, p. 112f.
51   *op. cit.*, p. 135.
52   *op. cit.*, p. 113.
53   *op. cit.*, p. 166.
54   *op. cit.*, 108f.
55   *op. cit.*, p. 116.
56   *op. cit.*, p. 138.
57   *op. cit.*, p. 126.
58   See, for example, G. C. Field's above-mentioned critical notice of *OSE* (*Philosophy*, Vol. XXI, 1946), p. 271f.
59   *PH*, p. vf.
60   *op. cit.*, p. vi (italics in original).
61   *LSD*, p. 248.
62   *OSE*, Vol. II, p. 85.
63   'Indeterminism in quantum physics and classical physics', *British Journal for the Philosophy of Science*, Vol. I, 1950–1, pp. 117–33 and 173–95.
64   *CR*, p. 339.
65   *PH*, p. 13.
66   *Science and the Modern World*, p. 120.

### Chapter Five  Freedom and values

1    *OSE*, Vol. I, p. 200f.
2    *PKP*, Vol. I, p. 27.
3    See *PH*, p. 35f, and *OSE*, Vol. II, p. 222.
4    *CR*, p. 343.
5    *CR*, p. 342.
6    *CR*, p. 24.
7    *OSE*, Vol. I, p. 120.
8    *CR*, p. 344f.
9    *OSE*, Vol. I, p. 124f and p. 265.
10   *OSE*, *loc. cit.* and p. 265; also vol. II, p. 160f.
11   *OSE*, Vol. I, p. 125.
12   *OSE*, Vol. I, p. 126.
13   See, for example, *OSE*, Vol. I, p. 265; and other passages mentioned in relation to the paradox of democracy.
14   *CR*, p. 350.
15   *CR*, p. 345.
16   *Op. cit.*, p. 83f.
17   See *Collected Poems* (Macmillan, London, 1952), p. 359.
18   *Philosophical Papers* (Oxford University Press, 1970 edn), p. 180.
19   *CR*, p. 341.

20   *CR*, p. 52.
21   *CR*, p. 347ff.
22   *OSE*, Vol. II, p. 369.
23   *OSE*, Vol. II, p. 386.
24   *OSE*, Vol. II, p. 390f.
25   *OSE*, Vol. II, p. 392f.
26   *Reason and Commitment* (Cambridge University Press, 1973) p. 22f.
27   *Faith and Philosophical Enquiry* (Routledge, London, 1970) p. 239.
28   St. John's Gospel, ch. 10, v. 10.

# References

**A. Works by Popper cited in the text**

*The Logic of Scientific Discovery* (Hutchinson, London, 1959, revised editions, 1968 and 1972) a translation, with additional material, of *Logik der Forschung* (Vienna, published 1934, but with imprint '1935').

*The Open Society and its Enemies* (Routledge and Kegan Paul, London, 1945, revised editions 1952, 1957, 1962 and 1966).

'Indeterminism in quantum physics and classical physics', *British Journal for the Philosophy of Science*, Vol. I, 1950–51, pp.117–33 and 173–95.

*The Poverty of Historicism* (Routledge and Kegan Paul, 1957, corrected edition, 1961).

*Conjectures and Refutations: The Growth of Scientific Knowledge*, (Routledge and Kegan Paul, London 1963, revised editions 1965, 1969 and 1972).

*Objective Knowledge; an Evolutionary Approach* (Oxford University Press, 1972).

'Autobiography' and 'Replies to my Critics' in *The Philosophy of Karl Popper* (edited by P. A. Schilpp, Open Court Publishing Co., Illinois, 1973). The autobiography has also been published separately under the title *Unended Quest* (Fontana, London, 1976).


**B. Other works cited in the text**

Austin, J. L. *Philosophical Papers* (Oxford University Press, 1961, 1970). *How to do Things with Words* (Oxford University Press, 1962, 1971).

Braithwaite, R. B. 'An empiricist's view of the nature of religious belief' (*The Philosophy of Religion*, ed. B. Mitchell, Oxford University Press, 1971, pp.72–91).

Collingwood, R. G. *An Autobiography* (Oxford University Press, 1939, Pelican edn, London, 1944).

Descartes, R. *Meditations* (trans. by J. Veitch, Everyman's Library, London, 1912).

Feyerabend, P. 'Against method' (*Minnesota Studies in the Philosophy of*

*Science* Vol. IV, University of Minnesota Press, 1970, pp.17–130).

Field, G. C. *Plato Today* (Oxford University Press, 1949).

Findlay, J. N. *Hegel: a Re-examination* (Allen and Unwin, London, 1958).

Hegel, G. W. F. *The Philosophy of History* (trans. by J. Sibree, Willey Book Co., New York, 1944).

*The Philosophy of Right* (Meiner ed, Hamburg, 1955).

Hume, D. *A Treatise on Human Nature* (ed. L. A. Selby-Bigge, Oxford University Press, 1888).

Kaufman, W. (ed) *Hegel's Political Philosophy* (Atherton Press, New York, 1970).

Kuhn, T. *The Structure of Scientific Revolutions* (University of Chicago Press, 1962, 1970).

Lakatos, I. *The Methodology of Scientific Research Programmes* (ed J. Worrall and G. Currie, Cambridge, University Press, 1978).

Levinson, R. B. *In Defence of Plato* (Harvard University Press, 1953).

Magee, B. *Popper* (Fontana, London, 1973).

Nielsen, K. *Scepticism* (Macmillan, London, 1973).

Phillps, D. Z. 'Religious beliefs and language games', *Ratio* Vol. XII, 1970 (reprinted in *The Philosophy of Religion*, ed B. Mitchell, Oxford University Press, 1971, pp.121–42).

*Faith and Philosophical Enquiry* (Routledge and Kegan Paul, London, 1970).

Ryle, G. *The Concept of Mind* (Hutchinson, London, 1959).

Schilpp, P. A. (ed) *The Philosophy of Karl Popper* (2 vols, Open Court Publishing Co., Illinois, 1973).

Strawson, P. F. *Individuals* (Methuen, London, 1959, 1964).

Trigg, R. *Reason and Commitment* (Cambridge University Press, 1973).

Whitehead, A. N. *Science and the Modern World* (Cambridge University Press, 1926, 1953).

Wild, J. *Plato's Modern Enemies and the Theory of Modern Law* (University of Chicago Press, 1953).

Wittgenstein, L. *Philosophical Investigations* (trans. by G. E. M. Anscombe, Blackwell, Oxford, 1953, 1958).

*Remarks on the Foundations of Mathematics* (ed G. H. von Wright, R. Rhees, and G. E. M. Anscombe, trans. by G. E. M. Anscombe, Blackwell, Oxford, 1956).

*The Blue and Brown Books* (Blackwell, Oxford, 1958, 1969).

*On Certainty* (ed G. E. M. Anscombe and G. H. von Wright, trans. by D. Paul and G. E. M. Anscombe, Blackwell, Oxford, 1969).

*Lectures and Conversations on Aesthetics, Psychology and Religious Belief* (ed C. Barrett, Blackwell, Oxford, 1970).

# Index

Adler, A., 15, 53
Aristarchus, 69
Aristotle, 118, 136
Austin, J. L., 98, 115–16, 117, 118,
    183
Ayer, Sir Alfred, 59

Barrow, I., 70
basic statements
    grounds for accepting, 107, 113
    Popper's definition of, 62
Berkeley, G., 18, 39
Bible, The, 93, 127
Braithwaite, R. B., 24
Broad, C. D., 7

Christianity, 201, 202
closed societies, 144–5
Collingwood, R. G., 6
conjectures, and refutations,
    progress via, 148, 189
    scientific theories as, 16, 22,
        30–31, 33, 34, 52–3, 78, 107
conspiracy theories of history, 157
convention, the role of,
    in the acceptance of statements as
        true, 107–9, 128–9
    in our definitions of philosophy, 2,
        3–5
    in the demarcation of science, 56
    in scientific method, 64
Copernicus, N., 69
    correspondence theory, 90, 117,
        126

Darwin, C., 45, 47, 125, 147, 165
democracy, 178–9, 191
    paradox of, 178
Descartes, R., 41, 49, 106, 146, 152
determinism, 156, 167–8, 182
dialectic, 40, 41, 154, 208
    Popper's critique of, 148–51

economism (Marx's), 155–6
Einstein, A., 14, 16, 19, 53
empiricism, 44, 45, 70
epistemology, 8, 43, 75, 142, 147
essentialism, 136–7
evolution, 125

fallibilism,
    Popper's account of, 81
    and the quest for truth, 91, 94,
        106, 113, 133, 198
    and scepticism, 95, 104, 129
falsifiability, 16, 25, 51–3, 57–8
fascism, 16
Feyerabend, P., 69–70, 74, 75
Findlay, J. N., 150
freedom, 6, 155, 207, 209
    political, 16, 146
    relativity of, 181–3
freedoms, the Popperian, 183–4
    conditions for realising, 184–93
Freud, S., 15, 53, 165

Galileo, 37, 69

Hegel, G. W. F., 165, 166

on dialectical progress, 146–9
the historicism of, 148, 152–3
Popper's attack on, 146, 149–50, 208
Heraclitus, 12–13, 147, 148
historicism
    and Hegel, 145–54
    and Marx, 154–65
    and the open society, 166
    optimistic and pessimistic forms of, 138
    and Plato, 135–45
    Popper's conception of, 16–17, 132
    Popper's refutation of, 167
    and reform, 185–6
    relation to Popperian epistemology, 133–5
    and religion, 135
Hume, D.
    the atomism of, 39
    and induction, 14, 15, 22, 24, 38, 44, 49, 51, 52, 78

indeterminacy, 187
induction
    Hume's critique of, 14, 22, 24
    the myth of, 43, 48
    Popper's dismissal of, criticised, 59–60
    the problem of, 38–41
instrumentalism, 37
interventionism, economic, 163, 164

Kant, I.,
    and the categorical imperative, 205
    as a critic of Hume, 40, 41, 44, 45, 78
    as illustrating Popper's conception of philosophy, 13–14, 22, 25
    Copernican revolution, 14, 40
    on philosophy, 146, 147
Kaufman, W., 146, 152
Kneale, W., 57–8
knowledge, 8, 14, 17, 20, 22, 37, 38, 45, 47, 137
Kuhn, T., 67–8, 80, 172

Lakatos, I., 71–3, 74, 76
language; language games, 23, 25, 26, 28–9, 32, 64, 84
Laplace, P. S., 167, 168
Leibniz, G. W., 170
linguistic tools, 29, 32
Locke, J., 125
logical positivism, 51, 54
Lucas, J. R., 85

Magee, B., 180
Marx, K.
    compared with Plato, 135, 139
    and dialectic, 147, 154–5
    and economism, 60
    the historicism of, 154–9, 166
    Popper's criticism of, 156, 160–65
Marxism
    as paradigm of historicism, 154
    as purported science, 15–16, 53, 77
    vulgar Marxism, 156–7
materialism, 76–7, 155–6
Maxwell, Clerk, 122
metaphysics
    contrasted with science, 55, 57, 77, 79
    Strawson's account of, 8
Mill, J. S., 155
minimal government, 180
moral relativism, 193–4, 197–8
    conditions for avoiding, 198–207
moral values
    the discovery of, 195–7
    and social policies, 193

natural selection, 47
Nazism, 146
Newton, I., 14, 69, 71, 78, 170
Newtonian science, 14, 39, 69, 71, 72, 73, 78
nominalism, methodological, 137

Oedipus effect, 170
open society, 144–5, 181
    and freedom to criticise rulers, 177, 184, 185, 187, 188, 194, 206

limitations of the, 185–93

Parmenides, 13
Phillips, D. Z., 24, 200
philosophy
  common ground between the
    Wittgensteinian and Popperian
    accounts and extra-
    philosophical problems, 6–8
  Popper's account of: illustrated in
    Plato, 11–13; in Kant, 13–14;
    in Popper's philosophy of
    science, 14–17
  Popper's 'crisis-and-response'
    account of, 20–21
  Wittgensteinian analysis of these
    illustrations, 21–5
Plato
  and essentialism, 136–7
  and historicism, 138–9, 144
  as illustrating Popper's conception
    of philosophy, 11–13
  and open and closed societies,
    144–5
  the political programme of, 140,
    143, 144
  in relation to Socrates, 141–2
  theory of Forms or Ideas, 11–13,
    22, 25, 138
politics, 16, 18, 162
probability, 67
problems, the genesis of, 65–7
pseudo-science, 49, 77
psycho-analysis, 14–15, 72, 77
Pythagoreans, 11–12, 21

rationality, 205–9
reinforced dogmatism, 149, 155
relativism,
  arguments for, 85–90
  arguments against, 90–103
  inherent in Popper's
    epistemology, 64, 129, 130–31
  intellectual, 82, 83
  moral, 175, 193–207
  Popper's repudiation of, 81, 82
relativity theory, 87
religion, 126–7, 135

philosophy of, 24, 31, 33, 34–5
Russell, B. A. W., 44
Ryle, G., 88, 141

scepticism
  criticisms of, 92, 105–14
  Hume's, 39–40, 42
  in Popper's epistemology, 104,
    129, 130
science
  demarcation of, 14, 56–7, 77
  and metaphysics, 76–9
  Popper's 'conjectures-and-
    refutations' account of, 14–16,
    51–5
  Popper's account criticised: by
    Kneale, 57–8; Ayer, 59–60;
    Kuhn, 67–9; Feyerabend,
    69–71; Lakatos, 71–5
social science
  the historicist conception of, 132
  and Marxism, 158
  and natural science, 175
  Popper's view of the function of,
    176
Socrates, 141, 142
state, the, 135–9, 157, 186
statement-identification, 99–102
statement-making, 97–9
Strawson, Sir Peter, 8, 20, 92, 109,
  110

Tarski, A., 37, 63, 82, 90, 116, 126,
  129
theism, 40, 76–7
theology, 39, 55, 79
totalitarianism, 16, 89–90, 140–41
truth
  as the goal of science, 37, 49, 50,
    79
  J. L. Austin on, 115–16, 183
  and relativism, 82–95
  Tarski's correspondence theory
    of, 37, 63, 82, 90, 116–19, 126,
    129

Utilitarianism, 180
Utopianism, 135, 154, 165

verification, 50, 53, 55, 64
verisimilitude, 127–9


Whitehead, A. N.
  the organic philosophy of, 40, 41,
    147
  on philosophy, 151, 152
  on scientific progress, 122–3, 124,

    173
Wittgenstein, L.
  on certainty, 106–7
  on language-games, 84
  on language-learning, 109, 151
  on philosophy, 9–10, 23, 24, 33,
    34, 36
  the philosophy of religion of, 24
world 1, world 2, world 3, 105–6